The Pagan Christ

TOM HARPUR

THE PAGAN CHRIST

Recovering the Lost Light

Walker & Company
New York

To the memory of
Professor Alvin Boyd Kuhn, Ph.D. (1880–1963),
a man of immense learning and even greater courage

Originally published in Canada in 2004 by Thomas Allen Publishers, Toronto, Canada.
First published in the United States of America in 2005 by
Walker Publishing Company, Inc.

For information about permission to reproduce selections from
this book, write to Permissions, Walker & Company,
104 Fifth Avenue, New York, New York 10011.

Library of Congress Cataloging-in-Publication Data
available upon request
ISBN 0-8027-1449-8

Book design by Gordon Robertson

Visit Walker & Company's Web site at www.walkerbooks.com

Printed in the United States of America

2   4   6   8   10   9   7   5   3   1

*The very thing which is now called the Christian religion
existed among the ancients also, nor was it wanting from
the inception of the human race until the coming of Christ
in the flesh, at which point the true religion, which was
already in existence, began to be called Christian.*

— ST. AUGUSTINE, Retractiones

But we have this treasure in earthen vessels.

— ST. PAUL, 2 CORINTHIANS 4:7

*Do you not know that you are the temple of God,
and that the Spirit of God dwells in you?*

— I CORINTHIANS 3:16

*Though Christ a thousand times in Bethlehem be born,
But not within thyself, thy soul will be forlorn;
The cross on Golgotha thou lookest to in vain
Unless within thyself it be set up again.*

— ANGELUS SILESIUS (1624–1677)

Contents

Author's Note

Thousands of souls in the Pagan world were on fire with the pure flame of divine passion of the Christly love centuries before Jesus ever lived.
— ALVIN BOYD KUHN, A Rebirth for Christianity

Before we begin, there is something you must know about the title of this book: the word "Pagan" is almost totally misunderstood today. The deeply pejorative sense of the word—entirely the result of centuries of Christian prejudice and bias—is illustrated at once by the *Concise Oxford Dictionary*'s almost brusque definition: "heathen, unenlightened or irreligious (person)." But the citation goes on to admit that in its origin, the word was totally neutral. It comes from the Latin *pagus*, a country district. A Pagan, a *paganus*, initially was a peasant. The term was soon adopted by emerging Church authorities to denote all who were not orthodox Christians. As we shall see, the "Pagans," who were persecuted, decried, killed, and ultimately utterly vanquished by the Church, held views of "the Christ within" that the Church was to plagiarize blatantly—and then cover up with book burnings, anathemas, and murder. Ironically, centuries later the Church was finally forced to turn to the "Pagan" Aristotle and his teacher, Plato, to save its theological bacon. The monumental work of St. Thomas Aquinas—which is the foundation of Roman Catholic theology and is based upon the writings of Aristotle, including his whole theory of natural law—testifies to that.

Acknowledgments

To the Canada Council: my sincere appreciation for the award and its support in the research and writing of this work.

Authors are often asked how long it takes them to write their books. The honest answer, in most cases, is what I would certainly say with regard to this one: a lifetime. *The Pagan Christ* flows from all I have experienced and read over that lengthy span. Consequently, I owe a huge debt to past teachers, friends, my many book and column readers over the years, and a host of other writers and thinkers far too numerous to name. In particular, though, I wish to thank the Reverend Larry Marshall, who first introduced me to the writings of Dr. Alvin Boyd Kuhn. When he originally sent me some samples of Kuhn's writings, I did with them what I usually do with the avalanche of religious and spiritual material that would pour over the desk of anyone specializing in this field for a major world-class newspaper—I put them to one side. Thankfully, however, he remained persistent. He sent more manuscripts and kept asking how I liked what had already come. At last, like the wearied judge in the Gospel parable of the woman who wouldn't take no for an answer in her quest for justice, I relented and undertook to read some of it as a way out. It was a startling revelation beyond anything I had imagined possible, a key turning point on my spiritual path. Reading at first in sheer disbelief, and then more and more seeing the radical truth of what was being so learnedly and powerfully set out before my eyes, I began to devour Kuhn's writings and then those of his two major sources, especially the Egyptologist, poet, and social reformer Gerald Massey. Marshall was a constant resource, encourager, and friend throughout the research and writing of *The Pagan Christ*. He read the second rough draft and made many helpful suggestions. I cannot thank him enough. Thanks as well are owed to Bill Denyar for his reading and gentle criticism of the initial draft.

Patrick Crean, the publisher at Thomas Allen, showed his warm enthusiasm for this project from the outset. A vote of thanks go to him for his courage and his overall wise counsel, especially in the final stages. To my editor, Jim Gifford, special gratitude is due for his thoroughness, his "tough love" approach to the text, and his quiet but steady pressure on me to make my own voice heard above the essential chorus of the major ancient and modern sources. Thanks too belong to Alyssa Stuart, the senior publicist at Thomas Allen, and to the rest of the support staff there.

Finally, my wife, Susan. There is no adequate way to express what she has meant to me in the creating and completing of *The Pagan Christ*. Her technical and editorial skills, honed by twenty-eight years of work at the *Toronto Star*, were an incredible and continuous asset to one who is quite honestly a techno-moron, a word the novelist Robertson Davies once used to describe himself to me in an interview. Susan played a crucial role at every stage, but her contribution really goes far beyond that. I'll say no more. She knows, and that's enough for me.

—TWH

1

DISCOVERY

A Bible Story I'd Never Heard Before

*My point, once again, is not that those ancient people
told literal stories and we are now smart enough to take
them symbolically, but that they told them symbolically
and we are now dumb enough to take them literally.*

— JOHN DOMINIC CROSSAN, *Who Is Jesus?*

ONE DAY, in the late sixties, while I was teaching at the
Toronto School of Theology's Wycliffe College, a very
bright English student at Victoria College, in the University of Toronto, came to my study with an urgent matter to
discuss. She was the daughter of a friend of mine and was enrolled
in an undergraduate course taught by Northrop Frye, a course for
which he was justly renowned. Her problem was that her rather
conservative evangelical faith was being deeply challenged. The
towering scholar, later to become internationally known in particular for his classic books on the Bible, was telling his classes
with all his usual wit and verve that the Bible was not a document
concerned with history but a vast collection of sublime myths and
metaphors. Though I was far from following any form of fundamentalism, I remember trying to reassure her—not without
difficulty—that there was indeed a profoundly historical core to

it all. That had been my background, and it suited the college's ethos as well. At that time, I knew very little of Frye's actual thinking, apart from her report. Fifteen years passed before I read the newly published *Great Code* and then its sequel, *Words with Power*, and came to a much fuller understanding of what Frye truly had to say and what Bible language really was all about. That experience and his words were in the back of my mind all through the months of research that went into the writing of this book. I found myself in particular recalling Johan L. Aitken's lines in his introduction to Frye's last work, *The Double Vision*. "In a legendary undergraduate course," Aitken wrote, "Frye reminded his students that when the Bible is historically accurate, it is only accidentally so: reporting was not of the slightest interest to its writers. They had a story to tell which could only be told by myth and metaphor: what they wrote became a source of vision rather than doctrine." In all my reading ever since, I have found that observation to be wise beyond any view of Scripture I had ever read before. It's an understanding that is vital to this exploration.

Let me say that I write here, as in all my work, as a journalist with special training in theology and religion. I have the great responsibility of sharing the "story" that follows with as wide an audience as possible, because what I describe and document in the following pages is one of the most far-reaching tragedies in history. It is the premise of this entire account that very early on, in the third and fourth centuries C.E., the Christian Church made a fatal and fateful error. Either deliberately, in a competitive bid to win over the greatest numbers of the largely unlettered masses, or through wilful ignorance of the true, inner sense of the profound spiritual wisdom it had inherited from so many ancient sources, the Church took a literalist, popularized, historical approach to sublime truth. What was preserved in the amber of allegory, it misrepresented as plodding fact. The transcendent meaning of glorious myths and symbols was reduced to a farrago of miraculous or irrelevant, or quite unbelievable, "events." The great truth that the Christ was to come *in man*, that the Christ principle was potentially in every one of us, was changed to the exclusivist teaching that the Christ had come *as a man*. No other could match him, or even come close. The Dark Ages—and so much more—were the eventual result.

While most of what is laid out in this book will possibly surprise and stir both faithful and outsider alike, that is not my primary intention. This book is not about seeking controversy or headlines; it is a sincere and earnest search for spiritual truth. Certainly it is in no way meant as an attack upon Christianity—or any other religion, for that matter. Quite the opposite, in fact. In the end, it is about the realization of a richer, more spiritual faith than I ever knew before.

I want to affirm with the utmost emphasis and sincerity from the very outset that the evidence investigated here, the discoveries I have made, and the inner struggles and deep insights that have flowed from them have made a joyous and life-changing imprint upon me. When I first began my investigation, I thought to myself, Can any of this be true? Several months later, I found myself asking instead, What if it is true? The implications were enormous. It meant, you see, that much of the thinking of much of the civilized West has been based upon a "history" that never occurred, and that the Christian Church has been founded on a set of miracles that were never performed literally. Finally, though, I said to myself, because of the sheer weight of the evidence before me, Yes, I believe it's true. And that has made all the difference, a huge and immensely positive difference for my understanding of my faith and my own spiritual life. Simultaneously, it has transformed my view of the future of Christianity into one of hope.

Just to anticipate a little, here's why I can say that with conviction. You will find that the allegorical, spiritual, mythical approach to the Bible and to Christian faith—that is, the true, spiritual

Christianity, before official Christianism took over—solves the enigmas of Scripture and the Christos story as nothing else can do. Bible stories come alive with amazing new freshness, believability, and power. Our own potential for Christhood, and for experiencing the indwelling spirit of God here and now, sounds forth in a clear and relevant message for everyone. Hope for a truly cosmic faith is kindled and fanned into full flame. There is a theological grounding given for our own instinctual yearning for a faith that resonates with our own "matter," the natural world. Our fresh (yet ancient, more universal) understanding of the Jesus theme opens up doors to other faiths that orthodox Christianity as it is now can never hope to pass through. And that's not all. Seen in their new light, the rituals of Easter and Christmas, along with Christian symbols such as the cross and the Eucharist, glow with renewed significance and depth.

In all honesty, however, this has not been a simple or easy journey for me. Having come from a Judeo-Christian background and commitment and dedicated my life to making known spiritual truth, I had never before encountered in depth the kind of challenges to my own faith I explore here. Certainly very little of what follows was ever presented to me by the institutional Church during my ten years of university training for the Anglican priesthood long ago. Nor was it ever once seriously discussed by any of my colleagues during the roughly ten years I spent as a professor of the New Testament and Greek at a prominent Canadian theological college. It was assumed by all throughout that traditional Christianity had always been more or less what it is today. Its superiority over other religions was seldom, if ever, seriously challenged.

Of course, I had read the great anthropologist Sir James George Frazer's *Golden Bough*, written between 1890 and 1915, with its comparative religions findings; I had read Plato and Aristotle in Greek at the University of Toronto and again at Oxford, and I had studied both Orphism and the Mystery Religions. Yet few, if any,

of the Egyptian parallels to the Gospel writings examined here
ever came into my view. The similarities that existed between
Christian beliefs and the earlier Pagan religions were always quickly
passed over in seminary as "foreshadowings" of the Good News
proclaimed by the New Testament. Like the various "prophecies"
and prototypes in the Old Testament, similarities in previous religions were represented as having been wholly "fulfilled" in Jesus.
Nobody even suggested that the opposite might be true, that the
Bible in general and the New Testament in particular actually copy
or repeat motifs laid down many centuries, and in some cases many
millennia, before. I was aware of Sigmund Freud's harsh-sounding
dictum that the Bible was a "total plagiarism" of the Sumerian and
Egyptian mythologies, but I had dismissed this as a gross distortion
typical of the founder of modern psychiatry's well-known bias
against all religion. I had also once read Dr. Anna Bonus Kingsford's opinion that the "Hebrew sacred books" were all "Egyptian
in origin," but I had quite arbitrarily dismissed it as nonsense.

When I started my ministry in a parish, and even when I was
teaching at the seminary, I had absolutely no idea of many of the
startling truths you are about to encounter. For example, I didn't
fully understand the nature and relevance of what I now call "a true
myth" for early religious thinkers—that myth is more eternal in its
meaning than history. It would have been news to me that Moses
is an Egyptian name—as in Ramose or Thutmose—and even that
there was a Jesus in Egyptian lore many thousands of years ago. His
name was Iusu, or Iusa, according to Gerald Massey, and that
means "the coming divine Son who heals or saves."[1] I knew nothing then of an Egyptian Christos, or Christ, named Horus. He and
his mother, Isis, were the forerunners of the Christian Madonna
and Child, and together they constituted a leading image in Egyptian religion for millennia prior to the Gospels. Erik Hornung says
there was "an obvious analogy between the Horus child and the
baby Jesus . . . long before Christianity, Isis had borne the epithet

'Mother of the God'"[2] What a different kind of preaching and teaching I would have done had I realized that this mythical Horus anticipated by thousands of years most of the sayings and the miracles of Jesus Christ—that he too had a supernatural birth, and that in one of his roles, he was "a fisher of men with twelve followers." It would have made a profound difference to me to know that piercing the literal sense of the Bible to reveal its hidden, allegorical, and mystical inner core could free us up and offer new, transformative spiritual vistas and insights. For example, imagine my surprise at discovering, during the research for this book, that Martha and Mary figure in a story about the raising from the dead of El-Asar, or Lazarus, at an Egyptian Bethany about four thousand years ago. The "miracle" described in John's Gospel was never a historic event; instead, it was a recurring, deeply archetypal, and widely used symbol of God's power to resurrect the dead.

There is so much more to explore and share. Most potent of all has been the increasing knowledge I have gained of how the key early Christian doctrine, the incarnation of spirit in human flesh or matter in each of us, is in fact the oldest, most universal mythos known to religion. It was current in the Osirian religion in Egypt at least two thousand years B.C.E. But I anticipate.

In any event, I can promise the reader this: I have indeed found for myself, in the course of all the emotional and intellectual wrestling involved in coming to grips with this material, not just a deeper faith but a far more bracing, more intellectually honest, more tuned-into-the-universe-itself kind of belief system than I ever dreamed possible. I see my Christian faith with a transformed vision.

What I have written is not intended primarily for scholars, although I hope they will be deeply challenged and learn from it too. While I have the greatest respect for scholarship and will be drawing upon the work of experts in many fields—as well as my own training and experience—I have dedicated my entire professional career as a theologian and journalist to the attempt to make complex issues as simple as possible for ordinary, intelligent laypeople. The scholars have their libraries and their own hidden sources. Many of them, it seems, can communicate only with one another. Indeed, some of them may like it that way. But the result too often has been, and still is, that ordinary, traditional citizens, the majority of any society, have been ignored or left to pick up whatever crumbs drop from the academic table. This is never more true than related to matters of theology—to religious beliefs and doctrines.

Much, perhaps even most, of what is contained in this book has been known to some comparative religions scholars for years— ever since the 1799 discovery of the Rosetta Stone on the western bank of the mouth of the Nile River by Colonel Broussard, an officer in Napoleon's army, an event that made possible the first deciphering of the ancient Egyptian hieroglyphic writings. But some combination of fear, vested Church interests, and the belief that some things should not be left to the hoi polloi to discuss at all convinced many of these experts over the years to keep virtual public silence. They know the potential for controversy and hostility from the ecclesiastical and other powers that be, as well as from those many rank-and-file Church members who fear change more than anything else. Whenever any of this material has been mooted seriously, others have rushed to crush it, dismissing it summarily or labelling it as rank heresy. They quote—usually out of context—whatever Bible verses seem to prop up their position. What the late comparative religions scholar and linguist Alvin Boyd Kuhn has called "the shadow of the third century" still makes its sinister presence felt.

The Church today stands at a crossroads. Many of its best thinkers are warning that it may have only one more generation before extinction because of its failure to communicate meaningfully with a postmodern age. Richard Holloway, former primus of the Scottish Episcopal Church, rightly notes that the religio-spiritual longing of modern men and women has never been stronger, but, he says, "The end of Christianity is coming because there is a system undergirding the traditional 'economy of salvation' which is more concerned with preserving its own power than exploring the truth."[3] My own thinking and experience confirm this. The answer to this crisis lies in a proper understanding of where and how everything began. However, engaging in this endeavour reveals some extremely disturbing facts.

The blunt truth is that seismic research by a few specifically neutral scholars, most notably Orientalists and Egyptologists, has been deliberately ignored by churchly authorities for many decades. Scholars such as Godfrey Higgins (1771–1834), author of the monumental tome *Anacalypsis*, the British Egyptologist Gerald Massey (1828–1908), and more recently, and most important, the already cited American specialist in ancient sacred literature Alvin Boyd Kuhn (1881–1963) have made it clear in voluminous, eminently learned works that the Jewish and Christian religions do indeed owe most of their origins to Egyptian roots.

Certainly a full appreciation of the huge contribution such experts as Higgins, Massey, and especially Kuhn have made to finding a fresh understanding of religion in general and Christianity in particular is long overdue. These men and their scholarship challenge present Christianity to the core and yet, without question, offer a radically fresh and hope-filled way ahead. They were men far in advance of their time. Through it all, though, they believed firmly in the presence of a divine power or cosmic mind behind and throughout the universe, and in the survival of the soul after death. I personally owe them a lot more than I can ever say.

Godfrey Higgins will always have a firm place in comparative religions studies because of his massive, two-volume *Anacalypsis: An Enquiry into the Origins of Languages, Nations, and Religions*. It was to have a profoundly formative influence upon Alvin Boyd Kuhn many years later. It stands as one of the most learned and far-ranging studies of the origins of religion I have ever encountered. First published (in only two hundred copies) in 1833, it was the final product of many long years of study.

Gerald Massey was a man of vivid genius and poetic fire who distinguished himself as a social reformer, a poet, and especially an Egyptologist. His poetry won the admiration of both Tennyson and Ruskin. His fame, however, rests mainly on six monumental volumes that dealt at length with the mythology and religion of ancient Egypt. He studied the extensive Egyptian records housed in the British Museum and taught himself to decipher the hieroglyphics. Although he was a capable lecturer, his speeches and books were not widely circulated. The record shows that his controversial work was considered taboo in what were regarded in his day as respectable literary and religious circles. He was nevertheless light-years ahead of his time.

I have found the writings and research of Dr. Alvin Boyd Kuhn to be the most erudite, most eloquent, and most convincing—both intellectually and intuitively—of any modern writer on religion I have encountered in a lifetime dedicated to such matters. To meet him through his books and monographs is to be confronted by a towering polymath whom history has yet to recognize fully in all his brilliance.

Kuhn's second book, *The Lost Light*, published in 1940, was a stunning, exhaustive exposition of the allegories, parables, and personages of biblical Christianity and of the basic foundations of all religion. It is unquestionably his single greatest contribution to a rational, convincing, highly illuminating understanding of what the ancient wisdom was really all about and where religion, especially Christianity, should be going today. I have a signed first edition of this book on my desk as I write this. Printed on the title page are the words "This book will be to religion what Darwin's work has been to science," a quotation from the president of the National Library Board of America. Kuhn's books have never been given the wide recognition they so deeply deserve. He simply stepped too often and much too hard on too many powerful toes, particularly those of the vested religious institutions and their hierarchical keepers.4

Far from being an original contribution to the world of religious thought, as these scholars have convincingly shown, Christianity was turned in the early centuries into a literalist copy of a resplendent spiritual forerunner. I will clearly document that there is nothing the Jesus of the Gospels either said or did—from the Sermon on the Mount to the miracles, from his flight as an infant from Herod to the Resurrection itself—that cannot be shown to have originated thousands of years before, in Egyptian Mystery rites and other sacred liturgies such as the Egyptian Book of the Dead.

Everything—from the star in the east to Jesus' walking on water, from the angel's pronouncement to the slaughter of the innocents by Herod, from the temptation in the wilderness to the changing of water into wine—already existed in the Egyptian sources. Egypt and its peoples had knelt at the shrine of the Madonna and Child Isis and Horus for many long centuries before any allegedly historical Mary lifted a supposedly historical Jesus in her arms. But for all those centuries before the translation of the Rosetta Stone by Champollion in 1822, the ancient key to all this Egyptian material had been lost. Centuries of blissful ignorance went by. Now, since the translation of the books of old Egypt—the Egyptian Book of the Dead, the Pyramid Texts, the Amduat, and the "Book of Thoth," for example—there is irrefutable proof that not one single doctrine, rite, tenet, or usage in Christianity was in reality a fresh contribution to the world of religion. Kuhn puts it tersely when he says that the entire body of Christian doctrine is simply a revamped and mutilated Egyptianism. These may seem extremely blunt words, but a full reading of his works reveals the mountain of undeniable evidence he has to back them up.

The cross, as we shall see, was a feature of ancient religion for a vast span of time prior to the Christian era. But imagine my surprise when I discovered that something universally believed to have been a purely Christian innovation—the Greek monogram comprising the first two letters of the word for Christ (*chi* and *rho*), letters often superimposed on each other in church ornamentation—was also pre-existent to Christianity. It appears on the coins of the Ptolemies and even those of King Herod the Great almost forty years B.C.E. Herod was made king of the Jews by the Romans in 40 B.C.E., and he reigned until 4 B.C.E. The Emperor Constantine the Great put this monogram on the labarum, or standard, of his legions after his famous victory at the Milvian Bridge three hundred years later. Thus he linked the Church to his political and military power, and all who rebelled against the new Catholic or universal orthodoxy were labelled heretics.

In his introduction to *Who Is This King of Glory?*, one of his deliberately neglected and yet most learned exposés, Kuhn says that the entire Christian Bible, Creation legend, the descent into and exodus from Egypt, ark and flood allegory, Israelite "history," Hebrew prophecy and poetry, and the imagery of the Gospels, the Epistles, and Revelation are now proven to have been transmitted from ancient Egypt's scrolls and papyri into the hands of later generations who didn't know their true origin or their fathomless meanings. He asserts that: "long after Egypt's voice, expressed through the inscribed hieroglyphics, was hushed in silence, the perpetuated relics of Hamitic (Egyptian) wisdom, with their cryptic message utterly lost, were brought forth to the world by parties of ignorant zealots as a new body of truth." Only by fully acknowledging and regaining its parenthood in that sublime Pagan source will Christianity rise at last to its intended true nobility and splendour, he argues.

As we shall shortly see, the Church of the third and fourth centuries, when challenged by its Pagan critics as to the real sources of its gospels, dogmas, and rites, reacted with fierce hostility, systematically hunting down and eliminating all traces of its Pagan past. It hounded anyone, whether Christian or not, who bore witness to the old truths. It closed down the traditional, "Pagan" philosophical schools, persecuted those involved in the various popular Greco-Roman Mystery Religions, burned hundreds of thousands of books, and hurled the charge of heresy—with its penalty of excommunication—at any who threatened to question the orthodox party line. Many were put to death. The Pagan inheritance was everywhere hotly denied. This was the beginning of a violent process that was to recur over the centuries and eventuate in a Christianity that Frye once bluntly described as "a ghost with the chains of a foul historical record of cruelty clanking behind it."[5] Studying this attempt to squelch the truth in detail for the first time was a profound shock for me.

Today there is no longer any excuse for any hierarchy to ignore the truth of what has actually transpired. The record is now plain for all to see. Not only did the early Christians take over almost completely the myths and teachings of their Egyptian masters, mediated in many cases by the Mystery Religions and by Judaism in its many forms, but they did everything in their power, through forgery and other fraud, book burning, character assassination, and murder itself, to destroy the crucial evidence of what had happened. In the process, the Christian story itself, which most likely began as a kind of spiritual drama, together with a "sayings" source based upon the Egyptian material, was turned into a form of history in which the Christ of the myth became a flesh-and-blood person identified with Jesus (Yeshua or Joshua) of Nazareth.[6] The power of the millennia-old Christ mythos to transform the whole of humanity was all but destroyed in the literalist adulation of "a presumptive Galilean paragon." Centuries of darkness were to follow.

I have laboured to present this work as clearly as possible, yet in places some hard work will be required, and readers must be prepared to think on their own and to be open to fresh ideas. It might well be a good idea to keep a Bible at hand, in case you want to check a reference for yourself, but this isn't essential. Keep in mind throughout that however negative—even shocking—the evidence may seem at times, a vast hope shines through it all. The overwhelmingly positive conclusions finally reached point toward an exhilarating new approach to faith and to a sorely needed, truly spiritual Christianity in this still very new millennium. My goal throughout is not to summarily dismiss the deep beliefs held by many millions in North America, Europe, and increasingly now in the Southern Hemisphere, where the vast majority of today's Christians live. But I do want these people to think deeply about their faith anew. Once the "surgery" is over, you will see, with me, how the Bible is wonderfully illumined afresh, how a rational, cosmic faith not only is possible but indeed is the only thing that makes sense in our fast-changing, pluralistic world. You will learn how any future faith must and can be fully grounded in nature and its cycles. The Jesus story will come alive and strike your heart and intellect as never before. Traditional rituals such as Holy Communion, baptism, and the Church's key festivals of Christmas and Easter will have new power once we understand their true meaning in the light of the ancient wisdom. The near-universal belief in a glorious destiny beyond the grave will be grounded once and for all in something more solid than a merely pious or emotion-based faith. Belief in the Christ within will be established as the key to personal and communal transformation. Our journey begins.

2

SETTING THE STAGE

Myths Aren't Fairy Tales

*On the intellectual side of religion and spirituality we are
still dwelling in the lingering shadows of medieval night,
hypnotized and victimized by superstition of the weirdest types
flaunted from pulpit and seminary. This beclouded day of
gloom will continue as long as we have not the acumen
to dissociate sublime myth, allegory, drama and
symbol from the dregs of history.*

—ALVIN BOYD KUHN, Who Is This King of Glory?

*Those who lack discrimination may quote the letter of the
Scripture, but they are really denying its inner truth.*

—THE BHAGAVAD-GITA

THE DISCOVERIES AND REVELATIONS in this book
have had a profound effect upon my own personal spiritual journey. It is hard for me even now to believe that
throughout all my previous training in and inquiry into the spiritual and religious dimensions of life, I could have missed something so important. Indeed, the uncovering of these truths has
been unquestionably the most transformative experience of my

life. My hope is that my excitement and inspiration will be passed on to you. We begin by taking a closer look at myth.

The Power of Myth

One would easily suppose that with the enormous popularity of the widely broadcast six-part television series *The Power of Myth*, featuring the late Joseph Campbell in conversation with Bill Moyers, and with the extensive writings on this topic by Campbell, there would be a general public awareness of the centrality and importance of mythology for human culture and progress. The series, which has often been repeated and reposes on the video shelves of many thousands of people the world over, made plain, in the simplest of terms, the essential ability of myths to change states of consciousness and to impart sublime truths accessible in no other way. It showed, among other things, how each one of us is affected by the myths not only of the past but of the culture around us today.

Nevertheless, it is safe to say that there are, at this moment, few words in our language less comprehended, or for that matter valued, than the word "myth." Mention "myth" or "mythology" to the average person, and he or she will assume that you are speaking of remote, insubstantial, irrelevant matters. In our culture, the word is synonymous with, at best, fairy tales and, at worst, outright lies and deception. If you pay attention, you'll be amazed at how often you'll read or hear someone say, "It's only a myth."

Since this book will frequently deal with myth, it is of paramount importance that this disastrous distortion and misunderstanding be met head on. Inasmuch as the arguments advanced will lead inexorably to the conclusion that the entire Gospel story of Jesus—not to mention about 95 percent of the rest of the Bible—is a myth or a collection of the same, it is imperative that the true meaning of myth receive detailed attention.

Here are three brief quotes from Kuhn to underline this salient point in my argument:

- "What was known of old . . . is that the myth as employed by ancient illuminati in Biblical scripture is not fiction, but the truest of all history!"
- "The myth is the only true narrative of the reality of human experience. It is the only ultimately true history ever written . . . as it is the actual experience of life in its evolution. Real as history is, it is finally less true than the myth. The myth is always and forever true; actual history is never more than an approximation of the truth of life."
- "Myth was the favourite and universal method of teaching in archaic times."

Missing What's Really Going On

A too often forgotten truth is that you can live through actual events of history and *completely miss* the underlying reality of what's going on. What history misses, the myth clearly expresses. The myth in the hands of a genius gives us a clear picture of the inner import of life itself. As Campbell repeatedly made clear in his many books and in the interviews with Moyers, the deepest truths about life, the soul, personal meaning, our place in the universe, our struggle to evolve to higher levels of insight and understanding, and particularly the mystery we call God can be described only by means of a story (mythos) or a ritual drama. The myth itself is fictional, but the timeless truth it expresses is not. As Campbell puts it, "Myth is what never was, yet always is." It's a means of expressing the inner structure or meaning of all history. It has the incredible power to fire the imagination and the spirit in such a way as to lift our consciousness ever upward to higher states of evolution. If you examine the best-known Greek myths, for example, you will see that each one has within it a deep truth about the human condition that remains timeless even though the event never happened. There are the simple examples of Narcissus, who fell in love with his own reflection, and Icarus, who through hubris and carelessness flew on his artificial waxen wings too close to the sun. We all know what insights Freud garnered from the Oedipus saga. Whether it's the prodigal son or the good Samaritan in the New Testament, the truth and relevance of these tales have nothing whatever to do with their having been actual happenings in history. This is why, in Kuhn's view, "Mythology is the repository of man's most ancient science."

This will be extremely difficult for some to grasp just at first. It was for me as well. But anyone who wants to understand religion, religious ideas, and religious documents—that is, scriptures of any kind—must realize that the divine, the mysterious, the ineffable, the workings of the spirit in the human heart or in the cosmos at large cannot be adequately expressed other than by myth, allegory, imagery, parable, and metaphor. Literal, descriptive narrative inevitably leads to either idolatry or utter nonsense. Thus myths are not some fictional embroidery or dispensable addition to the major faiths; they are their very essence. Strip them away and there is little that is precious left. Christianity does not need to "demythologize" its story; it needs to "remythologize" it, as we shall see.

Concealing Sacred Truth from Those Who Would Abuse It

There was another reason for the use of myths by ancient sages and scribes: they were a device for concealing sacred, precious wisdom from profanation by the vulgar or the malicious. There was a determination in the earliest circles of the very wise to prevent the special spiritual knowledge, or gnosis, from falling into unworthy hands, those who would misuse, desecrate, or pervert it in any way. By not being what they seemed on the surface—historical narratives or descriptions—and by ample use of symbolism and other devices, the myths kept the traditions alive for those who were truly seeking spiritual enlightenment, those who meant business. Sallustius, a fourth-century philosopher, in his treatise *On the Myths*, says that "to conceal the truth by myths prevents contempt of the foolish, and compels the good to practice philosophy." It was not in any way a class issue or a case of discrimination, except that it did demand a minimum level of intellectual acumen and education from a sincere seeker. The principal determinant of those admitted to the meaning of the myths or initiated into the widely popular Mystery Religions, where they were dramatized and experienced, was genuine zeal for the divine. Commenting on this esoteric approach, the great second-century theologian Origen said that ordinary people see only the exterior symbol: "It's allowed by all who have any knowledge of the scriptures that everything there is conveyed enigmatically, i.e., esoterically." Once the early Church turned to literalism and an exoteric, bottom-line rendering of the faith, Origen was condemned as a heretic and his books were banned.[1] To read them was to risk instant excommunication. The Church forgot or ignored the fact that St. Paul himself used the esoteric, allegorical approach.[2]

Ancient peoples did *not* believe their myths. They believed *in* them, in the sense that they believed in the truth beneath the stories. As Professor Kuhn notes, "Never did intelligent people believe them; they believed what they represented, symbolized, adumbrated." This distinction is tremendously important because, as we shall soon see, it was the total misreading of the myth, of the allegories and the drama, that resulted in Jesus' being made into a historical God-Man—an event that distorted Christianity from earliest times and effectively aborted the real power of the myth to transform the life of every individual. Once one man became the total embodiment of God-made-flesh, the rest of humanity were left looking beyond themselves to a matchless paragon of virtue instead of realizing their own Christ-power within. The impetus for moral and spiritual transformation thus was virtually nullified. This eventually led to the colossal blunder, perpetuated from the third century onward, of mistaking myth, drama, ritual, allegory, and other forms of symbolic representation for objective history, and following this by turning the body of myths into alleged, literal occurrences.

In *Shadow of the Third Century*, we read: "The sacred scriptures are written in a language of myth and symbol and the Christian religion threw away and lost the very soul of their meaning when it mistranslated this language into alleged history instead of reading it as spiritual allegory." The result was a pathetic, blind faith in a kind of emotional and superstitious supernaturalism. The evidence of this is all around us today in extreme, literalist, ultra-conservative forms of Christianity. Jesus becomes a magician or Superman figure, quite removed from the real universe in which we live. In his book *Miracles*, C. S. Lewis struggled manfully to justify the Gospel miracles in rational terms, but he ended in a sad failure on philosophical and other grounds. His basic error was in treating as history what never was history—and indeed was prefigured at least five millennia earlier in the Egyptian mythology. As Gerald Massey impatiently exclaims in his book *Luniolatry* (Moon worship), "The insanity lies in mistaking myth for human history or Divine Revelation. . . . The Gospels do not contain the history of an actual man, but the myth of the God-Man, Jesus, *clothed in an historical dress*." Sublime myth literalized makes for quite grotesque history. We shall see the evidence for this shortly. It's one of the chief reasons why the traditional interpretation of the Bible often makes so little sense to modern men and women— and especially to the young.

The Central Christ Myth

All of this brings us to the central Christos myth, which in its many different forms lies at the heart of every ancient religion. The work of Massey and Kuhn, reinforced by modern mythologists, firmly establishes that the single vast theme (in fact, the central teaching) of all religion is indeed the incarnation of the divine in the human. Moreover, while the sun is the source of all that is in our solar system, it is also by its light alone that we are able to see and know everything that exists, and for that reason, it was a natural symbol in antiquity for the ultimate being, for God. Thus the radiant figure of the sun god, who really represented at the same time both the divine and also humanity divinized, was at the core of the Christ mythos in ancient times. In the various sun gods, from Hercules of Greece to Horus, or Iusa, of Egypt, humans could see pictured their own history, their destiny, and their eventual conversion into angels of light. The same is true of the Gospel Jesus figure.

Significantly, modern science is confirming that every cell in our body is literally shot through with particles of the sun. At the Sudbury Neutrino Observatory in Ontario, the deepest, cleanest research site in the world, scientists have ascertained that untold billions of solar neutrinos pervade the entire universe. They are able to pass through the earth itself and all substances, including lead. More than a hundred billion neutrinos will pass through your hand as you read this sentence![3]

The following is the best summary I know of what Kuhn's reasoning and years of research on the Christ concept come down to in the end: "The vitalizing item of ancient knowledge was the prime datum that man is himself, in his real being, a spark of divine fire struck off like the flint flash from the Eternal Rock of Being, and buried in the flesh of body to support its existence with an unquenchable radiant energy. On this indestructible fire the organism and its functions were 'suspended,' as the Greek Orphic theology phrased it, and all their modes and activities were the expression of this ultimate divine principle of spiritual intelligence, energizing in matter."

I had studied some of these insights while reading Greats (Classics) at Oxford years ago, but nobody ever brought it all together in a meaningful synthesis like this.

The ancients placed at the myth's centre an ideal person who would symbolize humanity itself in its dual nature of human and divine. This ideal person—the names were Tammuz, Adonis, Mithras, Dionysus, Krishna, Christ, and many others—symbolized the divine spark incarnate in every human being, the element "destined ultimately to deify humankind." Rooting their religion firmly in the bedrock of nature itself, the ancient sages saw the successive phases of our divinization being enacted daily, monthly, and yearly in the solar allegories of rising and setting, waxing and waning (of the moon, which mirrors the sun's movements), and on the larger scale, in the precession of solar equinoxes and solstices. Ancient religion was solar and lunar based. It is called sun worship, but it was much more spiritual than this suggests or sounds. The ancient sages of Egypt, Chaldea, and Sumeria were wise and spiritual enough not to wholly identify their deity with even so glorious a manifestation as the sun. God, they understood, was far beyond the sun in glorious reality; but since one can speak of God only by means of metaphor in the end, the solar disk was the most powerful, most fitting symbol they could conceive of. What's crucial to remember is that when they extolled the sun's splendour, they saw it as symbolic not only of God but ultimately of our own divinity as well. The sun god was the embodiment, or model, of what each of us, through spiritual evolution, was finally meant to become.

Since myth and ritual always go hand in hand, the entire evolutionary history of humankind was accordingly programmed by these same theologians and depicted in a great drama that was repeated in mystery plays aimed at raising people's consciousness and allowing them to experience the emotional catharsis involved in living through a symbolic dying and rising again "to newness of life." All the subsidiary myths, allegories, parables, rites, and fables were formulated to support and supplement this central play, or acting out of the one truth—*that we are embodied souls or spirits destined, through the love of God, for eternity*. Like the sun setting in the west, we too have descended into mortal forms through incarnation. As it rises daily in the east with renewed power and vigour, so we will rise again. In other words, what the central Christ (or sun god) represents, we too one day shall be, and not just in theory or according to some mythical ideal, but in a final, resurrected reality. This is a spirituality full of hope and power.

What is amazing is the universality and similarity of these ancient myths, though they are found in widely disparate cultures and date from the very mists of antiquity. Whether Chaldean, Sumerian, Persian, or Egyptian—or indeed, as we shall see, from Central Africa or the Americas—they seem to have come from a single highly advanced source of intellectual understanding. It's almost as though long ago, there was one virtually cosmic religion that eventually and gradually deteriorated over eons. Some eminent scholars take this view, but no one really knows for certain. One thing is rock solid, however—our modern assumption that ancient equals primitive couldn't be more mistaken. Far distant civilizations still stun us with their engineering and architectural feats—the pyramids and palaces of old Egypt or the "cathedral" of Stonehenge—and the same is true in the realm of the spirit.

We have seen how the ancients used allegory and myth to express their thinking about God and other religious themes. But apart from their profound study of the only Bible originally available to humans—the whole "book" of Creation around them and in the cycles of nature—where did these brilliant insights and convictions come from? The answer seems to be that they came from deep within. Through prolonged meditation and inner searching, the ancients discovered archetypal images and symbols that corresponded to what they saw and experienced in the natural world. They came to know, for example, the reality of the Christ (or atman, or soul) within by inward exploration. They discovered what God had already in compassion planted there: the divine, God's own "image." Since the language of our unconscious is based on symbols—as Jung and many others have discovered—it was natural to express such profundities in ageless imagery, metaphor, and allegory.

What is of the utmost importance, though, is that through the myths and the esoteric (or inner) symbolism, the reality of the faith of these ancient peoples still shines brilliantly today. The evidence shows that their belief in God, in the eternal Christ "seed" or principle in every human being, and in the certainty of a radiant life to come was as strong as or stronger than that of any literalist or fundamentalist believer today. The Egyptian texts, as we shall see, glow with a life-transforming power and a lofty morality to match. The Ten Commandments, for example, are all anticipated in the teachings from the Hall of Judgment, where the soul was weighed in the balance at life's end.

Here is a summary of what the spiritual Christ of both the pre-Christian and the earliest Christian gnosis, or experience, was and how such a reality operates in us today:

1 "The Christos is the name give to the incarnate presence of God within.
2 The Christos, though known by many names, is present within all humanity; it is common spiritual property, but not all Christians and non-Christians recognize or acknowledge it in their lives.

3 To release the potential power of the Christos within, every-one must realize his or her innate spiritual nature and power.

4 Doctrines, creeds, dogmas, rites, and rituals have tended to replace this awareness of an innate spiritual essence, although they could still be used to help us celebrate the presence of the Christ within.

5 The Gospels are really dramas about the Christos, with Jesus in the starring role as a dramatic personality. Jesus is the symbolic personification of the Christos.

6 Jesus' birth, death, and resurrection are subjective events of the Christ within that each of us is meant to experience. The Christ is born within the manger of our hearts; the Christ within gives "his" life for us in the same way that a seed must die in order to germinate. The Resurrection is our being raised to new life out of the tomb of our carnality and world-liness, and in the end, as the creed says, we are reborn to "the life of the world to come."

7 It is through our permission that the Christos is unleashed to spiritualize our nature. We don't become God, but each of us is a fragment of God with divine potential.

8 Religions should provide opportunity for people to commit their lives not to a personal, historic Jesus (in the case of Christianity) but to the eternal Christ, however this divine presence is described.[4]

All of these themes will recur as we move along.

3

CHRISTIANITY BEFORE CHRISTIANITY

Where It All Began

*The very thing which is now called the Christian religion
existed among the ancients also, nor was it wanting from the
inception of the human race until the coming of Christ in
the flesh, at which point the true religion which was
already in existence began to be called Christian.*

— ST. AUGUSTINE, Retractiones

THIS ASTOUNDING STATEMENT by St. Augustine, one of the most brilliant thinkers in the earliest centuries of the Church, utterly refutes the traditional view that Christianity, though of obvious Jewish roots, virtually fell from the skies as a radically new, unique, all-surpassing religion destined to fulfill or eclipse all other faiths. St. Augustine here unequivocally states that "from the inception of the human race," the Christian religion has been around, and that it was held "among the ancients also." Elsewhere, speaking of Socrates (who antedated Christianity by about five hundred years), he said that he was as grand a Christian as any churchly saint or martyr. Indeed, he said that Socrates' Pagan brand of Christianity was as lofty and pure as the kind he himself knew. Few Christians are aware that Augustine himself received the Christian doctrine of the Trinity from the Pagan philosopher Plotinus (c. 205–270 C.E.), who "fed his mind on the attributes of the Pagan divinities and was steeped in Hellenistic rational religion and esotericism."

Significantly, St. Augustine's words are echoed at considerable length by the Church historian Eusebius (c. 260–340), the most important—though highly biased—early historian of Christianity. "The religion published by Jesus Christ to all nations is neither new nor strange," Eusebius writes. "For though, without controversy we are of late, and the name of Christians is indeed new; yet our manner of life and the principles of our religion have not been lately devised by us, but were instituted and observed . . . from the beginning of the world, by good men, accepted by God; *from those natural notions which are implanted in men's minds.*" This latter concept is crucial. It explains the archetypal nature of the Christos symbolism as it occurs throughout this investigation.

Indeed, in his famous book *Ecclesiastical History*, Eusebius, the bishop of Caesarea and one of the major shapers of the emerging Christian orthodoxy he championed, says that the Gospels of the New Testament were really the old dramatic books of the Essenes, from pre-Christian days.[1] Of a group of Essenes called Therapeutae (healers), in Egypt, he writes: "These ancient Therapeutae were Christians and their writings are our Gospels and Epistles."

Even the second-century theologian and historian Justin Martyr conceded as much when he wrote that whatever things were rightly said among the ancients "are now the property of Christians!" He had important and numerous reasons for making such a claim, and he is frequently at great pains to show that Christianity in no way differed from Paganism. In a further statement, addressed directly to Pagan critics of his faith, Justin Martyr argues that in "declaring the Logos, the first begotten Lord, our master Jesus

Christ, to be born of a virgin mother, without any human mixture, and to be crucified, and dead, and to have risen again and ascended into heaven, *we say no more than what you say of those whom you style the sons of Jove.*"

Celsus, a famous Pagan philosopher with whom Origen waged a well-known, detailed debate, said: "The Christian religion contains nothing but what Christians hold in common with the heathen; nothing new." For this, Origen had no rebuttal. As well, Ammonius Saccas (*c.* 175–240), the great founder of Neoplatonism (born of Christian parents himself) and the teacher of Origen, stoutly maintained that Christianity and Paganism differed on no essential points.

The Evidence

The words from these early witnesses pack a huge wallop for orthodox theology. But they truly sink in only when one takes the time to examine meticulously the evidence on which they stand. The evidence of close similarities between Christianity and other ancient world faiths is massive, detailed, extremely specific, and quite incredibly far-flung, stretching from the Vedic wisdom of India to the Norse myths of Scandinavia, the legends of the Incas, and the original spirituality of the indigenous peoples of North America. The Spanish conquistador Hernando Cortez (1485–1547), after his conquest of Mexico in 1519–21, complained in his diaries that the devil had positively taught to the Mexicans "the same things which God had taught to Christendom." Early explorers in contact with North American Natives had similar experiences.

Without exception, every element of the allegedly "new," uniquely revealed religion was extant before the first Christian century in the traditions, practices, and literature of many other lands and people. When the Abbé Huc became the first Christian to enter the region of Turkestan, he was filled with consternation when he found the Tartary natives celebrating the Eucharist with bread and wine. Francisco Pizarro was amazed when he found Aztec and Mayan rites and beliefs similar to those of the Roman Catholic system. The truth is that nobody of any acumen can observe the hundreds upon hundreds of resemblances between material in the Bible and very specific passages in many pre-Christian books and scrolls and believe that this is all purely accidental. Kuhn states bluntly that "no one can make the search and discover these numberless resemblances without forming the conviction that the Bible writings are rescripts, often . . . corrupted, of antecedent wisdom literature." As I read the evidence, checked and rechecked the sources, I gradually realized the truth of this assertion.

In his highly detailed 830-page *Anacalypsis*, Godfrey Higgins, a giant of ancient learning, says, "One thing is clear—the mythos of the Hindus, the mythos of the Jews and the mythos of the Greeks are all at bottom the same; and what are called their early histories are not histories of humankind, but are contrivances under the appearance of histories to perpetuate doctrines . . . in a manner only understood by those who had a key to the enigma."[2]

Gerald Massey, to whose lifelong study of ancient myths and symbolism both Kuhn and I owe an enormous debt, stated, "The human mind has long suffered an eclipse and been darkened and dwarfed in the shadow of ideas the real meaning of which has been lost to moderns. Myths and allegories whose significance was once unfolded in the Mysteries have been adopted in ignorance and reissued as real truths directly and divinely vouchsafed to humanity for the first and only time! The early religions had their myths interpreted. We have ours misinterpreted. And a great deal of what has been imposed on us as God's own true and sole revelation to us is a mass of inverted myths."[3]

Parallels between Jesus and the Buddha

A number of authors have commented on the parallels between the Buddha and Jesus.

Here is a paragraph from Oliver Wendell Holmes's introduction to Sir Edwin Arnold's famous account of the life of the Lord Buddha, *The Light of Asia*:

> If one were told that many centuries ago a celestial ray shone into the body of a sleeping woman, as it seemed to her in her dream, that thereupon the advent of a wondrous child was predicted by the soothsayers; that angels appeared at this child's birth; that merchants came from afar bearing gifts to him; that an ancient saint recognized the babe as divine and fell at his feet to worship him; that in his eighth year the child confounded his teachers with the amount of his knowledge, still showing them due reverence; that he grew up full of compassionate tenderness to all that lived and suffered; that to help his fellow creatures he sacrificed every worldly prospect and enjoyment; that he went through the ordeal of a terrible temptation in which all the power and evil were let loose upon him, and came out conqueror of them all; that he preached holiness and practiced charity; that he gathered disciples and sent out apostles to spread his doctrine over many lands and peoples; that this "helper of the worlds" could claim a more than earthly lineage and a life that dated long before Abraham was—of whom would he/she think the wonderful tale was told? Would he/she not say that this must be another version of the story of the One who came upon our earth in a Syrian village during the reign of Augustus Caesar and died by violence during the reign of Tiberius? What would this person say if told that the narrative was between five and six centuries older than that of the Founder of

Christianity? Such is the story of this person [the Buddha]. Such is the date assigned. The religion he taught is reckoned by many to be among the most widely prevalent of all beliefs.

Since Holmes was living in staid New England about the 1830s, and since none of the newly translated Egyptian hieroglyphic material had yet been published—indeed, the whole of comparative religious study still was in its infancy—it was quite daring of him to draw this close parallel. What is worth noting, however, since it shows the frequent inertia of humanity in the face of unorthodox truths, was that his words appear to have had little or no effect upon the prevailing climate of thought among Christians in general at that time.

The Buddha, when he prepares to depart, promises (like Jesus) to send the Paraclete, "even the spirit of truth which shall lead his followers into all truth."[4] The Buddha had his transfiguration when he went up a Sri Lankan mountain called Pandava, or Yellow-white. "There the heavens opened and a great light came in full flood around him and the glory of his person shone forth with 'double power.' He shone as the brightness of the Sun and Moon." This exactly parallels—but predates by six centuries—the Gospel story of Jesus' transfiguration on Mt. Tabor.

What is true of actual events in the Buddha's life—and I could provide many more instances—is also true of his sayings. Jesus said that whoever looked upon a woman with lust has already committed adultery in his heart. The third commandment, according to the Buddha, is "Commit no adultery; the law is broken by even looking at the wife of another man with lust in the mind."

Among other sayings assigned to the Buddha is one dealing with the wheat and the tares, as in the Gospels. You may remember that on one occasion (Matthew 13:24ff), Jesus told a parable about a farmer who sowed "good seed" in his field. While he was asleep, an enemy came and sowed poisonous seeds (tares) in the

same spot. When the crop grew, the man's servants wanted to
pull the weeds out. The owner, however, warned them not to do
so because of the risk of tearing out the "wheat" as well. He told
them to wait until the harvest (final judgment), when the tares
could be uprooted and burned while the grain went safely into the
barn.

Another saying involves the parable of the sower, the only
parable found in all three synoptic Gospels. In this story, Jesus
describes how a sower cast his seed broadside and it landed on a
variety of soils—some good, some stony, some thick with thorns
—with a range of predictable results. So it was, he said, with those
who received the word of God. The Buddha told it earlier.

The Buddha similarly related the parable of the hidden treasure
that was to be stored safely where a thief could not break in, and the
story of a rich young man who was told to sell all he had and give it
to the poor. It's also reported that Buddha said, "You may remove
from their base the snowy mountains, you may exhaust the waters
of the ocean, the firmament may fall to earth, but my words in the
end will be accomplished." Jesus said, "Heaven and earth shall
pass away but my words shall not pass away." The great scholar
Joseph Warschauer pointed out not only that every one of Jesus'
answers to Satan in the temptation in the wilderness comes from
Deuteronomy in the Hebrew Bible (Old Testament), but also that
an encounter between the Saviour figure and the principle of evil
is fully paralleled in Zoroastrian (Persian) and Buddhist literature and the Egyptian scriptures. The well-known Sermon on
the Mount was by no means first told in Matthew's Gospel. It
belonged, in one form or another, to a whole body of ancient,
arcane, or secret religions. There is, for example, not a single
word or saying in it that cannot be paralleled or found explicitly
in the Jewish Mishnah, Midrash, or Talmud. Having once been a
professor of the New Testament, I was aware of that, but not of all
the other parallels. The Hermetic Books of Egypt contain some of

the most ancient wisdom of any books in the world.[5] The Seventh Book of Hermes is entitled "His Secret Sermon on the Mount of Regeneration." The blunt truth is that the bulk of the sayings attributed to all the masters or gods in all the early religions were once oral teachings in the ancient myths and in the various Mystery Religions "ages before they were ever written down."[6]

Other Parallels

The sayings of Jesus are not the only item from a common ancient source. Studies show that there are close "parallel cycles" of allegorical "events" in the mythic and dramatic representations of thirty to fifty earlier gods (or Christs) in the ancient sacred bibles of the world. The parallels in the birth and life of Lord Krishna, the Hindu Christ, are now well known. The Persian prophet Zoroaster was born in innocence and of a virgin birth, from a ray of divine reason (Logos). Eventually, he was suspended from wood or "from the tree"—the cross or tree of the later Calvary. There is also the story of Salivahana, a divine child born of a virgin in Ceylon (Sri Lanka). He was the son of Tarshaca, a carpenter. His life was threatened in infancy by a tyrant who afterwards was killed by him. His story shows such close affinity to that of Jesus that it would be hard to deny a common source for both. Many of the other circumstances, with slight variations, are also the same as those told of Lord Krishna.

The central teaching of Christianity was and is the doctrine of the Incarnation (i.e., that God left the glories of heaven and became a human being like any of us). As John's Gospel puts it, "The Logos or Word became flesh." One could go on to illustrate this affirmation by citing endless New Testament quotations, references, and illustrations, but surely it needs no further elaboration. That's what the whole faith is about, pure and simple. As the Nicene Creed says, "For us men and for our salvation he came down from heaven and was incarnate by the Holy Ghost of the Virgin Mary, and was made man." But, and this is of tremendous significance, the thoroughgoing studies of ancient religions done over many years by the scholars I refer to here have established with certainty that incarnation—the indwelling of God or divine essence in the human, every human—*is the central teaching of all ancient belief systems everywhere*. It became clear to me as I investigated further that ancient cults focused all their efforts upon the cultivation of the god within man. This, in the final analysis, is the nucleus of the only true Christianity. It was true of the Sumerians and the Chaldeans; it was true of the Egyptian dynasties for untold millennia; it was true for the authors of the Old Testament (the Psalmist prayed, "Take not thy holy Spirit from me"), for Pythagoras and Plato, and for all the varied Mystery Religions of the Greco-Roman world in the four centuries B.C.E. and beyond. It was at the core of nearly all Paganism. As I saw the evidence for this continuing to grow and delved more deeply into it, a whole new world of understanding began to open before me. I remembered once reading in Plutarch (c. 45–125 C.E.) that all the ancient Greek wise men—Solon, Thales, Pythagoras, and Plato— had in their day gone to Egypt and been instructed by the priests in the ancient wisdom. But the full impact of that escaped me at that time.

It was in Egypt that the Greeks, and the peoples of the entire Middle East, learned of the doctrine of God in man—the Incarnation. By about the year 1425 B.C.E., there had been painted in the tomb of Pharaoh Tuthmosis III, deep inside a stone mountain where the sun never penetrates and the darkness is perpetual, a complex mosaic that tells a story that was already then at least a thousand years old. This mysterious painting, all done in ancient Egyptian hieroglyphics or sacred picture writing, is called *The Book of What Is in the Duat* (or the Amduat). The mural is divided into twelve panels that represent the hours of the sun's passage through the heavens each day. But as the complex figures show, the story being told is really that of each person's spiritual journey from natural man or woman to heir of God. What's important for our discourse here is that the one supreme being, Ra (pronounced *rah*)—often depicted as a sun disk or a human being—is shown enclosed inside a tabernacle, or canopy. The canopy for the ancient Egyptians symbolized the flesh. In other words, the painting clearly shows God incarnate in the flesh—as a person, as representing "every man." This is the very concept that Paul echoes when he says, fifteen hundred years later, that we are God's temple, or tabernacle, "and that the Spirit of God dwells in you." A spectacular copy of the Amduat was on display in the United States in 2002 as part of a touring exhibit called *The Quest for Immortality: Treasures of Ancient Egypt.*[7]

From all his years of study of Egyptian myths and symbols, Kuhn says that the essence of this ancient religious outlook was that where mind and body meet "is our holy mount." Our life, according to the old wisdom, stretches from the western gate of physical birth (the setting of the sun symbolizes entry into matter), across the dark nocturnal sea of earthly experience, to the eastern horizon of bursting light. In this life, we are on the "mount of the horizon," the Hill of the Lord, our Mt. Sinai, and with veiled face, we may come close enough to deity to hear his voice, his uttered, manifested Word of Truth (though, like Moses, we can not face his full glory).

The sole *and crucial* difference between the ancient myths and Christianity is that Christianity eventually concentrated this universal concept into a single historical person. (The debate over whether Jesus of Nazareth, called Christ, was a historical person is not as cut and dried as many suppose, but I will discuss that contentious issue later.) What was being symbolized, allegorized, imaged, and clothed—even at times deliberately hidden, to avoid "casting pearls before swine"—in all kinds of sacred myths and stories, like that of Jonah in the belly of the great fish or Daniel in the lion's den, was the truth of the God-presence in every human life. By the middle to the end of the second century C.E., however, the Jesus story had been turned into a literal "history" of the god-hood of one individual alone. Only through him and his alleged "perfect offering" of himself in sacrifice to the Father could human-ity achieve salvation. Any book, any academy or school, any thinker who ran counter to this official rendition of the ancient religion clearly testified to by Augustine was ruthlessly opposed—and where possible, destroyed. Fraud, forgery, deceit, and vio-lence, as we shall see shortly, became the tools the orthodox used to crush the "heretics." The heretics were simply the losing side. The victors got to tell the story—their way.

The Saviour Theme

Consider this: comparative religions studies reveal that almost every traditional faith the world over rests on a central story of the son of a heavenly king who goes down into a dark lower world, suffering, dying, and rising again, before returning to his native upper world. Acted out in a moving, multi-faceted dramatic ritual, the story tells how this king/god wins a victory over his enemies, has a triumphant procession, and is enthroned on high. Compara-tive religions scholars have made lists of thirty to fifty such avatars or saviours, including Osiris, Horus, Krishna, Bacchus, Orpheus, Hermes, Balder, Adonis, Hercules, Attis, Mithras, Tammuz of Syria, Thor (son of Odin), Beddru of Japan, Deva Tat of Siam, and many more. Kersey Graves, in his book *The World's Sixteen Cruci-fied Saviours*, quotes a prophecy of the Persian Zoroaster: "A virgin should conceive and bear a son, and a star would appear blazing at midday to signalize the occurrence." Zoroaster told his followers, "When you behold the star, follow it wherever it leads you. Adore the mysterious child, offering him gifts with profound humility.

He is indeed the Almighty Word which created the heavens. He is indeed your Lord and everlasting King."[8]

In their 1999 work *The Jesus Mysteries: Was the "Original Jesus" a Pagan God?*, two British scholars, Timothy Freke and Peter Gandy, examine the close parallels between the Greco-Roman Mystery Religions and early Christianity. Their data prove to anybody but the most closed-minded that the old "similarity or contiguity in time is not the same as a causal or imitative link" line of rebuttal will no longer wash.

Freke and Gandy show that Christianity and the Mystery Religions of the preceding and contemporary periods share virtually all the same beliefs, doctrines, rituals, and rites. To give just one example, in the case of those based upon the Osiris/Dionysus myth, the "hero" is the saviour of mankind, God incarnate, born of a virgin in a cave on December 25; he has a star appear at his birth, is visited by magi from the East, and turns water into wine at a wedding; he heals the sick, casts out demons, and performs miracles; he is transfigured before his disciples, rides a donkey into a special city, is betrayed for thirty pieces of silver, and celebrates a communal meal with bread and wine; he is put to death on a cross, descends into hell, and is resurrected on the third day; he dies to redeem the world's sins; he ascends into heaven and is seated beside God as the divine judge. He represents the Christos, or the divine soul, of every human being.[9]

Literal or Mythical?

The only difference—and it was quite radical—between the Jesus story of the New Testament and the many ancient myths depicting what seems the identical combination of concepts and characteristics is that nobody among the ancients, prior to the full-fledged Christian movement, believed for one moment that any of the events in their dramas were in any way historical. What counted were the deep, timeless spiritual truths behind or beyond the fictional packaging. There was one primal, central myth—originating undoubtedly in Egypt—and all the rest flowed from that. In Christianity, however, the myth was eventually literalized. Jesus was historicized. The consequences of this were to prove very damaging over the centuries to come. A believer had to put his or her trust in Jesus alone to know both divinity and ultimate resurrection. That's the kind of religion on which I, like many of you, was raised. The pre-Christian Christianity spoken of by Augustine had become "Christianism" instead.

Christianity, as its millions of followers have been traditionally taught, is about the arrival in history of the Messiah, the Son of God, as an actual person. But in Egyptian religion—and all the other so-called primitive faiths already mentioned—the "messianic son," symbolled by the sun itself, came ever mythically "as the manifestor and witness for the Father," who had sunk his own life in matter to reproduce himself in his next generation. According to the historian Herodotus, the "father of history," the Egyptian Jesus, known as Iu-em-hetep, was one of the eight great gods who were described in the papyri as having existed almost twenty thousand years ago. [10] He bore different names as specific cults changed. But to the sages of old time, the coming was a constantly recurring and purely symbolic event. The ancient messiah was an anthropomorphic, representative figure that came from age to age, cycle to cycle. In the Egyptian Ritual, he came symbolically each day, but he also came periodically; he came "regularly and continuously." His solar and lunar symbols came cyclically and in eternal renewal with the seasons. The solstices and the equinoxes marked his waxing and waning presence. This Egyptian "messiah" was not expected at any historic date, at any epoch. Rather, symbols of his spiritual coming manifested themselves in natural phenomena by the day (sunrise and sunset, for example), the year, or the lunar cycle. *The constant repetition of the symbols was the assurance of their unfailing fulfillment*. They meant that an elevation of distinctly divine consciousness was gradually coming into rulership in humanity, a kingdom of goodness, truth, and beauty, a kingdom of love.

It is now clear to me that for the ancients, the final fulfillment of this coming, or advent, would have meant stopping dead the march of the universe. And for one person to be saved here and now, in some static fashion for all eternity, he would have had to drop out of step with the rhythmic pulse of life. To them, salvation meant to consummate the present evolutionary cycle and keep marching on with nature until full divinization was realized. There was no manic expectation of some supernatural, apocalyptic "second coming." It was happening to those who opened themselves to it here and now, step by step. Significantly, here the King James translation of the "end of the world" has done a lot of harm. The Greek text always uses words that explicitly signify the end of the age, cycle, or eon, not the end of the cosmos itself.

Christliness

In the pre-Christianism Christianity, it was believed that the coming of the Messiah, or Christ, was taking place in the life of every person at all times. Each person had his or her evolutionary solstice, his or her Christmas, and, eventually, his or her Easter too. The symbols for all of this, taken from the book of nature, were annuals; the actual events they typed (symbolized) in mankind's history were perennials. In nature, every process was seen as typical and repetitive. But also it was, and is, typical of all other processes, and of life in its entirety. The Christ portrayed in nature and then personified in dramatic form in the Egyptian rituals stood for the "sun" of divinity in human beings. The Gospels' "life" of Jesus turns out in the end analysis, then, to be a somewhat garbled and fragmentary copy of an Egyptian prototype who was a purely dramatic figure portraying the divinity in man. We will look more thoroughly into this dimension of the story in chapter 9. Significantly, Meister Eckhart (1260–1327), the German Dominican mystic who died before he could be fully tried for heresy by the archbishop of Cologne (he died while appealing to the pope), once wrote that the Christ was not a historical person, per se, but rather "the collective soul of humanity."

We can sum it up this way: the primary truth of human culture presented by all sage religions of antiquity is that there resides deeply embedded in the core of our basic constitution a nucleus of what, for want of a better designation, must be called a divine spark, or "sun." The glow of Christliness—a thing Kuhn describes as at once both chemically radioactive and intellectual—in us is, indeed, as Paul himself says, our "hope of glory." All the sun symbolism of religion, ancient and modern, is an attempt to express this one salient truth. All the Christs of antiquity were denominated as sun gods. We all share in this one primordial "fire."

Sun Worship and Christianity

Most Church members have no idea of the period of overlap between ancient "Pagan" sun worship and what was gradually developing as "orthodox" Christianity. Constantine, for example, generally recognized as the first Christian emperor, gave toleration to Christianity in or about 313 in the Edict of Milan, after his victory at the Milvian Bridge, where he had his legendary vision of *in hoc signo vince* (conquer in this sign, the sign of the cross). But his coins continued to bear the inscription *sol deus invictus* (unconquerable sun) for many years. He refused baptism until he was on his deathbed in 337 so that he could die having committed no fresh crimes. He had good reasons to worry. Even though he had summoned some 318 bishops to Nicaea in 325 to solve the Arian controversy* and thus achieve political and religious unity for the empire—the result was the still-repeated Nicene Creed—he remained a violent man. Having, he thought, settled the doctrine of the Trinity once and for all, he returned home from Nicaea and murdered or caused to have murdered his son, Crispus; his wife, Fausta (boiled alive and suffocated in her bath); his brother-in-law, Licinius, and his son (flogged to death); and several others.

Constantine never quite gave up the hope of further uniting the empire in the adoration of the one sun god who combined in himself the Father-God of the Christians and the much-worshipped (solar god) Mithras. Significantly, according to the Catholic Encyclopedia, Pope Leo the Great (pontiff from 440 to 461) witnessed that in his day, it was the custom of many Christians to stand on the front steps of St. Peter's in Rome "and pay homage to the sun by obeisance and prayers."

The February 2003 issue of the well-known and respected magazine *Bible Review* carried an illustrated article, "Faces of Jesus," which described a famous ceiling mosaic of Tomb M, underneath St. Peter's in the Vatican. It dates to the third or fourth century C.E. The mosaic shows the vine of the Greek sun god, Dionysus, reinterpreted as the vine of Jesus Christ and surrounding a large image of Christ, as the sun god, riding in a sun chariot being pulled across the heavens by four white horses.[11] Thus Jesus was quite literally the "sun of righteousness" for many members of the Church for several centuries. The well-known Christmas carol "Hark, the Herald Angels Sing" has this line from Scripture: "Risen with healing in his wings." A common depiction of the sun in ancient times shows it as winged on two sides. The Christian

---

* Arius was the author of the key "heresy" debated at the Council of Nicaea. His position was that Jesus Christ was created by God the father and so was inferior to him.

Sabbath, *Sunday*, is a direct relic of this solar phenomenon. The Pagan name for it was *dies solis* (the day of the sun). The phrase "Our Lord, the Sun" was used in prayer by Christians up to the sixth century, and was even embedded in the Church's liturgy until it was changed to "Our Lord, the God."

The Ultimate Christian Symbol

The symbol of the cross—"the old, rugged cross," as the familiar hymn puts it—will forever in traditional Christianity be associated with the shame, suffering, sacrifice, and ultimate victory of Jesus Christ on the first God's Friday (Good Friday). But it has to be noted that inasmuch as it was by far the earliest and most universal of all religious icons, the cross had quite a range of wholly different meanings for untold millennia before the dawn of official, literalist Christianity (Christianism).

Egyptologists, for example, report that the sign of the cross was commonly found on the breasts of mummies, and that the cross was frequently placed in the hands of the dead as "an emblem both of incarnation and of new life to come." It was even carved on the back of the scarab (a gem or brooch representing the dung beetle), another symbol that meant eternal life.

The ankh, a cross with a circle or loop at the top, was widely used in ancient Egyptian culture as a sign of eternal life, but crosses of all types, from swastikas to the cross of Plato's mythical divine man "stamped upon the universe," are evident whenever so-called primitive religion is studied. (Incidentally, the swastika symbol, tainted forever by its appropriation by the Nazis, was found in ancient Hindu, Mexican, and Buddhist traditions, and many others. The name comes from the Sanskrit world *svastika*, meaning a mystical cross denoting good fortune. Some authorities say it was meant to represent the sun with its rays.) Conservative scholars, eager to debunk any dependency of Christianity upon Paganism, usually attempt to explain away the extraordinary dissemination of the cross through the world prior to Christianity by calling it a primordial symbol related much more to other symbols such as the centre, the circle, and the square. It's most obvious use in this respect would be to divide a circle into four even parts, for example. Yet other scholars have produced a mass of evidence for a radically different point of view.

Spirit into Matter

Kuhn contended that the single most important religious event in all human history was the awakening of self-reflective consciousness. At that precise moment, we stopped being purely animals and became "quickened" as true human beings with intellects and souls. A solely religious version of this same evolutionary phenomenon can, of course, be found in the classic creation myths of the first two chapters of Genesis.

The birth of all religious impulses ultimately is traceable to this momentous creation event—the awareness that the "horizontal" line of our animality had been intersected by the "verticality" of self-reflective reason and a profound sense of the divine, the Christos within. The cross, Kuhn convincingly argues, symbolized spirit plunged into matter. As we have seen, the technical term for this is incarnation. It is the interaction between spirit and matter that is the key to how the entire universe works, but nowhere is this more vitally true than in our own humanity.

The cross, then, in all its shapes and forms, depicted allegorically this primal experience and reality. Hence its universality. It was a constant symbol of our rootedness in the earth on the one hand and our destiny with God on the other. Later mystic philosophers found it to be the ideal "plus sign" because, as a symbol of addition, a process of expanding by adding on, it signified the

whole way to human development. Placed on an angle, as the multiplication sign, the cross again mystically represents the motion
and impulse given to all life by the intersection of spirit (the verti-
cal) with matter (the horizontal). It's what pulses through the
universe as the initial simplicity of the one becomes the infinite
multiplicity of the many.

The evidence is overwhelming that in Paganism and early
Christianity, the cross was always a symbol of life, never of death
(except as "death," in its symbolic sense, means incarnation). To
be in the body was to be put—even impaled or crucified—on this
cross of fleshly existence. This is the powerful meaning behind
Jesus' command "Take up your cross . . ."—that is, accept the discipline and ambiguity and suffering involved in being a fully aware
human being. (The Greeks said that the body is the tomb of the
soul, and they had a word play on it: *soma* [body] = *sema* [tomb].)
It also symbolized the cross of life on earth, because its four arms
represent the fourfold foundation of the world, the four elements
(earth, water, air, and fire), and the underpinning of the human
temple, or being.

It needs to be better known that the true sign of Christianity
for the earliest centuries of Church history was not a crucifix—a
cross bearing the figure of Jesus—but either a bare cross or one
with a lamb fastened to it. In the entire iconography of the catacombs, no figure of a man on a cross appears for the first six or
seven centuries of the era. It will come as a surprise to many that
the first known figure of a god on a cross is a likeness of the sun
god Orpheus from some three centuries B.C.E. The crucifix on
the amulet on the cover of *The Jesus Mysteries*, by Freke and Gandy,
clearly depicts this image.

Not until 692, in the reign of Emperor Justinian II, was it
decreed by the Church (through the Trullan Council) that the
figure of the historical Jesus on the cross should supersede that of

"the lamb, as in former times." Hence the erroneous—and to be quite honest, overly prominent—display of the crucifix throughout the Roman Catholic world today. The bare cross is a more accurate symbol of the original faith.

The Irony

There is a somewhat grotesque irony at play here. For just over one billion Roman Catholics—and for the secular world looking on—the central icon of the living God today is a human figure impaled and in agony on an instrument of torture, suffering, and pain. Small wonder that such a belief system makes so much of suffering while remaining sadly indifferent to the suffering that several of its teachings cause. Vatican edicts on birth control and other "hormone issues" are cases in point. Religion and spirituality are supposedly about life—abundant, evolving, transforming, ultimately triumphant life. An empty cross can convey all that. But a crucifix symbolizes the opposite. Gerald Massey, who, like Kuhn, began his researches with no animus whatever toward religion in general or the Christian Church in particular, waxes highly indignant about this issue. As a victim of cruel child labour and grinding poverty, he knew first-hand the frequent, hard-hearted indifference of the superficially pious and devoutly orthodox "upper and middle classes." Massey knew full well that the history of Christianity shows plenty of evidence of great individual acts of charity, and of powerful movements based upon compassion and a love of social justice, but he was adamant that the centrality of the crucifix—of a personal, historic Jesus on a cross—had unconsciously fostered a belief that "suffering is good for you," that you must resign yourself and, above all, comply and conform.

The Hope

Learning about the depth and background of all these symbols in the pre-Christian era, and about how the literal, surface meaning is only a veneer over their essential truth, has been a truly liberating experience for me. It has made clear to me that the concepts at the heart of Christianity really flow from the deep well of the unconscious, having been planted there by God. For example, the idea of the Christ within—the fully realized spiritual human being—is now to me an unmistakable, Jungian-style archetype in our human psyche. The same is true of the other religious symbols described here. Implanted deeply by the Creator, they belong to us uniquely as human beings, however they are named, and they are full of promise and hope for a meaningful, twenty-first-century faith.

Remember, above all, that the fact that most of the material in the Jesus story was previously extant in other sacred literature of the ancient world in no way detracts from its power and relevance for our lives today. If something is true or portrays a deep reality, it remains true forever. Things are not true simply because someone somewhere first said them, or because they are collected in books such as the Bible. They are true because they ring with full authenticity on the anvil of our souls.

4

THE GREATEST COVER-UP OF ALL TIME

How a Spiritual Christianity Became a Literalist Christianism

There are many things that are true which it is not useful for the vulgar crowd to know; and certain things which although they are false it is expedient for the people to believe otherwise.

— ST. AUGUSTINE, City of God

The following two strong statements truly compelled me to pay close attention—to sit up and think more deeply:

- "Christianity evolved and took historical form as the result of a corruption of high wisdom already extant, and not as the promulgation of new light and wisdom previously unknown."
- "Christianity only gained favour and held the allegiance of the masses of the populations of the West for centuries because it succeeded in accommodating its message to the prevalent levels of general unintelligence. In doing so it inevitably distorted its truths into ludicrous caricature and baneful forms of error and falsehood."

THE ALVIN BOYD KUHN BOOK that has made by far the greatest impression upon me, given my past training and overall general commitment to the idea of the high nobility of Christianity as a religious movement, has been *The Shadow of the Third Century*. Its 522 studiously researched pages on the lies, fraud, deceit, and violence that conspired to turn Christianity into what Kuhn calls Christianism came as a profound surprise and shock. I can only hope that all sincere seekers after truth will go beyond this present, necessarily brief, summary to read it fully for themselves. There's no question whatever in my mind that those who do so will be as deeply affected as I was. Kuhn shows clearly that the truth about early Christian history has been sadly suppressed. Indeed, he claims—and then proves—that the trail of unbelievable and quite deliberate skulduggery runs throughout almost the entire history of ecclesiastical Christianity. Reading his arguments and checking his sources for myself, I realized that other investigators had missed the truth before because they were not cognizant of (or were unwilling to face) the fact that a conspiracy had operated over a span of centuries. They ignored what were piously seen as unfortunate excesses or momentary lapses and kept following the official party line.

His case rests upon the undeniable fact that the religion that started under the name of Christianity in the first century did not long retain its original deeply spiritual nature and substance. I was quickly forced to realize that it was not by any means the same religion in the fourth century that it had been in the first. Despite beginning as a more or less sincere effort of genuine religiousness and mysticism fed by many sources and expressed in many forms, it had plunged rapidly down the grade of deterioration "until in the fourth century it had completed its dire transformation (transmogrification) into Christianism."

I have carefully examined the major evidence so thoroughly documented by Kuhn, and I have found these facts:

- Christianity began as a cult with almost wholly Pagan origins and motivations in the first century, "and by the fourth it had utterly turned its back on Paganism and repudiated every hint of . . . connection with it, loading it with contempt from that day to this."
- Books that were highly regarded in the movement at the start and for some time thereafter were condemned and violently repudiated within less than two centuries.
- Several doctrines that were held in great esteem in the initial period, such as the doctrines of reincarnation and a universal salvation, were later refuted.
- Nearly all the original thinkers who had shared in the building of the new movement—its very pioneers and leaders—had, even before the fourth century, been pronounced heretics and were reviled by those who had swept in and grabbed control of the policies.
- The mystical/allegorical method of interpreting the sacred Scripture, used at the beginning by Paul and such eminent scholars as Clement of Alexandria and Origen, was replaced by a wholly literal/historical approach.

Let me expand a little on this last point. This whole process of drastic change hinged on the crucial decision to take the ancient esoteric wisdom of so-called Paganism—the pre-Christianism Christianity of which both St. Augustine and Eusebius wrote— and make it exoteric (i.e., plain, open, and simple for the ignorant and unlearned masses). This decision had no doubt a worthy aim, and on one level, fuelled by the Roman gift for organization and crowd control (not to mention the ready use of force whenever deemed necessary), it was a great success. But the price, both intellectually and practically, was terrible.

In a powerful passage, Kuhn says that by the time the Pagan doctrine of the birth of Christhood in man had been put forth exoterically, for lowly mental grasp, as the literal birth of a baby on December 25, it was no longer true. By the time the crucifixion of divine mind power on the "cross" of existence in the fleshly body of every member of our species had been concretized and historicized as the literal agony of a quivering body of one man on a wooden cross, it was no longer true. By the time the dismemberment of the unit power of Christhood (with each human given a portion for his divine transfiguration from within) had been made "comprehensible" as the actual breaking of a literal loaf of bread into fragments, it was a false belief. Indeed, "by the time the descent of the Monad [the One God and Source of All Being] from the Logos of divine intellection into the water (matter) of the human body had been 'clarified' and 'simplified' to poor mental capacity as the baptism of a man in the Jordan River, it was a delusion and a snare to uncritical thought. Instead of enlightening him it would hallucinate him, because his ability to lift it from the concrete to the spiritual sense was non-existent. And by the time the incarnation doctrine had been 'made plain' as the descent of God's radiant being into the physical corpus of one man, so that simple minds could see it, it was an outright mockery of truth. . . . Crude conception ends by taking the concrete images for the factual substance of truth."

The earliest Church Fathers themselves admit that they took the high, symbolic, esoteric (or secret) wisdom that the Christian movement had inherited from Paganism—from Platonic philosophy and the Mystery Religions—and explained it, or rather downgraded it, by means of vulgar fables for the illiterate mob. One fifth-century pope even exulted, "What profit hath not this fable brought us." In his *Anacalypsis*, Godfrey Higgins comments, "Their explanations to the vulgar are suitable to the vulgar, and were meant merely to stop their enquiries." Indeed, Higgins, who also began his prodigious studies with no bias whatever against Christianity, says concisely that while the Fathers confessed—and, for close to two hundred years, upheld—the existence of an inner profundity of meaning and high range of mystical experience that could be shared only with initiates and "genuinely tested and accredited competents," they were soon spreading these inner teachings abroad to the general public, "and in the process reducing the rich and sumptuous feast of wisdom to such a hash and porridge as the ignorant masses could find in some way digestible. Thus came Christianism which was the wreckage of Christianity."

I found it particularly convincing that the great historian of that period, Sir Edward Gibbon, in his *Decline and Fall of the Roman Empire*, observed: "The most extravagant legends, as they conduced to the honour of the Church, were apprehended by the credulous multitude, countenanced by the power of the clergy, and attested by the suspicious evidence of ecclesiastical history."[1]

In short, in the view of these scholars, the Church converted a whole mass of romantic legends or myths into so-called history, a multiplication of "fictitious stories." What emerged was in many ways a cult of ignorance. Not surprisingly, today's ultra-conservative Christians are not very pleased with Gibbon. Most have yet to hear of Higgins, Massey, and Kuhn. But they need to hear them if Christianity today is to be more a part of the solution to the world's problems and less a part of the problems themselves. The still-potent aura of Christian triumphalism needs to be shattered by the hard facts of history for a new order of global religious harmony to emerge. Here is a humbling assessment by Kuhn of the real state of affairs: "The universal tradition in all Christendom has had it that the new faith sprang into existence out of conflict as the bearer of the victory of light over darkness. Alas and again alas, it was not so. It came out waving the banner of darkness as victor over the light. But it all but put out the light of the world."

This statement about putting out the "light" may seem like an exaggeration of the worst kind—until you read the full story and comprehend it. I discovered in my research that like Massey and Kuhn, a host of other scholars have documented such a horror story of book burning, forgery, and deliberate fraud over the late second, third, and fourth centuries that anyone unfamiliar with it can scarcely take it all in. "Picture the anomaly of the Christian host emerging from the struggle allegedly carrying the victorious banner of light, while with hot feet it stamped out the blackened ashes of the books of the Alexandrian library," wrote Kuhn. "Picture this bearer of the standard of new light . . . burning in 553 C.E. the books of its most truly exalted theologian, Origen, and invoking anathema [curses of excommunication] on anyone found reading them."

Charles B. Waite, in his *History of the Christian Religion to the Year 200*, tells how Eusebius, whose *Ecclesiastical History* is the principal source for the history of Christianity from the apostolic age until his own day, was a most conspicuous liar. What's almost equally bad is that Eusebius frequently made many sloppy mistakes. "No one has contributed more to Christian history, and no one is guilty of more errors," Waite charges. "The statements of this historian are made, not only carelessly and blunderingly, but in many instances in falsification of the facts of history. Not only the most unblushing falsehoods, but literary forgeries of the vilest character darken the pages of his . . . writing." I had heard not a word about any of this during my years of training for the Anglican priesthood.

Waite cites authorities who confirm this scandal by asserting that Eusebius indeed had "a peculiar faculty for diverging from the truth." He was always ready to supply by fabrication what was wanting in the historical record. In other words, this great world religion actually rests on a foundation of falsehood and forgery.[2]

Few mainline Church members today are aware of just how extremely critical Sir Edward Gibbon is in *Decline and Fall* of all these early Christian frauds, deceptions, and forgeries. Gibbon candidly asserts that Eusebius, whom he calls the "gravest" of the ecclesiastical historians, "indirectly confesses that he has related whatever might redound to the glory, and that he has suppressed all that could tend to the disgrace, of religion." This is not history—it is the kind of chronic revisionism more often associated today with repressive political systems. Anyone truly familiar with Gibbon's scrupulously careful account knows that he found everything about Christian "history" until 250 totally untrustworthy and "suspicious." He wrote, "The scanty and suspicious materials of ecclesiastical history seldom enable us to dispel the dark cloud that hangs over the first age of the church."

Gibbon testifies, for example, to the "vulgar forgery" of the deliberate insertion of two admittedly spurious passages regarding Jesus Christ into the text of the Jewish historian Josephus. He also produces reliable authorities to show that even in such an important matter of historical record as the number of Christian sectaries martyred under several Roman emperors, the Christians "outrageously falsified the figures." The gross overstatements were to increase the sympathy that martyrdom naturally arouses, he explains.

In an article on evolution, the historian Alexander Wilder says that men like Irenaeus, Epiphanius, and Eusebius (all early Christian apologists) "have transmitted to posterity a reputation for such untruth and dishonest practices that the heart sickens at the story of the crimes of that period." The duplicity, he notes, is all the worse since the whole Christian outline rests upon it. Gerald Massey bluntly charges that the "Christian scheme or schema, as it is aptly called in the New Testament, is a fraud."

Here is specific, shocking confirmation of an otherwise seemingly grotesque evaluation from one of the most respected Fathers of the Church, St. Gregory of Nazianzen (329–389), in a letter to the esteemed St. Jerome. Nicknamed "The Theologian," Gregory wrote to his friend and confidant, "Nothing can impose better on the people than verbiage; the less they understand, the more they admire. Our [Christian] Fathers and Doctors have often said, not what they thought, but what circumstance and necessity forced them to."

The whole aim of these third- and fourth-century Machiavellian machinations was to obscure and conceal all traces of the deep connection between the "new light" of Christian revelation and its Pagan past. "And when Eusebius recorded his memorable boast that he had virtually made 'all square' for the Christians, it was an ominous announcement of what he had done to keep out of sight the mythical and mystical rootage of historical Christianity," charges Massey. "The Gnostics had been muzzled and their extant evidence as far as possible masked. He and his co-conspirators had done their worst in destroying documents and effacing the telltale records of the past, to prevent the future from learning what the bygone ages could have said directly for themselves."[3] They made mute all the Pagan voices that would have "cried aloud their testimony" against the unparalleled imposture then being shaped and perfected in Rome. They in fact succeeded in reducing the first four centuries to total silence on all matters of the most vital importance for any proper understanding of the Christian religion. Massey's last sentence in this passage, however, is the most significant of all. He writes, "The mythos having been at last published as a human history, everything else was suppressed to support the fraud."

Whether such dishonest practices were always motivated by malice, ignorance, misplaced zeal, or deliberate conspiracy can be keenly debated by scholars. What cannot be gainsayed by anyone is that the history of the early centuries of the Christian religion witnessed the perpetuation of an "extensive series" of what all later historians refer to as "pious frauds." Many, if not all, of the Christian apologists of the period admit this unashamedly themselves.

This very admission of widespread basic dishonesty greatly strengthens the case that the entire transformation of earlier myth into a seemingly historical "reality" was itself a lie. This lie is perhaps mitigated somewhat if we remember what G. R. S. Mead wrote in his *Fragments of a Faith Forgotten*: "It must not be supposed that the re-writers and editors of the old traditions were forgers and falsifiers in any ordinary sense of the word. Antiquity in general *had no conception* of literary morality in its modern meaning, and all writing of a religious character was the outcome of an inner impulse." Mead goes on to add that the mythologizing of history and the historicizing of mythology were "common to the times" and, at one point or another, to all ancient peoples. If the literal truth of objective events is not really your main theme or interest, but the experience of the inner spiritual life is, it can partly explain to a modern reader what was often actually going on. (In my experience, no modern theologically trained literary critic has done more to clarify these issues than Northrop Frye.) In his *Anacalypsis*, Higgins says that it was common for priests in ancient religions to attribute to their opponents absurd opinions they never held—simply to disgrace them. He adds, "This has always been considered by priests a mere allowable ruse in religious controversy."

The German scholar John Laurence von Mosheim, in his celebrated *History of the Christian Religion*, says of the Gospel of Hermas, "At the time he wrote, (most likely) between 140 and 155 c.e., it was an established maxim with many of the Christians that it was pardonable in an advocate for religion to avail himself of fraud and deception if it were likely they might lead to attainment of any considerable good. Of the list of silly books and stories to which this erroneous notion gave rise from the second to the 15th century no one who is familiar with Christian history can be ignorant."

Gibbon's harsh judgment was that *as long as they contributed to the glory of the Church*, the legends and forgeries were lauded by the mob, welcomed by the hierarchy, and supported by the dubious "evidence" of alleged ecclesiastical history. As a specific example, Gibbon notes in his work *Vindication* that the thirty-second chapter of the *Twelfth Book of Anselm, Evangelical Preparation*, bears for its title this scandalous proposition: "How It May Be Lawful and Fitting to Use Falsehood as a Medicine and for the Benefit of Those Who Want to Be Deceived."[4]

The greatest preacher of the early Church, John Chrysostom (the golden mouth), who lived from about 347 to 407 and was both bishop of Constantinople and a famous doctor of the Church, observed in his commentary on 1 Corinthians. 9:19, "Great is the force of deceit, provided it is not excited by a treacherous intention." Few today can read this without some recoil and surprise.

Centuries later, even such a distinguished churchman as Cardinal John Henry Newman, in the *Apology for His Life*, appeared to put his stamp of approval on this kind of dishonesty for the glory of the faith. He writes, "The Greek Fathers thought that when the cause was just (*justa causa*) an untruth need not be a lie." With such logic, one can justify almost anything.

This is just a small sampling of a mass of evidence set out by Kuhn and others that the early Fathers held it as a "distinct proposition" that pious frauds were not only justifiable but even laudable. To enforce their claims to exclusive salvation, they filled all ecclesiastical literature "with the taint of the most unblushing mendacity." Since "heathenism" had to be combated, prophecies about Christ by Orpheus and the Sybils were forged, and "lying wonders" were multiplied. Heretics had to be convinced, so false interpolations and complete forgeries were made. The whole process continued until eventually the very sense and love of truth "seemed blotted out from the minds of men." As we shall see, even the texts of the evolving New Testament were tampered with.

Higgins bluntly declares that every ancient author, without exception, has come to us through the medium of Christian edi-

tors who have "either from roguery or folly, corrupted them all."
He writes, "We know that later in one batch all the Fathers of the
Church and all the Gospels were 'corrected,' that is, corrupted by
the united exertions of the Roman See, Lanfranc, who became the
Archbishop of Canterbury in 1070, and the Benedictine monks of
St. Maur."

A similar revision had occurred centuries earlier. Victor Tunu-
nensis, an African bishop of the sixth century, wrote a chronicle
ending at the year 566. It records that in the year 506 at Constantinople, by order of Emperor Anastasius, "the holy Gospels, being
written by illiterate Evangelists, were censured and corrected."
One of the Church Fathers, a Bishop Dionysius, complained that
even his own writings "had been falsified by apostles of the devil."
No wonder, he added, "that the Scriptures too were falsified by
such persons."[5] Even Origen had noted that already the differences between copies of the Gospels in his day were "considerable," partly because of the carelessness of individual scribes but
also partly because of the impious audacity of "those who added or
removed what seemed good to them in the work of 'correction.'"[6]

Obviously, you have to regard with deep suspicion any group or
movement, however noble its declarations, that proceeds to win its
"case" by silencing, excommunicating, or murdering its assumed
opponents. Yet most Christians today are totally unaware that
Church history conceals a horrendous, lengthy record of precisely these kinds of tactics by the proponents of what eventually
became "orthodox," credal belief. What's more, the kind of big-
oted fury unleashed in the third and fourth centuries against
Pagans, "heretics," and nonconformists of all types set a ruthless
precedent for centuries to come. The comparatively modern
Church historian G. R. S. Mead cites, for example, the burning of
the manuscripts of French rabbis during the notorious Inquisition
and the vandalism of fanatical crusaders, "who left smouldering
piles of Hebrew scrolls behind them in their path of blood and

fire." Kuhn argues that the official burnings of Hebrew books began at Montpellier, France, in 1233, with the commitment to the flames of all the works of Maimonides (1135–1204), the renowned Jewish philosopher and theologian. In the same year at Paris, some twelve thousand volumes of the Talmud were burned, and in 1244, eighteen thousand other various works were thrown into fire, he records.

Epiphanius (315–403), the rigidly conservative bishop of Salamiz, in an attack upon the "Sabellian heretics" (who found they couldn't follow the majority view of the Trinity), wrote that "the whole of their errors . . . they derive from . . . that which is called the Gospel of the Egyptians."[7] Kuhn remarks, "Priceless in value would be that same Gospel of the Egyptians *if Christian fury had not destroyed it.*" Another priceless book, *The True Logos* by Celsus, one of the most noted Pagan philosophers of the second century, was likewise burned. The brilliant Gnostic philosopher Basilides (*c.* 135–150) taught at Alexandria in the second quarter of the second century and claimed to know of a secret tradition transmitted by St. Peter himself. He was highly regarded even by so eminent a Christian theologian and Church Father as Clement of Alexandria (*c.* 150–215). Yet according to Eusebius, his irreplaceable, widely renowned *Interpretations upon the Gospels*— in twenty-four splendid volumes—were all burned "by order of the Church." Thirty-six priceless volumes written by Porphyry (*c.* 232–303), one of the most learned and brilliant minds of his era, were destroyed by the Church Fathers. Porphyry, a Neoplatonist philosopher who could not accept the divinity of Christ and who exposed numerous inconsistencies in the Gospels, had tried official Christianity for a brief time but found it sadly wanting. Fifteen of his burned books formed a special series called *Against the Christians*. Scholars would give a lot to have them now.

In his book *Pagan and Christian Creeds*, Edward Carpenter, an English philosopher, writes bluntly, "The Christian writers . . . not

only introduced new doctrines, legends, miracles and so forth—
most of which we can trace to antecedent Pagan sources—but they
took pains to destroy the Pagan records and so obliterate the evidence of their own dishonesty." J. M. Robertson, in *Pagan Christs*,
agrees with Carpenter and gives as an example the treatise of
Firmicus (*c.* 350), which was deliberately mutilated at a passage
accusing Christians of following the practices of the widely popular cult of Mithras. [8]

Kuhn, in his inspiring but at times difficult tome *The Lost
Light*, explains that the story of the destruction of not only books
but also cities, monasteries, and temples—indeed, of the early
pre-Christian Gaelic civilization in Britain, Ireland, Brittany, and
Gaul—is also a sorry narrative of Christian fury. A Christian mob
destroyed the Gaulish city of Bibracte in 389, and Alesia was destroyed before that. Bibracte had a sacred Druid college with forty
thousand students, and it offered courses in philosophy, literature,
grammar, law, medicine, astrology, architecture, and esoteric religion. Arles, with a seat of learning founded two thousand years
B.C.E., was sacked by Christians in 270. These acts of outrage in
all probability included the tragic destruction of scrolls and books
that might well have completely illumined our understanding of
the mysterious rock monuments at Stonehenge. Instead, it today
still lies wrapped in a miasma of questions and ignorance.

The utter destruction of the untold thousands of irreplaceable
books and scrolls of the incredible library at Alexandria by a
Christian mob stands as perhaps the greatest single testimony to
the overwhelming hatred of learning and education held by the
rank-and-file majority who flocked to the new religion. [9] They
were looking, as I have already described, for an exoteric (or literal) religion suited to the lowest common denominator.

This vast store of ancient knowledge, with its museum and the
temple of Serapis (the Serapeum), was first established by Ptolemy I, a former boyhood friend of Alexander the Great and later

one of his leading generals, between 300 and 290 B.C.E. It housed priceless classics in every field of human endeavour, from medicine to theology, including works by the great Greek playwrights Euripides, Aeschylus, and Sophocles. It had been partly burned by accident during a punitive attack on the harbour by Julius Caesar in 47 B.C.E., and it was then targeted for destruction by Emperor Aurelian in the third century. He reigned 270–275 C.E. In 400 the Serapeum, to which most of the books had by then been moved, was burned to the ground on the orders of Theophilus, the bishop of Alexandria. Then there were riots led by a mob of Christian monks in 415, in the reign of Emperor Theodosius, and with the knowledge or connivance of Bishop Cyril, who had succeeded Theophilus as the patriarch. All that remained of the library, museum, and temple was finally left in smoking ruins.

Tragically, this same mob, led by a monk named Peter the Clerk, then attacked and murdered the most brilliant woman philosopher, astronomer, and mathematician of antiquity, the widely renowned Hypatia.[10] The daughter of the distinguished Platonic philosopher Theon and the leading lecturer at the library and museum, Hypatia represented the highest standard of Pagan erudition and grace—and was a prime example of the equality of women in the supposedly inferior religion. She was taken by the mob to a church called the Caesareum, where she was stripped, stoned with roofing tiles, and torn apart; her flesh was scraped from the bones with oyster shells, and she was then burned at a spot called Cinaron. Socrates Scholasticus (380–450) records, in his *Ecclesiastical History*, that this happened during Lent, in the fourth year of Cyril's episcopate. Some authorities question whether Cyril was directly involved in Hypatia's death, but he was known to be jealous of her popularity and was a hot foe of anything other than the new, orthodox Christianity, or Christianism. Cyril ruthlessly hunted down heretics, Pagans, and Jews, looting their homes and possessions. The *Oxford Dictionary of the Christian*

Church says that if Cyril didn't order Hypatia's murder, it "was certainly the work of his supporters." This same source says that whatever one thinks of the "methods adopted" by Cyril in fighting the perceived enemies of the Church, "his distinction and ability as a [Christian] theologian are beyond dispute." (Apparently, you can be a good theologian while acting out the worst kind of violence.) Incidentally, the great library of Alexandria has recently been reopened, with great pomp and pageantry, nearly sixteen hundred years after its destruction.[11]

All of this mayhem was a further deliberate attempt to "blot out all links" between the Christian body of doctrine and any Pagan material. The top Church authorities were not content with the original, specious allegation that Satan had been behind all the amazing resemblances—they even talked of "anticipated plagiarism," charging that the devil stole the rites, doctrines, and dogmas centuries before they became accepted by the Church— so they destroyed as far as possible the entire Pagan record to obliterate the evidence of their own dishonesty. Whole treatises on Mithraism—a vigorous rival to early Christianity—were obliterated. The library of Apollo at Rome was torched and burned to the ground. Commenting on this whole shameful phenomenon, Sir Gilbert Murray (1866–1957), the great classical scholar, said, "The polemic literature of Christianity is loud and triumphant; the books of the Pagans have been destroyed!" Rome's Emperor Theodosius I, who reigned from 379 to 395, had made a number of heresies illegal, and Paganism was virtually outlawed. His successor, Theodosius II, promulgated the Theodosian Code, which specifically placed thirty-six heresies under a total ban and completely anathematized Paganism, Pagan temples, and astrologers as well. In 529, Emperor Justinian, in the name of Christianity, finally closed the doors of Plato's famous Academy in Athens, put the philosophers to flight, and forced any who failed to escape to be baptized.

The Church's initial attempts to blame obvious similarities between Christian doctrines and the Pagan originals on the work of the devil struck me at first as too outlandish to be believed. Then I read what the otherwise esteemed Christian apologist Justin Martyr had to say about it. He described the Lord's Supper as told in the Gospels and then declared that "the wicked devils have *imitated* [it] in the Mysteries of Mithras, commanding the same things to be done. For, that bread and a cup of water are placed with certain incantations in the mystic rites of one who is being initiated you can either know or learn [emphasis in original]." Tertullian (160–220), originally from North Africa and eventually the first Roman theologian to write in Latin, also said that the devil "by the mysteries of his idols" imitates even the main part of the divine [Christian] "mysteries." He writes, "He baptizes his worshippers in water and makes them believe that purifies them from their crimes! . . . Mithras sets his mark on the forehead of his soldiers; he celebrates the offering of bread; he offers an image of the resurrection . . . he limits his chief priests to a single marriage; he even has his virgins and ascetics."

The concluding proof that the later medieval and our modern views of Christianity are not identical to those held at the very outset lies in the sad truth that one of the most influential and most learned of the Fathers, a man whose scholarship was central to the early Church's self-understanding, was excommunicated as a heretic. It was done within three hundred years of his death by a Church that had so very quickly lost the light of its original inspiration. Origen, a pupil of St. Clement of Alexandria, believed in and taught reincarnation, karma, and universal salvation as Christian doctrines. He was opposed to a literalist approach to Scripture and to the reduction of the profundities of spiritual truth to the vulgarities of simplistic exotericism (i.e., literalist, common, bottom-line thinking). He paid the price. One of his most significant observations—an observation that the Church needs to hear and ponder anew today—was that a literal understanding of a "Christ crucified" was a doctrine "only fit for children" in the faith.

What I have just documented, as concisely as possible, is the calculated destruction, corruption, and accompanying cover-up of an ancient, honourable, and highly spiritual religion. It was a crime of major magnitude that the Church still refuses to acknowledge, let alone ask divine forgiveness for. The most important thing to remember at this point is that there can be no genuine hope of recovery and renewal for either an individual or an institution without an honest facing up to the past. Sweeping any of this under the carpet of ignorance, excuses, or platitudes can never lead to the healing and the future we all seek. To use again the metaphor I employed at the start, no surgery is ever pleasant, but at times surgery alone holds out the hope of a healthier future for the patient.

The hope that still gleamed brightly through for me as I first read about this ominous, dark, and shameful record was the same light that the prologue to John's Gospel says shines on forever in the darkness, "and [that] the darkness has never succeeded in putting out." This same light, according to St. Paul, has shone into each of our hearts through the indwelling spirit of the Christ. That crucial, optimistic part of our story is yet to come.

5

IT WAS ALL WRITTEN BEFORE—IN EGYPT

Part I:
Ancient Egyptian Religion

All that went into the making of the Christian historical set-up was long pre-extant as something quite other than history, was in fact expressly non-historical, in the Egyptian mythology and eschatology. For when the sun at the Easter equinox entered the sign of the fishes (Pisces) about 255 B.C.E., the Jesus who stands as the founder of Christianity was at least 10,000 years of age and had been travelling hither as the Ever Coming One through all preceding time. . . . During those 10,000 years, that same incarnation of the divine ideal in the character of Iusa [or Horus], the Coming Son, had saturated the mind of Egypt with its exalting influence. Little did men of that epoch dream that their ideal figure of man's divinity would in time be rendered historical as a man of flesh.

— ALVIN BOYD KUHN, Who Is This King of Glory?

MANY of you, if you're like me, have always been intrigued by the mystery surrounding ancient Egypt. But the average person won't have a working understanding of

Egyptian religion, mostly because the symbolism has often been so poorly explained. Even modern Egyptologists in their scientific approach have tended to miss or dismiss its inner meanings. This short account will help the reader see the background for all that follows. [1]

Like the Christians many millennia later, the ancient Egyptians believed in a God who was self-created, self-existent, immortal, invisible, eternal, omniscient, almighty, and inscrutable; he was the maker of the heavens and the earth, sky and sea, men and women, animals, birds, fish and creeping things, trees and plants, and the incorporeal beings who were the messengers (angels) that fulfilled his wish and word.

The whole of Egyptian religion and theology was based on this belief. (One hymn from the pyramids says, "Oh, thou divine Child, who didst create thyself, I am not able to describe thee.") In an amazing fashion this belief persisted from the very beginning. True, a seemingly polytheistic set of ideas and beliefs also was cultivated from time to time, but more as personifications of natural forces and powers—much as in Hinduism. The idea of monotheism, as I read it, was never lost sight of; on the contrary, it has been reproduced in the religious literature of all periods. This is particularly true of the various re-editings of that corpus known as the Egyptian Book of the Dead. The word used of other deities was not actually our word "God" but Neter, a spiritual aspect of the one God.

In his work *Egyptian Religion*, Sir Wallis Budge, the controversial keeper of Egyptian and Assyrian antiquities in the British Museum a century ago, describes the ancient Egyptian as standing easily "first among the nations in his capacity for development, and in his ability for evolving conceptions about God and the future life, which are claimed as the peculiar product of the most cultured nations of our time."

Siegfried Morenz, in his well known book, *Egyptian Religion*, says that in spite of differences "we can speak of an Egyptian religion which . . . has one fundamental point in common with Christianity: the reality of a God who is *in* man and *above* men.

In the light of this present book, what was particularly important was the Egyptian belief in an anthropomorphic divinity, or Christ ideal, whose life in this world and the world beyond was typical of the ideal life of man. The chief embodiments of this divinity were, of course, Osiris and his son, Horus. Neither, however, was ever regarded as historical.

A list of the names of all the gods of Egypt would fill pages. But all these gods were only forms, attributes, or phases of Ra, the solar god, who himself was the supreme symbol or metaphor for God. "The educated classes in Egypt never placed 'the gods' on the same high level as the one God, and they never imagined that their views on this point could be mistaken," Budge states.

Ra was undoubtedly the oldest of the gods worshipped, "and his name belongs to such a remote period that its full meaning is unknown. He was in all periods the visible emblem of God," says Budge. A hymn inscribed in the tomb of Seti I (*c.* 1370 B.C.E.) reads, "Praise be unto thee, O Ra, thou exalted power . . . thou One who bringest into being that which has been begotten, behold (thy) body is Horus." In other words, Horus, the son of Osiris and Isis, is himself an aspect of Ra. Indeed, Budge says, "We find everywhere the attempt being made to emphasize . . . that every god [Neter], whether foreign or native, was an aspect or form of Ra."

Here are some typical descriptions from the ancient text:

- God is One and alone and none other is existent with him.
- God is the One creator who has made all things.
- God is a spirit, a hidden spirit, the spirit of spirits, the divine spirit.
- God is from the beginning. . . . He was when nothing else had being. . . . He shall endure to all eternity.

- God is truth. . . . God is life. . . . He liveth life to humanity and he breathed the breath of life into his nostrils. [2]
- God is father and mother, the father of fathers. . . . He is creator of the heavens and the earth.
- He is the primeval Potter who turned men and gods into being out of his hands.

There are also passages (which remind me of those in Isaiah 40) where the Egyptian text says, "The heavens rest upon his head and the earth supports his feet." I am also reminded of the Psalms in the following: "God is merciful unto those who reverence him and he heareth him that calleth upon him. He protects the weak against the strong and hears the cry of him that is bound in fetters." And in a passage reminiscent of Genesis, chapter 1, we learn that the Egyptian believed in a time when nothing existed—neither heaven nor earth—except for the boundless primeval water, Nu, which was shrouded in thick darkness. "At length the spirit spoke the word and creation was the result."

It is clear that at one time "the Egyptian's greatest hope seems to have been that he might not only become divine, the son of God by adoption, but that Ra would actually become his father." He or she would become the actual child of God.

From the earliest period on, the Egyptian believed that Osiris was of divine origin; that he suffered betrayal, death, and mutilation at the hands of the powers of evil; and that after a great struggle with these powers, he rose again. Because he had conquered death, the righteous too might conquer death. He was so exalted that he became the equal and even, at times, the superior of Ra, the sun god. At his birth into the world, a voice was heard saying, "The lord of all the earth is born." Budge notes, "The worship of Osiris was so widespread and the belief in him as the god of resurrection so deeply ingrained . . . that he represented the ideal of a person who was both god and human and he typified to the Egyptians in all ages the being who by reason of his sufferings and death as a human could sympathize with them in their own sickness and death." I think immediately of this passage in the Epistle to the Hebrews: "For in that he himself has suffered being tempted, he is able to help them that are tempted."

Osiris was divine, yet in the myth he became a human who lived on the earth, ate, drank, and suffered a cruel death, then triumphed over death through help of the gods (Horus) and attained everlasting life. Budge adds, "But what Osiris did, they could do, and what the gods did for Osiris they must also do for them. . . . They like him would rise again and inherit life everlasting." Horus was so closely associated with Osiris that at times they are virtually interchangeable. We are reminded at this point of the Jesus of John's Gospel. He said, "I and the Father are one."

Thus to Osiris this hymn was sung: "Let thy heart be content, for thy son Horus is established upon thy throne." In another line from the same hymn, we catch what seems like a forecast of Handel's *Messiah*: "Homage to thee, O thou king of kings, lord of lords, and prince of princes."

What is most significant is that no matter how far back researchers go, there is no time "that there did not exist a belief in the resurrection, for everywhere it is assumed that Osiris rose from the dead." Eventually, Osiris "became the cause of the resurrection of the dead; and the power to bestow eternal life upon mortals was transferred from the gods to him. . . . He who was the son of Ra became the equal of his father and he took his place side by side with him in heaven." One is reminded of the statement in the Apostles' Creed "and he ascended into heaven and sitteth on the right hand of the Father." He thus became not just the equal of Ra but, in many respects, "a greater god than he."

In another phase of the same complex of stories, Horus is all that Osiris was. In one litany from the Egyptian Book of the Dead, it says, "Thy son Horus is triumphant. . . . The sovereignty over the world has been given to him, and his dominion extends to the uttermost parts of the earth." Both were "the god-human, the being who was both divine and human."

Budge writes, "In Osiris later on, the Christian Egyptians found the prototype of Christ, and in the pictures and statues of Isis suckling her son, Horus, they perceived the prototypes of the Virgin Mary and her Child." Somewhat naively, he adds that nowhere in the world did Christianity find people whose minds were so thoroughly prepared to receive its doctrines as the Egyptians!

Regarding the great goddess Isis, he argues that what appealed most to the Egyptians was her role as "divine mother." In this character, "thousands of statues represent her seated and suckling her child, Horus, whom she holds upon her knees."

In *The Secret Lore of Egypt*, Erik Hornung says "there was a smooth transition from the image of the nursing Isis, Isis lactans, to that of Maria lactans. The miraculous birth of Jesus could be viewed as analogous to that of Horus, whom Isis conceived posthumously from Osiris, and Mary was closely connected with Isis by many other shared characteristics."[3]

The Eye of Horus

For those who may be feeling that Horus, the Egyptian Christ, is some remote and obscure figure from the mists of mythical antiquity, I'd like to show that his story still touches the life of virtually every dweller on our planet, regardless of nationality, colour, or clime. The Horus myth tells that he was determined to avenge his father's murder at the hands of his wicked uncle, Seth. In the battle, Horus' eye was torn out and shredded into fragments, but Thoth, who personified divine intellect and was the inspirer of laws for the ancient Egyptians, healed and restored it fully. The complete, renewed eye thus came symbolically to denote wholeness, healing, and health. It was used eventually in the hieroglyphic script to represent unharmed wellness and unity. The symbol then became a mystical sign used by Galen, the famous Greek physician of the second century, to impress his patients, and its pictograph gradually evolved into the shape of Rx, which is today the symbol for a prescription in every country the world over, whatever the language.

Have you ever closely examined an American one-dollar bill? There, too, you will see the eternal eye of Horus/Osiris—and a pyramid as well. Several of the American Founding Fathers, most notably George Washington, belonged to the Masonic Order. The Masons base most of their inner rituals on symbols and ceremonies that originated with the building of the great pyramids of Egypt and other Egyptian esoteric lore.

The Afterlife

In Egyptian religion, the belief that the deeds done in the body would be analyzed and scrutinized by the divine powers after death belongs to the earliest period of that civilization. This belief remained essentially the same in all generations and throughout all periods. Each soul was dealt with individually, most often by being "weighed in the balance"—a concept many carvings depict. We see scales with the individual's heart in one pan and a feather (symbolic of righteousness or moral law) in the other. The goal was to gain admission to the realm of Osiris.

The place of judgment was called the Hall of Maat (or Mate, the plural). This word originally referred to a reed or stick used for measuring. The name was then transferred to two goddesses, Isis and Nephthys, who were also called the Mate because they stood by at the judgment representing straightness, integrity, what is true and right. Significantly, both Massey and Kuhn trace the New Testament name Matthew to this root concept; whether this be so or not, it is undeniable that of the four Gospels, Matthew's is

supremely the Gospel of judgment (see especially the great parable of the sheep and goats in Matthew 25). It is also the Gospel
where the new Torah, or Law of Righteousness—the Sermon on
the Mount—is found.

In the Hall of Maat, the deceased person recited a negative
confession in a series of addresses to a "jury" of forty-two gods.
He or she named each god and said, "I have not committed such-
and-such a sin." Sins included robbery, false witness, cheating on
weights and measures, fits of anger, lying, fornication, blasphemy,
and other similar offences.

As Budge observes, the religious and moral concepts underlying this confession are "exceedingly old," and they give us a clear
picture of the high values marking what the ancient Egyptian
believed to be his or her duty to both God and neighbour. After
the judgment, Horus, who has all the attributes of Osiris, leads the
deceased to his father's throne and asks that he or she be accepted
into the divine presence "and be like unto the followers of Horus
forever."

The deceased then says, "I have given bread to the hungry man
and water to the thirsty man and clothing to the naked person,
and a boat to the shipwrecked mariner." These words are haunt-
ingly echoed many centuries later in the chapter from Matthew
just cited above: "For I was hungry and you gave me meat; I was
thirsty and you gave me drink; I was a stranger and you took me
in; naked and you clothed me."

It cannot be said too often that what is most striking at all
stages and in all forms in the study of Egyptian history, literature,
and art is the frequency of the allusions to future life. Belief in one
god is ancient there, but as Budge often points out, belief in a life
to come is older yet—"at least as old as the oldest human remains
found in Egypt." The Egyptians believed that those who once have
lived in this world have "renewed" their life beyond the grave,

"and that they still live and will live until time shall be no more."
The souls of the blessed, complete with spiritual bodies, "dwelled
in heaven with the gods and they partook of all the celestial enjoy-
ments forever."

The ancient Egyptians believed that a person consists of body,
soul, and spirit. In spite of what some have taught about the meaning of mummification, the Egyptian texts are quite specific: the
soul and spirit of the righteous pass from the body and live with all
the beatified and the gods in heaven. But the physical body did
not rise again, and it was believed never to leave the tomb. In the
fifth-dynasty inscription, about 2350 B.C.E., it says, "The soul to
heaven, the body to earth."

Budge, however, stumbles over why the Egyptians continued
to mummify their dead when they didn't expect the body to rise
again. He is at a loss to explain it. He notes that in all the Egyptian
texts, there is never once an explanation given for the mummification process. Kuhn, however, believes the mummy's meaning is
quite clear. Its secret lies in the ancient Egyptian belief in incarnation, the God-become-flesh in every person, as already explained
in chapter 3. The mummy was to be a constant reminder of incarnation and its eternal significance. The body was the vehicle for
the divine spirit. Just as it was soaked in various medications and
spices to preserve it, so too each individual is "steeped" in, or
anointed with, soul energies that will endure to everlasting life.

The Egyptians believed in a bodily resurrection, but it was of
a purely spiritual kind. The body of the deceased changed into a
Sahu, or "incorruptible spiritual body" (shades of what Paul says
quite explicitly in 1 Corinthians. 15), which passed immediately
out of the tomb and went to heaven to dwell with God. According
to Budge, this belief in a spiritual body dates even to the prehis-
toric period. The ultimate destiny of the soul is to become wholly
divinized. In the Papyrus of Ani, the deceased says, "My soul is

God, my soul is eternity." Eventually, he or she becomes part of Ra himself. The Amduat, already mentioned, was part of this body of ancient sacred writings dealing with the same theme.

As early as the fifth dynasty, the dead were believed (as in the New Testament Book of Revelation) to suffer neither hunger nor thirst; they were robed in white linen and ate of the fruit of the Tree of Life. In chapter 52 of the Egyptian Book of the Dead, it is made plain that in heaven, relationships were recognized and rejoiced in. In one passage (c. 1000 B.C.E.), the deceased prays that his father and mother "be given unto me as guardians of my door, and for the ordering of my homestead." Budge points out, "He would not ask this thing if he thought there would be no prospects of knowing his parents in the next world. . . . Thus we are sure that the Egyptians believed they would meet their relatives in the next world and know and be known by them."

In spite of the highly spiritual tone of all this teaching, chapter 110 of the Book of the Dead shows that the Egyptians believed they would live a semi-material life in the age to come. Though spirits, they would sow and reap, eat and drink celestial foods, make love, and "do everything even as a person does upon earth."

Budge concludes his book with the following: "Thus we see by what means the Egyptians believed that mortal man could be raised from the dead, and attain unto life everlasting. The resurrection was the object with which every prayer was said and every ceremony performed, and every text, and every amulet, and every formula, of each and every period, was intended to enable the mortal to put on immortality and to live eternally in a transformed glorified body."

Part II:
Horus and Jesus Are the Same

So Moses was instructed in all the wisdom of the Egyptians.
—Acts 7:22

Out of Egypt have I called my son.
—Hosea 11:1

Egypt labored at the portrait of the Christ for thousands of years
before the Greeks added their finishing touches to the type (symbol)
of the ever-youthful solar god. It was Egypt that first made the
statue live with her own life and humanized her ideal of the divine.
The Christian myths were first related of Horus or Osiris, who was
the embodiment of divine goodness, wisdom, truth and purity. . . .
This was the greatest hero that ever lived in the mind of man—
not in the flesh—to influence with transforming force; the only
hero to whom the miracles were natural because he was not human.

— GERALD MASSEY, The Natural Genesis

We come now to the most critical section of our exploration—
the specific evidence that the Jesus story is not original as it comes
to us in the New Testament Gospels. Gerald Massey has traced
180 instances of close similarity or actual identity between Horus,
the Christ of old Egypt, and the Gospel Jesus. Reading first his
research and then Kuhn's elaboration of it, together with the com-
plementary work of scholars like Freke and Gandy on the period
intervening between Egypt and later Greek/Jewish develop-
ments, I was led inexorably to the conviction that Egypt was truly

the cradle of the Jesus figure of the Gospels. Here already was the story of how the divine son "left the courts of heaven," as Massey puts it, and descended to earth as the baby Horus. Born of a virgin (through whom he "became flesh," or entered into matter), he then became a substitute for humanity, went down into Hades as the quickener of the dead, their justifier and redeemer, "the first fruits" and leader of the resurrection into the life to come.

This mythical prototype has led me, and many others who have studied the discoveries that follow, to a deeper, more spiritual comprehension of what it means to say that Jesus is the Christ. It has been a deeply positive, consciousness-raising experience, one filled with fresh hope of a truly "reasonable" faith with eternal, universal roots. Rather than destroying deeply held convictions about God, the relevance of the Gospels, and immortality, this exploration has confirmed them for me and enriched them beyond measure.

In his sharp reply to the many angry critics who claimed that he was destroying belief in the deity of Jesus by pointing out} all the similarities, Massey exclaims: "It is not I that deny the divinity of Jesus the Christ; I assert it! He was and never could be any other than a divinity; that is, a character non-human and entirely mythical, who had been the divinity of various Pagan myths that had been Pagan during thousands of years before our Era."

The truth is that the miracles ascribed to Jesus on earth were already described in the pre-Christian religion. Of this, there is ample proof. Horus is, as we shall see, behind the very same miracles that are repeated in the Gospels and were first performed as mysteries in the divine netherworld, according to the myths.

Once the historicization and literalization of the central character in the Jesus myth had taken place, and what had begun as a series of dramas based on a symbolic or mythical redeemer was firmly locked into the four Gospels as actual histories of a god in disguise, the charge of the Pagan enemies and critics of Christianity was sounded. You have stolen all our beliefs and rites, they claimed, and by making them out to be concrete, historical events, you have claimed them as your own. What you have written in your Gospels has all been written before by the sages and demigods whom we revere.

In my view, this verdict of the so-called Pagans is now unassailable. When you read, for example, about the saviour figure Horus explicitly making the kind of "I am" claims that conservative Christians loudly teach are wholly unique to Jesus—especially in John's Gospel—you see what these Pagan critics were saying.

Consider this: Horus (The Ritual: The Egyptian Book of the Dead *c.* 78) said, "I am Horus in glory"; "I am the Lord of Light"; "I am the victorious one . . . I am the heir of endless time"; "I, even I, am he that knoweth the paths of heaven." These together are strongly reminiscent (or rather, one should say prophetic) of Jesus' words, "I am the light of the world," and again, "I am the way, the truth and the life."

You, the reader, must eventually decide whether this "Pagan" charge of religious plagiarism on a monumental scale was warranted. It is still too early in our exploration for a final assessment. But judging by the utter ferocity of the reaction of the Church of the third and fourth centuries, we can conclude that this accusation was regarded by the Church authorities as a highly embarrassing, even lethal, rebuke. As we have seen, they first tried to ridicule the whole suggestion of their having "borrowed" from Paganism. When that failed, they took the bizarre tack that the devil had planted these similarities in the Pagan religions centuries before, in order to deceive potential converts. When that didn't cut it either, they became extremely provoked and violent indeed. All the signs point to a guilty, fearful conscience at work.

Angry "Christian" Mob Burns Precious Books

As already mentioned, at the end of the fourth century an angry "Christian" mob, stirred up by their fanatical leaders, stormed the famous, centuries-old library at Alexandria and burned it to the ground. Many thousands of absolutely priceless scrolls or "books" containing classical works and a irreplaceable store of ancient wisdom on all subjects, from mathematics, astronomy, theology, philosophy to medicine, were utterly destroyed. The last school of "Pagan" philosophy at Athens was closed by Church decree in 529, but the process of eliminating all competitors had been begun over two centuries earlier. Unfortunately, the Church has only rarely since that time been a sympathetic friend of dissident or even challengingly new ideas. The famous case of Galileo's forced recanting of his view that the earth moves around the sun illustrates the point.

The truth is that the Gospels are indeed the old manuscripts of the dramatized rituals of the incarnation and resurrection of the sun god Osiris/Horus, rituals that were first Egyptian, later Gnostic and Hellenic, then Hebrew, and finally adopted ignorantly by the Christian movement and transferred to the arena of history. They were not considered history until, in Christian hands, their esoteric meaning had been obscured and the wisdom needed to interpret them non-historically was wanting. Kuhn says quite starkly that we can now state, with little chance of refutation, that the Gospel "life" of Jesus had already been described, in substance, at least three thousand years before he came. An Egyptian Jesus had raised an Egyptian Lazarus from the dead at an Egyptian Bethany, with an Egyptian Mary and Martha present, in the scripts of that ancient land about two thousand years B.C.E. We will look at this Lazarus incident in much more detail shortly.

In an extraordinary revelation, Massey writes that carvings depicting scenes of angels announcing a deific advent to shepherds in the fields, of the angel Gabriel telling a virgin that she would be the mother of the Christos, of the Nativity in the cave, and of three sages kneeling in adoration before the infant deity were on the innermost walls of the holy of holies in the temple of Luxor at least seventeen hundred years B.C.E. The Virgin Mother had held the divine child in her arms in zodiacs on temple ceilings for millennia before the Galilean baby saw the light.

The temple of Luxor was built by Amenhotep III, a pharaoh of the eighteenth dynasty. There is a reproduction of the scenes I have just described and their accompanying hieroglyphics in Massey's book *The Historical Jesus and the Mythical Christ* (page 34 of the Kessinger edition). The temple of Luxor is indeed where they are still to be found today. Gerald Massey describes each illustration of the Nativity in great detail. His central thesis in this and his five other learned volumes on Egyptian religion and its parallels with Christianity is that all ancient religion began as astronomical and astrological in nature. All the great truths of the divine incarnation in matter, and of the eternal, ever-coming Christ into every individual, were engraved in the starry heavens above and symbolized by the cyclic movements of the heavenly bodies, particularly the sun (which, as we have seen, was the ultimate symbol of the full effulgence, power, and majesty of God). Massey shows that traditional Christianity is in fact, in its origins, what he calls "equinoctial Christolatry" (i.e., Christ-worship based on the symbolism of the solar cycle). The canonical Gospels, he contends, "inherited the leavings of primitive or archaic man, ignorantly mistaking these for divine revelations." Unaware that the original mythos of messianic mystery, the virgin motherhood, the incarnation and birth, the life and character, the crucifixion and resurrection of the saviour Son who was the word of all ages, the alpha and omega, was already part of Egyptian religion since earliest times, the compilers of the New Testament missed the point entirely that *the whole thing was meant allegorically*.

What all of this means is that the manger of the Christian story existed in Egyptian mythology as the birthplace of the messiah, or anointed one. Though sited in the zodiac at a spot known as Aptu or Abydus, it was also referred to as a cave. Indeed, Justin Martyr uses the "type," or symbol, of both a cave and a stable as the birthplace of Jesus. At the winter solstice, the ancient Egyptians would parade a manger and a child through the streets of major cities and towns. The birth of the Persian sun god, Mithras, also was held to have occurred in a cave at the winter solstice, sometime between 3000 and 2400 B.C.E. His birthday was celebrated on December 25. Mithraism, a contemporary and keen rival of early Christianity, had a Eucharist-type meal, observed Sunday as its sacred day, had its major festival at Easter (when Mithras' resurrection was celebrated), and featured miracles, twelve disciples, and a virgin birth.

The various names for the Christ in Egyptian literature—Iusa or Iusu (Jesus), Horus, Iu-em-hept, and Atum (Hebrew Adam)—are always associated with phrases meaning "the coming one" or he who is "the comer," because he represented the cyclic rebirth of the solar deity. He is the "ever-coming child" of the Virgin Mother, the great Isis, or a host of others. In his role as messiah, Horus announces himself with the words "I am Horus who steppeth onward through eternity. . . . Eternity and everlastingness is my name." He says he is yesterday, today, and tomorrow, and the name of his boat is *Millions of Years*. Spiritually, he was the symbol for the soul in every human being. In the Gospel, we remember, Jesus says, "Before Abraham was, I am." The Epistle to the Hebrews reads, "Jesus Christ, the same yesterday, and today and forever."

The evidence that Christianity was in its beginnings firmly rooted in an Egyptian-style, equinoctial mode of thinking still abounds today. The birthday of Jesus Christ was first celebrated by the earliest Church in the spring of the year. But in 345, Pope Julius decreed that the birthday (nobody knew any precise date for it, suggesting again that the entire thing was pure myth) should thenceforth be held on December 25, three days after the "death" of the winter solstice and the same day on which the births of Mithras, Dionysus, the Sol Invictus (unconquerable sun), and several other gods were traditionally celebrated. Few Christians today realize that in the fifth century, Pope Leo the Great had to tell Church members to stop worshipping the sun. The first ostensibly Christian emperor, Constantine, who converted to the new faith at the beginning of the fourth century, was still worshipping the sun god Helios many years later, as coins and other evidence reveal.

But the birth of the Christian Saviour is not the only event tied to so-called Pagan astronomical/astrological roots; the greatest Church festival of all, Easter Day, the moment of Christly Resurrection, is also similarly linked. Easter occurs on different dates each year because, like the Jewish Passover, it is based upon the vernal equinox, that dramatic moment when the hours of daylight and the hours of darkness at last draw parallel and then the light finally and triumphantly wins out. Thus Easter is always fixed as the first Sunday after the first full moon following the spring equinox. It's a cosmic, solar, and lunar event as deeply rooted in religious traditions originating from sun-god worship as one could conceivably imagine. Traditional Christianity, I have come to realize, has forfeited a great deal of its vital historical connection with the natural world and the cosmos as a whole by a deliberate downplaying of the significance of this solar–lunar connection.

Massey found numerous parallels between the stories of the Egyptian sun deities, Osiris, Horus, and Ra (all interchangeable), and that of the biblical Jesus. The "three kings," or magi, of the biblical account, for example, echo a triad of solar deities who symbolized the ancients' thinking about the three regions, earth, heaven, and a netherworld (and were later symbolized by the three stars of the "belt" in the constellation Orion). Among the other similarities he uncovered were the following:

- Like the "star in the east" of the Gospels, Sirius, the morning star in Egypt, heralded the birth of Horus.
- Horus was baptized in the River Eridanus (Jordan) by a god figure named Anup the Baptizer (John the Baptist), who was later decapitated.
- Like Jesus, Horus had no history between the ages of twelve and thirty.
- Horus walked on water, cast out demons, and healed the sick.
- Horus was transfigured on a mountain; Jesus took Peter, James, and John into "a high mountain" and was transfigured before them.[4]
- Horus delivered a "Sermon on the Mount," and his followers faithfully recounted the "Sayings of Iusa" (or Jesus).
- Horus was crucified between two thieves, buried in a tomb, and resurrected. His personal epithet was Iusa (or Iusu), the "ever-becoming son" of Ptah, or the Father.
- Horus was the good shepherd, the lamb of God, the bread of life, the son of man, the Word, and the fisher; so was Jesus.
- Horus was not just the path to heaven but the way by which the dead travel out of the sepulchre. He was the god whose name was written as the "road to salvation"; he was thus "the Way, the Truth and the Life." *Therefore, the key verse of conservative orthodoxy today was sourced in Pagan roots.*
- The Creed says that Jesus descended into hell, or (better) Hades, but so too did Horus before him. Both went to preach to the souls in prison. Both were "dead and buried," but only figuratively. Again, this is simply a metaphorical description of the descent of the divine into matter—into human beings, in fact. As Kuhn sharply observes, "It has absolutely nothing whatever to do with a literal hillside grave." The death of the god is his self-giving to mortals. That's why every ancient religion had at its heart a dying or dismembered/disfigured deity. One of humanity's first mythical saviour figures, Prometheus, was pinned by the wrists and ankles to a rock in the Caucasus

Mountains where his liver was torn out by a vulture.

- Jesus came in the name of the Lord. He was called Kyrios, or Lord. Horus too was "the Lord" by name.
- Like Jesus, Horus was supposed to reign for one thousand years (i.e., to usher in a millennium).
- Horus came to seek and to save what was lost. We are reminded of the Gospel parables of the lost sheep, the lost coin, and the "lost" son.
- In the Gospels, it is the women who announce the Resurrection. "The goddesses and the women proclaim me when they see me," shouts Horus as he rises from the tomb, "on the horizon of the resurrection."

Altogether, Massey discovered nearly two hundred instances of immediate correspondence between the mythical Egyptian material and the allegedly historical Christian writings about Jesus.[5] Horus indeed was the archetypal Pagan Christ.

Our close examination of the astonishing parallels between the Egyptian Christ figure Horus and the Jesus of the canonical Gospels declares in a dramatic and, to me, irrefutable manner our major premise—that Christianity in its final orthodoxy was simply a reissuing of an ancient wisdom in a literalized and highly exclusivist form. The result was a kind of plagiarism, but in a badly warped and weakened edition. What was timeless and universally applicable in the Horus myth eventually became tragically locked into a single person, time, and place; what had been esoteric and symbolic was made exoteric and historical. Instead of an ideal and divine principle—the Christ—working in every heart, all of God's evolutionary thrust for humanity was locked up exclusively in one personality—the "personal Jesus." Myth had been misread as biography. Countless millions ever since have had to look beyond, to an external, morally unreachable Saviour, instead of being empowered by the saving grace of the ever-coming Christ spirit within. This is what we need so badly to rediscover and apply. We can find that light as we move beyond the literal text of the New Testament and see the metaphorical and allegorical truth beneath it all.

The Spiritual Importance of the Number Twelve

In Luke's Gospel, we read how Jesus' parents took him to the temple for what today is called his bar mitzvah—his entry into adult responsibility to the Torah. But Horus and all the other Christ figures also came of age in a special rite at twelve. (Today, bar mitzvahs occur at the age of 13 for boys, and the equivalent for girls, the bat mitzvah, at age 12.)

Significantly, both Horus and Jesus were accompanied by twelve disciples, as were Mithras and Dionysus. After reading Massey and Kuhn, I discovered that this has a deeper spiritual meaning than appears at first sight. A vast flood of light is let in upon Gospel interpretation if it is understood that the twelve disciples of Jesus symbolized the twelve powers of spiritual light energy to be unfolded by man in twelve labours (or stages) of growth, all imaged by the twelve signs of the zodiac. Kuhn says that from the first it should have been seen, "without cavil," that the twelve apostles were so much more than agents used by a historical personage to found an earthly ecclesiasticism. For when the Gospel Jesus told them they would sit with him on the twelve celestial thrones and judge the twelve tribes of Israel, they moved at once from the realm of personal history into that of "cosmic hierarchism."

Egypt gave the twelve followers a more definitive name and function. The twelve were astronomical powers, rulers or "saviours of the treasure of light." Because light was the crowning product of all cosmic operation, the saviours of it were the culminating depositories of dynamic agency. They became the twelve great spirit-children of Ra's unimaginable might. With Horus, they became the twelve who accompanied the god to earth as sowers of the seed and later reapers of the divine harvest. In John, Jesus uses the same sowing and reaping metaphors to describe the mission of his twelve disciples. He says, "I tell you, look around you and see how the fields are ripe for harvesting." Without exposing you to a further mass of detail, let me say simply that the evidence seems incontestable that the twelve disciples represent twelve deific powers, and not men.

In the ancient gnosis, as the soul advances through the scale of evolution, he or she passes through twelve grades of being, adding to his or her estate the quality gained at each level, until his or her absorption of the essence of all nature is complete. These twelve qualities of perfected spiritual understanding are what are represented by the twelve astrological signs of the zodiac. In the ancient wisdom, the sun's journey through each sign, acquiring the special powers of each, symbolized the soul's round of the elements and the acquisition of the twelve intelligences. It all had as its basis the passage through the heavens of the solar god, who symbolized the unseen divinity behind and through all things. We are made up of body, mind, and spirit. For each of these there are four elements: fire, air, earth, and water. Combined in the one grand synthesis that constitutes a human being, these twelve aspects create the potential for Christ consciousness.

In the old religions of Egypt, Chaldea, and Greece, the twelve rays of genius in humans were variously represented by the Twelve Saviours of the Treasure of Light, the Twelve Reapers of the Golden Grain, the Twelve Harvesters in the Fields of Amenta, the Twelve Builders, the Twelve Carpenters, the Twelve Potters, the Twelve Weavers of the Pattern, the Twelve Fishermen, the Twelve Rowers of the Boat of Ra (with Horus at the prow), the Twelve Sailors in the Ship of Ra, the Sun. The Twelve Labours of Hercules, the Twelve Sons of Jacob, the Twelve Tribes of Israel, the Twelve Apostles, and the twelve knights of King Arthur's table all have the same zodiacal, evolutionary, and theological derivation.

And then there are the twelve months of the year. It was no accident that there were twelve gods with Odin in Norse mythology. The whole of the Bible, as anyone familiar with it knows, is permeated by the number twelve and multiples thereof.[6] Twelve times twelve times one thousand gives the figure of 144,000, the symbol for all the "elect" of God in the Book of Revelation.

Fish / Scarab / Beetle

The Egyptian Christ, manifested in the sign of Pisces, was fore-ordained to be Ichthys (the Greek word for "fish"), the fisherman, and to be accompanied by fishermen followers. Doctrinally, he was the "fisher of men." Horus, the best-known Egyptian Christ figure, was associated from time immemorial with the fish, and Massey's *Natural Genesis* features a reproduction of an Egyptian engraving showing Horus holding a fish above his head. Several of the early Christian Fathers refer to Christ also as Ichthys, or "that great fish," and the mitre worn by succeeding popes "in the shoes of the fisherman" is shaped exactly like a fish's mouth. It's well known that the Greek word *ichthys* forms an acrostic meaning "Jesus Christ the Son of God (Our) Saviour." Having been in Rome numerous times during my dozen years covering religion around the world for the *Toronto Star*, I have seen first-hand how frequently the outline of a fish occurs in catacombs as a Christian symbol. It also doubled as a sign of the Eucharist. Prosper Africanus, an early Christian theologian, calls Christ "that great fish who fed from himself the disciples on the shore and offered himself as a fish to the whole world." Commenting on this same passage from the end of John's Gospel, St. Augustine says that the broiled fish in the story "is Christ." The art found in ancient Egyptian tombs commonly shows fish, fishermen, nets, and fish traps of varying kinds. All have the same spiritual meaning.

Much more important, however, is the fact that the Egyptian

texts bear witness to an "only begotten god" (meaning begotten of one parent only), whose symbol was the beetle because in ancient science this creature was thought to be "self-produced, being unconceived by a female." Massey says, "The only begotten god is a well-known type [symbol], then, of divinity worshipped in Egypt. In each cult the Messiah-son and manifestor was the only-begotten god. This, according to the Egyptian text, is the Christ, the Word, the manifestor in John's Gospel." In fact, in one early version of the Greek text of the New Testament's Gospel of John, the phrase "the only begotten son of God" actually reads "the only begotten god"! Its very unorthodoxy makes it likely that it is the preferred, original reading.

The truth thus came forcefully home to me that this Egyptian Christ is indeed the express image of the Christ of John's Gospel, who begins in the first chapter without father or mother and is the Word of the beginning, the opener and architect, the light of the world, the self-originated and only-begotten God. I found that the very phraseology of John often echoed the Egyptian texts, which tell of he who was "the Beginning of becoming, from the first, who made all things but was not made." Some of the Fathers of the Church knew that the beetle was a symbol of Christ. Augustine, indeed, writes, "My own good beetle, not so much because he is only begotten (God), not because he, the author of himself, has taken on the form of mortals, but because he has rolled himself in our filth and chooses to be born from this filth itself"—like the dung beetle.

When the god Osiris came to earth as a saviour, he came as his own son, the child Horus. He was born "like or as a Word." The Egyptian texts say that he came to earth as a substitute. Indeed, an ancient Egyptian festival celebrating the birth of Horus was called "The Day of the Child in His Cradle."

When Horus comes to earth in the Egyptian story, he is supported or given bread by Seb, who is the god of earth, "the father on earth." He is thus the divine father on earth of the messiah-son, who manifests in time. Just as Joseph, the adoptive father of Jesus, provides shelter and food for his son, so Seb (Jo-Seph) cares for Horus. The consort of Seb is the mother of heaven, named Nu; Meri (Mary) is another Egyptian name for heaven, as well as the name for the mother of the messiah. Massey concludes, "Thus Seb and Meri for earth and heaven would afford the two mythic originals for Joseph and Mary as parents of the divine child." There are seven different Marys in the four Gospels. They correspond with uncanny fidelity to seven Marys, or Hathors, in the Egyptian stories.

Faced with such a body of facts, I had absolutely no question left. The evidence from Egypt seemed clearly beyond rebuttal. I believe we can say with total assurance that the Jesus who was administered to by seven women; betrayed by Judas; conqueror of the grave; the resurrection and the life; before Herod; in Hades and in his reappearance to the women and the seven fishermen; crucified on either the fourteenth or the fifteenth of the spring month, Nissan, and also "spiritually" crucified in "Egypt," as it is written in Revelation (11:8); as judge of the dead, with sheep on his right hand and goats on his left—is, as Kuhn has argued, "Egyptian from first to last, in every phase, from the beginning to the end." There is an undeniable irony and a profound, deep, undeniable truth in Hosea's prophetic saying "Out of Egypt have I called my Son." A deep irony indeed.

Once again it is absolutely critical to stress that my argument that the Christ of the Gospels had an antecedent in Egypt (and in many other places and cultures as well) is not part of any attempt to debunk orthodox Christianity. Nothing is further from my mind. My aim, instead, is to reveal the truly spiritual nature of the Christos archetype in all of human history and, ultimately, to explain what this will mean to us.

6

CONVINCING
THE SCEPTICS

Considered as those of a human being, the character and teachings
of the Christ in the Gospels are composed of contradictions and
opposites impossible to harmonize. In fact, the many hundreds of sects
and denominations of Christians who are today engaged in formulating
the theology of their assumed founder and in denying each other's inter-
pretation, do but inevitably represent the organic disunity from the
beginning, and reflect the fragmentary nature of the origins.

The general assumption concerning the gospels is that the historic
element was the kernel of the whole, and that fables accreted around
it; whereas the myths, being pre-extant, prove that the core of the
material was mythical, and it then follows that the "history" is
incremental. . . . The worst foes of the truth have ever been the
rationalizers of the mythos. They have assumed the existence of a
personal founder of Christianity as the fundamental fact. They
have done their best to humanize . . . the mythos by discharging the
supernatural and miraculous . . . in order that it might be accepted.
Thus, they have lost the battle by fighting it on the wrong ground.

— GERALD MASSEY, The Historical Jesus and the Mythical Christ

SINCE MOST, IF NOT ALL, of this material will be new and
even unimaginable to many readers, and since it is so critical to the major arguments I present throughout, I want to

expose any remaining sceptics to more relevant evidence. Remember, our ultimate goal is a renewed spirituality focused upon
and fuelled by the "Christ in you, the hope of glory," to quote St.
Paul. As he says, we can do all things through this Christ consciousness, which "strengthens us within." Our bodies are indeed the temples of God, whose Holy Spirit dwells in us always,
no matter how we feel on any given day. [1]

As we continue to examine the similarities between the words
and miracles of Horus and those of the Gospel Jesus, we will discover fresh, unsuspected insights and meanings in Bible texts that
once seemed worn, beyond belief, nonsensical, or simply inexplicable. Comparing the two representative Christs helps us move
out of old, and now irrelevant, paradigms toward the universality
of the much deeper message behind it all.

The Nativity and Early Years

Jesus' Nativity will always be associated with the ox and the ass
because of the stable and the manger. But these two animals were
also with the Egyptian Iusa, ages upon ages before. What this
earthy feature of the birth story is really about, in the true, esoteric
sense, is the coming of the divine into the basic animal nature to
create that wholly new reality—the human being (part animal,
part divine). Significantly, both these animals are in a way asex-
ual, or "crossovers," which suggests that ultimately the Christ in
us is a melding of the male and female principles. Indeed, the
Christ of Revelation has the breasts of a woman! Spirit (male)
and matter (female), when brought together, ultimately become
androgynous. This is the real meaning behind these words in Luke
20:34: "Those who belong to this age marry and are given in marriage; but those who are considered worthy of a place in that age
and in the resurrection from the dead neither marry nor are given

in marriage. Indeed they cannot die anymore, because they are like angels . . . being children of the resurrection."[2]

Notice that Horus, who says, as he presents himself to earth, "I am the baby born as the connecting link between earth and heaven," is paralleled completely by the infant Jesus, who came to bring "glory to God in the highest and on earth peace to all those of good will."

Immediately after the story of the birth of Jesus in Matthew, there is the threat from Herod that I alluded to in an earlier chapter. In the story of Horus, the life of the infant god is immediately threatened by an evil being called, significantly, Herut. Herut is "the serpent of many myths," Kuhn contends. The best other example is a serpent that tries to kill the infant Hercules, another saviour figure who died and went to heaven.

In the New Testament the angel of the Lord says to Joseph, "Arise and take the young child and his mother and flee into Egypt." At the birth of Horus, the god That says to the mother, "Come, thou goddess Isis, hide thyself with thy child." She is told to take him to a secluded spot in the marshes of Lower Egypt, called Kheb (or Khebt). Interestingly, the heroic Sumerian king, Sargon, had to be hidden, like Moses, in a reed basket by a river also to avoid being killed.

Jesus, all four Gospels declare, was baptized in the River Jordan by his cousin John, who was dubbed "the baptizer." John was later beheaded by the tetrarch Herod Antipas (4 B.C.E.–39 C.E.)— after Salome's famous dance—at the whim of his wife, Herodias, and his death signalled the beginning of Jesus' public ministry. Horus, as we have seen, was baptized in the River Eridanus (or Arutana) by the Egyptian John the Baptist, Anup, who was also later beheaded. Kuhn says that Horus in his baptism was "transformed from the word made flesh to the word made truth"—a change from the natural to the wholly spiritual.

Something I had never realized before was that each Christ figure of antiquity had his own special forerunner. In the case of Horus, Anup makes the path ready for his advent (although Horus preceded Anup in stature and authority). Anup, we are told, lived in the dark and empty reaches of Amenta—the Egyptian term for "earth"—until the day of his manifestation. In the Gospels, John the Baptist is said to have dwelt in the wilderness until the time of his "showing forth," or public appearance, in Israel. [3] Anup (also known as Anubis) is "the preparer of the way of the other world"; he is the power making straight the paths to the upper realms of heaven. This instantly calls to mind Matthew's description of John the Baptist (Matthew 3:3): "For this was he that was spoken of by Esaias [Isaiah], saying, The voice of one crying in the wilderness, 'Prepare ye the way of the Lord, make his paths straight.'"

The minor deity Anup, though distinguished, was only a star god—that is, a precursor to the much greater solar light, the sun itself. Similarly, John, though enormously important in the New Testament, was far surpassed by those enlightened by Jesus, according to the Gospels. The "least" in the kingdom of heaven, it says, is greater than he. In other words, to be in the spiritual realm, to be an incarnated soul, is to be greater than the one who symbolizes the natural animal-man. The baptism of Jesus is in reality a symbol, or glyph, of the incarnating process that all of us take part in. The water he descends into denotes matter (our bodies are about two-thirds water, and water is the symbol for matter in the ancient theology). The bird "like a dove" (traced in Egyptian lore to Tef, the breathing force) stands in general for the divine energy of the soul. In the ancient Egyptian planisphere, or chart of the heavens, the star called Phact, which was the dove, was in the position to announce the coming of each new solar year, and hence of the sun god Horus. Horus, according to the myth, was given the hawk as his distinctive symbol, and he is often depicted as a hawk-headed figure. But Kuhn points out that he also rose from his baptism as the dove, for he exclaims, "I am the Dove; I am the Dove!" Seven doves, representing the sevenfold nature of all deific emanations, are frequently found described in words or pictures in arcane or esoteric religions. In Didron's *Book of Iconography*, for example, the child Jesus is depicted in the Virgin's arms, surrounded by seven doves that symbolized the seven powers he was to spiritualize.[4]

Jesus and Horus received their baptisms at the age of thirty. My research revealed that there is a gap in the life history of all the ancient sun gods between twelve and thirty. Both numbers are symbolic; they stand for the completion and perfection of cycles, the end of an age, or stages of transition and transformation. "At 30, each emerges as the Adult God, or Homme Fait," Kuhn writes.

According to Luke's unique account, Jesus is twelve when he stays behind at the temple in Jerusalem and engages the scribes in questions and discussion. This was universally acknowledged by the ancients to be the age at which each individual becomes aware of his or her soul within. It is the dawning of maturity, when the falsetto voice of innocent youth dramatically changes to the authentic voice of adult responsibility, and children are endowed with responsible knowledge of good and evil. Horus was twelve when he had his eye—which had been stolen by Sut (who corresponds to Satan)—restored to him, a symbol of this basic rite of passage and of the dawning of the full intellectual faculty. These are the kinds of insights that excited and stimulated me most in this whole exploration.

Ministry, Teachings, and Miracles

In the Egyptian myth and symbolism, "the kingly force of life"— that is, the sun and the spiritual reality it stood for in each human being—was thought to be caught up in an ongoing struggle against elements seeking to limit or destroy its potency. (This is why the

December solstice was so crucial in all ancient religions.) Thus the Christos, Horus, who represented the spiritual light, is depicted as constantly engaged in a "great spiritual warfare" with various mythical creatures, including the seven-headed dragon of darkness called Sut (and a variety of other names). The Gospels similarly depict Jesus, the agent of light against darkness, involved in a running battle with his adversary, Satan.

The story of the Temptation of Jesus, as told in the Synoptic Gospels, vividly symbolizes this and again can be found in the Egyptian Ritual in an earlier form. Horus is seized in the desert of Amenta (earth) and taken up a high mountain, called Hetep, by his evil twin and arch-rival, Sut, for spiritual testing. Sut represents dark opposition to Horus, the "good light" at every step. But like Satan, he eventually is defeated. Jesus' cry about seeing Satan "fall like lightning" was preceded millennia before by Horus when, in ultimate victory over Sut, he says to Osiris, his father, "I have brought thee the associates of Sut in chains."

Of the three Gospel accounts of the Temptation, Luke's is particularly interesting, in that he alone concludes, "When the devil had finished every test, he departed from him until an opportune time." The contest, in other words, was meant to be understood as continuous. Once understood in its symbolic sense, it speaks at a much deeper, cosmic level of the yin and yang of existence, the struggle to balance the polarities of life—light and dark, up and down, centrifugal and centripetal forces, hot and cold—and so on. Ancient religion was deeply connected to the realities of the universe at all levels. But the struggle of Jesus and Satan (or Sut and Horus, allegorically understood) is really about our own daily struggle here and now. The Christ within us gives us the victory. As Paul says, "I can do all things through the Christ who strengthens me within."

Kuhn draws on his deep understanding of esoteric meanings and ancient languages to create a fascinating take on the whole concept of Armageddon, the supposed final conflict between the forces of Christ and Satan, or the Antichrist, at the end of all things. He argues that the term "Armageddon" has nothing to do with some final armed battle in the Middle East (or anywhere else) at some supposed "end of the world." He contends that it really stands for the ongoing struggle between essential evolutionary forces, symbolized by Christ and Satan, and that at its most basic level, it is "nothing but the whole battle of life" each of us is now waging day by day. Hell, for example, is right here, right now. The so-called Day of Judgment is an ongoing, present process in every life.

In the Egyptian Ritual, when the associates of Sut came and seized Horus, they suddenly saw a double crown on his forehead and fell on their faces. Gospel readers know that when Judas and his associates came to the Garden of Gethsemane to apprehend Jesus, he asked them (in John's version) whom they were looking for. When they said Jesus of Nazareth, he said, "I am he" (or, in the plain Greek, "I am"). Once he said that, they "stepped back and fell to the ground." Scene for scene, these two stories are the same.

According to all four Gospels, Jesus was a healer and an exorcist. Even the scholars of the controversial California-based Jesus Seminar (about which I will say more in another chapter) admit that much. As Matthew, chapter 15, describes it, "Great crowds came to him, bringing with them the lame, the maimed, the blind, the mute, and many others. They put them at his feet and he cured them." But I was surprised to discover that Horus had, much earlier, opened dumb mouths and performed other Jesus-like healings. The act of giving a voice to those unable to speak was of particular significance in the Egyptian record. The inner meaning was that Horus' spiritual influence caused their lives to express the words of power and truth. This is the allegorical essence behind Jesus' healings too. The Christ within gives each of us the power to find and express "our own true voice."

Horus restores sight to the blind, casts out demons, and makes the deaf hear. He is designated as "he who dissipates the darkness." He is hailed as a prince in the City of the Blind, as one who "comes to shine into their sepulchers and to restore spiritual sight to the blind on earth." He is also described as "open[ing] the eyes of the prisoners in their cells." This was echoed by Jesus in his first sermon in the synagogue at Nazareth, when he says, "He has sent me to proclaim release to the captives and recovery of sight to the blind."

Confronted by these similarities, I was forced to face the question that necessarily faces the reader now: What becomes of the Gospel healings in the light of all this antecedent material in the Egyptian scripts? There can be but one reply that is sincere: the New Testament miracles are virtually identical reproductions of ancient religious dramatizations, and not actual or historical occurrences. All of the Gospel miracles of Jesus are historically impossible, Massey says, because "they were already pre-existent as mythical representations . . . and depicted in the drama of the Mysteries." His point is that the miracles ascribed to Jesus in the Gospels had all previously been assigned to the pre-Christian Iusa/Horus, the divine healer who was quite obviously non-historical. Horus/Iusa—or Jesus—is the performer of all the miracles later repeated in the New Testament. "The miraculous of the gospels was the mythical of the Egyptian religion and subsequent Mysteries—all provably pre-extant," Massey concludes. But it's important to stress that they were all pointing to a living, healing God behind, beneath, and within all things. The incarnate God heals those who call upon his inner power. This is as true today as it was in ancient Egypt or in Palestine two thousand years ago.

That is the really significant aspect to keep in mind as we consider the relevance of all this to our life and faith today. The healings remain tremendously important. Spiritually, the message is that the Christ (or divinity) within each of us can be called upon to aid us in all our infirmities. In the Gospels, the disciples were fearful of an approaching storm, but Jesus was asleep in the stern of their boat; like them, we need to awaken the Christ within and draw upon that resource. The healings of the Gospels are not cancelled out. Far from it. They are seen in their true light, as illustrations of God's healing power yesterday, today, and always.

The God of Wine

Few stories in the Gospels are more familiar than what John calls the first "sign," or miracle, of Jesus: the changing of water into wine at a wedding in Cana of Galilee. "You have kept the good wine until now," says the surprised steward to the bridegroom as he tastes the results.

Traditional commentators have made much of the fact that the water used, according to John's account, had been set aside for "Jewish rites of purification" of the old era and had been transformed into an utterly new, much more potent entity. Not only is the evangelist saying here that what Jesus, as the Christ, offers is better than the traditional way, but he's also saying that Christ actually rivals and surpasses Bacchus (the Greek counterpart is Dionysus), the reigning god of wine in the surrounding Pagan culture. The Christ comes to intoxicate humanity with the divine wine or "more abundant life."[5]

Here again, the Egyptian Horus, we find, was the much earlier prototype of Bacchus. Like both Bacchus and Jesus, Horus was the vine, and his "season" was celebrated at the Egyptian Uaka festival "with prodigious rejoicing and a deluge of drink." The divine "mania," said by Plato to be even better than laborious reason, was the heady transport that resulted from imbibing the spiritual liquor of life. The Bacchic feast of intoxication was a symbol of the legitimate and blessed ecstasy of the soul on partaking of the heavenly wine, the gift of the divine presence within.

It was a sign of the gift of reason and spirit and the symbol of "life abundant."

As always, though rooted in natural symbols, what is being really dealt with, then, is profoundly spiritual in essence, often on several levels at once. The fermented potency of wine was, at its deepest spiritual level, a symbol of the presence of the incarnated God within the spiritually aware person—a direct contrast to the natural animal-human. "The juice of the grape was the 'blood' or essential energy of Horus or Osiris in the Egyptian Eucharist just as in the case of Jesus at the Last Supper," notes Kuhn. What is so important here, especially since these elements are so often lacking in today's Christianity, are the themes of transformation and inner power.

In other words, the wine offered by the "gods" for humanity's uplift is their own celestial nature and energy. The transformation of water into wine represented the power of the divine to mature the inert elements of sense and feeling in every one of us into spiritual character. Horus was given the title "the Jocund" when he "rose up full of Wine," and he was symbolized by the constellation Orion, with the goblet stars for his cup. Orion, as we have seen, constellated the figure of the heavenly Christ.

Writing on this same series of motifs, Godfrey Higgins observes that in places in the Egyptian scripts, Osiris himself was characterized as the vine and Horus as the *Unbu*, or branch. He comments, "The typical tree of life in the Greek [dependent on the Egyptian] planisphere is the grapevine." The grapes originated in or near the sign of Virgo, the mythical mother of the child who was to "rise up out of death to bring salvation to humans under the sign of the vine." In John, chapter 15, in a lengthy and detailed dissertation, Jesus says that he is "the true vine," and that his followers are the "branches," destined to bear much fruit. Horus played this symbolic role in Egypt long before. The imagery changes—the walls of old Egyptian tombs show vintners pressing new wine, and wine-making is everywhere a constant metaphor of spiritual pro-cesses—and yet the same reality, the Christ principle, is central.

The soul, or the portion of god within, causes the divine fer-ment in the body of life. It's developed there, as on the vine, by the sun of man's spiritual self. Astronomically, the vine and the mixing bowl were constellated as celestial symbols, the latter as the star cluster called the Crater (Latin for "bowl"), the sacra-mental cup, or grail. Anyone who has both studied John's Gospel for years and taught it to seminary students, as I have, has to be deeply impressed by the Egyptian wisdom and symbolism. Clearly, it shows that John is a reworking or copy of what came ages before.

Significantly, both Massey and Kuhn—and other authorities—testify that the surface of the coffin lid of the mummified Osiris (every deceased person was referred to as the Osiris) constituted the table for the Egyptian cult's Last Supper or Eucharist. It was the board on which the mortuary meals were served. The coffin bore the hieroglyphic equivalent for KRST. Massey connects KRST with the Greek word *Christos*, messiah, or Christ.[6] He says, "Say what you will or believe what you may, there is no other origin for Christ the anointed than 'Horus the Karast' or 'anointed son of God the Father.' . . . Finally, then, the mystery of the mummy is the mystery of Christ." The mystery of Christ is the mystery of you and me. The Egyptians, and all those who closely followed them later, believed that each of us is intended ulti-mately to be a Christ, anointed for an eternal destiny with God. Significantly, the authors of *The Jesus Mysteries* have dedicated their book to "the Christ in each of us." St. Paul quite boldly speaks of "putting on Christ," and of each of us having "the mind of the Christ." That was a kind of hopeful Christian understanding that was beginning to make more and more sense to me. I recalled how, in writing to the Galatians, Paul spoke of suffering the pangs of childbirth "until the Christ is formed within you."

Of Fishing, Fishermen, and Nets

In *The Lost Light*, and frequently in his other lectures and writings, Kuhn examines the numerous references in the ancient Egyptian material to fish, fishing, water, and all the images pertaining to them. We have already seen something of the power of the fish as a Christos symbol throughout ancient religion. But the symbolism changes and varies in a hundred different settings, always following the principle that "nature is meaningless nowhere," and that "every cosmic process had its reflection in nature, again in the spiritual life of man, and lastly (often) in the physiology of the body." Jesus, Horus, and many other "gods" came as fish. In India there is the fish-avatar Vishnu, and it was also a title for Bacchus and Marduk. Astrologically speaking, and this was crucial for ancient Christology, the Christos was represented as Pisces from roughly 255 B.C.E. to 1900. Aries, the ram or lamb, was the dominant Christ symbol in ancient religion for about twenty-four hundred years before that, and Taurus, the bull, preceded Aries. A complete "age," or cycle—where the sun moved through all twelve signs of the Zodiac—occurred approximately every twenty-six thousand years. That means the Christos type today, and for the rest of this millennium, would be Aquarius. In a Christly pattern, this is indeed the very beginning of the Age of Aquarius, the water-bearer. Notice that in the Aquarius' astrological pictographs, there are streams of water flowing from the jar—the stream of matter and of spirit.

The fish represented the immortal soul as "a breather in the water of worldly existence." Just as a fish almost miraculously can live and breathe wholly surrounded by water, the ancients taught, so too the soul can be entombed by flesh or matter and still survive. Escape from a purely natural life to a spiritual one was described in the Egyptian Ritual as "coming forth from the net" or coming forth from the Catcher of Fish. In fact, the ancients always portrayed true being as an escape from the waters of life (i.e., from matter)—hence the widespread use of the fisherman's net as an emblem of salvation.

A passage called "The Secret of Horus in An" is the mythic tale of how his mother, Isis, caught him in the water. The goddess Neith, on her behalf, fished him out with a net. This was a cosmic symbol of life first coming out of the water as part of the evolutionary process. Like the infant Moses (a sun god, in Kuhn's view), Sargon, and even ancient New Zealand gods such as Maui, Horus was drawn out of the water at birth. The meaning is profound.[7] Matter, symbolled by water, gives birth to spirit, or the Christ.

In Mark's Gospel, Jesus called four fishermen to follow him. In the Egyptian Ritual, the four fishers pulled the dragnet through the waters to capture Horus. They are described more fully as "fishers for the great prince who sits at the east of the sky," More proof that Horus was thought of as the rising sun and the Christos.

Walking on the Water

In the Egyptian material, Horus emerges from the rage of a nocturnal storm on the waters into the calm of a bright daybreak. Like Tammuz and many other mythical sun gods, he was said to "still the sea by his power." In one place, Osiris is said to keep souls from being drowned in the symbolic waters of incarnation. As already cited, Jesus, in one Gospel, sleeps in the stern of a boat as a great storm overtakes him and his disciples and threatens to sink the ship. He rebukes the waves with a "Peace, be still" command. On another occasion, the disciples are in a boat being buffeted by contrary winds, and Jesus comes toward them "walking on the sea."[8] Again the sea (ever the symbol of the unruly powers of matter) was calmed. Rationalists have attempted to explain this incident away by saying that Jesus must have been walking on a sandbar or along the shore itself, and in the uncertain mists of

morning—it was about the "fourth watch" (i.e., just at dawn)—
the disciples made an innocent and forgivable mistake. But this
line of approach rests on just as literalist an understanding of the
passage as the fundamentalist's assumption that Jesus was indeed
contradicting the basic laws of nature.

The reference to the "fourth watch" is deeply significant in the
ancient wisdom as well. From an evolutionary point of view, we
humans move from the mineral stage to the vegetative stage to the
animal stage; accordingly, it is in the middle of the fourth phase, of
animal-human development—the "fourth watch"—that incarnation, or the advent of divine, self-reflective consciousness, takes
place. Three and a half was a terribly important number in the
ancient lore for this very reason, and those with a deeper interest
can examine for themselves the Book of Revelation (especially
chapter 11) to find several instances of its use. Of course, twice
three and a half, the number seven, is the single most important
figure in the whole of ancient religion. It stands for perfection, for
the very principles (or *archai*) upon which the cosmos itself has
been built. Hence, the seven "days" of Creation, the seven notes
of the scale, the seven colours of the prism, and so on, throughout
not just the texts of ancient Bibles but the whole of the universe.

In the Egyptian Ritual, the Manes, or deceased person, prays,
"Grant that I too may be able to walk on the water as thou walkest
on the Nun [the primordial, quantum 'soup' out of which the universe was born] without making any halt." Elsewhere he cries out,
"I fail; I sink into the abyss of the flowing waters." The correspond-
ing story in Matthew 14:25–30 tells how Peter asked to join Jesus
walking on the water but, having got out of the boat and felt the
great power of the wind and the waves, began to sink, crying out in
fear, "Lord, save me!" This story is an almost exact copy when it's
understood in its true, esoteric (or symbolic) meaning. Through
insights such as this, I was finding the New Testament come alive
to me as never before.

Once again, Horus anticipated all of this. It was written of him, "He hath destroyed the water-flood of his mother. . . . He hath dispersed the raging rain storm!" And again, "He hath dispersed for thee the rain storm, he hath broken for thee the tempests." What such passages are actually about is the power of the Christ within each of us to still the strong, restless power of the elements in our lower animal nature, symbolized by the wild and roiling sea. Instead of a literal story about a kind of magician, we have a relevant and potentially transformative wisdom to apply to our daily life.

The Egyptian Ritual assigns various names to the ship of Horus as it crosses the sea of this lower life. Horus himself says in one place, "Collector of souls is the name of my barque." He was described as collecting souls for Ra, and in so doing, he was thought to be reunifying the dismembered Osiris through his "Horus spirit." The deeper meaning—because there are always several layers—is that all humanity is to be gathered together in a new bonding of love and goodwill. As the ship sails along, "it will collect again the divine fragments scattered abroad in the descent [of the god] to earth." The symbolism of Noah's ark and the later likening of the church to a ship (the word "nave," the main body of a church, comes from the Latin word for "ship") all echo these earlier ideas.

Rising in Three Days

The Gospels, indeed the entire Bible, follow the Egyptian emphasis upon the number three as well. Even a cursory examination of the Jewish and Christian scriptures reveals how often the number three occurs. For example, when Jesus stayed behind at the temple after his bar mitzvah, Mary and Joseph searched for him "for three days." In Matthew 15:29–32, Jesus is said to have had compassion for the hungry crowd because "they continue with me three days."

His message to that "fox" Herod was that "on the third day I shall be perfected." Three-day symbolism is found all through the Old and New Testaments.

So we find that Horus, like Jesus at his Resurrection, rose in a new body of light on the third day. Osiris also is said to "die" at the winter solstice and be "reborn" at the spring equinox, again as Horus, on the third day at Easter. Like Jesus, the Egyptian saviour shared the experience of human suffering and death. However, as we have seen, later Christianity took this story literally instead of spiritually or mythically.

The chief significance of the number three here is that it "represents the period of incubating life"—a special time when something new is about to break forth. But it was based solidly on Egyptian lore, founded as always upon keen observation of the natural world. The ancient sages had observed that the moon, the monthly manifestor of the reflected light of the sun, went through a cycle of twenty-eight days, which always included a three-day period when the sun lit up no part of the orb's surface visible to us from earth. This critical period of waiting to see the "birth" of the new moon (and also, by proxy, of its lord, the sun) was a symbol of both heavenly and human gestation and dramatic renewal. The full moon was a monthly symbol of the maturation of the divinity, or Christos, in everyone.

That's what was also behind the symbolism of Jonah's being held three days in the belly of the great fish and, however distantly, of Jesus' saying about the temple being destroyed and in three days "I will raise it up" (a prophecy that, again, was really about dying, resurrection, and new life).

Other Familiar Roles

- Jesus was the Good Shepherd whose voice the sheep know and who goes out into the wilderness to bring back the one that is lost. In John, chapter 10, this whole theme is worked and reworked in a spiralling fashion typical of the Gospel's style. Not only is he shepherd and gatekeeper for the flock, but he is the gate itself. Horus was the Good Shepherd centuries, even millennia, before, however. He says to the flocks of Ra in the desert of Lower Egypt, "Protection for you, all you flocks of Ra." Part of Osiris' regalia was a shepherd's staff, or crook, precisely like the one carried today by the pope and bishops of the Catholic, Orthodox, and Anglican Churches.

- Both Horus and Jesus are described as coming forth as the Winnower. Matthew's Gospel tells how John the Baptist predicts that Jesus will hold a fan (the New Revised Standard Version, or NRSV, calls it a winnowing fork) in his hand, "and he will clear his threshing floor and will gather his wheat into the granary; but the chaff he will burn with unquenchable fire." Esoterically, this unusual symbol is a clear pictograph for the principle of the mind. Intellect is to sweep out the chaff of sensuality and free the golden grain. Those who were initiated into the greater mysteries in the Greco-Roman world were washed with water and then breathed upon and symbolically "fanned and winnowed" by the purifying wind or spirit. This was really the same as the dual baptism of water and fire in the Gospels. In Egypt, the fan, called the Khi, was the sign of air, breath, and spirit. In Egyptian and Greek religion, the divine brings us intellect, which is what keeps us from being smothered by sensation. This understanding is in stark contrast to millions of ultra-conservative Christians, who seem so often to view reason as "a tool of the devil" and pride themselves on acting on "faith alone."
- Passages in the Gospels dealing with judgment of sinners (and also the drama of Jesus' Passion narrative, specifically the trials before Caiaphas, Herod, and Pilate) reflect, with uncanny

accuracy, scenes from the Egyptian Great Hall of Justice, where those who have sided with Sut against Horus are separated from the sheep and transformed into goats. I am again reminded of Matthew, chapter 25, and the parable of the sheep and the goats at the end of the age. In the King James Version, or KJV, it begins, "When the Son of man shall come in his glory and all the holy angels with him, then shall he sit upon the throne of his glory: And before him shall be gathered all nations: and he shall separate them one from another, as a shepherd divideth his sheep from the goats: And he shall set the sheep on his right hand but the goats on the left." Notice that it is Matthew alone who has Jesus saying that the very hairs on a person's head are numbered in God's sight. In the Egyptian Ritual, every hair is weighed on the scales of justice. Many chapter headings are sayings of deceased persons that repeat sayings originally ascribed to Horus. Horus indeed is the divine speaker of yore, just as Jesus in the Gospels is presented as the one whose words are life.

- Massey places those people in the Egyptian myth "that sat in darkness" and saw a great light in what is called Amenta (i.e., the earth itself). When Horus brings the divine light, he is declared to "descend from heaven to the darkness of Amenta as the Light of the World." In John's Gospel, chapter 9, Jesus says, "As long as I am in the world, I am the light of the world." The evangelist then uses the story of the healing of the man who was blind from birth to illustrate this truth. In a deeper, more spiritual sense, we are all blind from our birth in a material body (i.e., "in matter"), until our eyes are opened and we realize what and who we really are: bearers of the Christ within.

- Jesus said he was the bread of life, a theme underlined heavily in chapter 6 of John's Gospel. There, Jesus says, "I am the living bread that came down from heaven. Whoever eats of this bread will live forever; and the bread that I will give for the world is my flesh. . . . Unless you eat the flesh of the Son of Man and drink his blood, you have no life in you." And again, "For my flesh is true food and my blood is true drink. Those who eat my flesh and drink my blood have eternal life."

Clearly the "bread" is, then, the divine principle of light and life. The "blood" is the pledge of the same life and energy poured out for human benefit. But Jesus was not the only divine person who offered his body and blood symbolically for the nourishment of mortals. Massey says Horus "also gave his flesh for food and his blood for drink." Needless to say, the language is pure allegory. As I first read this, I could not help thinking that if this had been fully understood by the Church of the late second, third, and fourth centuries, a lot of bloodshed over the true nature of the Mass or Eucharist could later have been avoided. A lot of misunderstandings and hardships remain today because Churches such as the Roman Catholic Church still insist on taking the Eucharist passages in the Bible so literally. That's one of the chief reasons that Rome refuses to engage in intercommunion with Anglicans, Lutherans, and other Churches that take a more symbolic approach.

Horus declared, in the Egyptian Ritual, "I am the possessor of bread in Anu. I have bread in heaven with Ra." He is both the bread of life and the divine corn. Like Jesus, who was of the same consubstantial essence as the divine Father, according to John's account, Horus is symbolically "the flesh and blood of his father Osiris." In his Christological character, Horus said, "I am a soul and my soul is divine. I am he who produceth food. I am the food that perished not." Jesus said, "I am that bread of life. . . . Whoever eats of the bread that I shall give him will never hunger." Both are speaking about the same deep spiritual realities.

- The concept of being born twice, once naturally and then again spiritually, is a feature not just of John's Gospel—with its oft-quoted "You must be born again," or, better, "You must be born from above"—but of almost all early religions, including Hinduism. In the Egyptian cults, those twice born are born first of the "water" of human nature and then again of the spirit. The Ritual text calls out to the glorified soul: "Hail, Osiris, thou art born twice!"9

- Both Horus and Jesus make a series of lengthy addresses to their fathers. Horus, indeed, gives roughly forty of them in all. The most famous of Jesus' Gospel monologues of this type constitutes the whole of John, chapter 17. It is certainly not historical but part of the myth. It, like most of the discourses John attributed to Jesus, reads quite differently from anything Jesus says in the three Synoptic Gospels. It ends, significantly, "Now, I come to thee. . . . Glorify thy son." In fact, he asks the Father to restore to him the glory he had with him "before the world was." Horus pleads in a similar manner for Osiris to "let the state of the shining ones be given to me. The elect arrives at the Aged One on the confines of the Mount of Glory where the crown awaits."10 This is a clear statement of the return of the solar ray of the Logos. He was, from all time, in the bosom of the universal father, Ra, and he suffered death in order to glorify humankind, whom Ra gave him to uplift in nature. Like Horus, Jesus asks to be restored to his pristine effulgence, or glory. The similarities are so striking that when I first examined them, I could hardly believe what I was reading.

- When Horus rises up in his glory, he lifts all other people with him. I was powerfully reminded here of Jesus' words about being "lifted up" and drawing "all people" unto him. Paul, of course, says, "Now is Christ risen from the dead and become the first-fruits of them that slept." Likewise Horus, "the Lord of Resurrection," is the first of those who slept in darkness to wake as "a soul most mighty."

- Horus, as a symbolic sun deity, was often portrayed in the iconography as a little, old, ugly man (representing the dying or setting sun, and also the waning sun of autumn). As the rising sun in the east, however, he was pictured as ruddy, strong, and youthful. Jesus, in Gnostic monuments in the Roman catacombs, is portrayed either as vigorous, young, and of a beautiful countenance or, to use Isaiah's words, as an afflicted, elderly "man of sorrows and acquainted with grief."

As the Horus of the incarnation—symbolized by the sun on the western horizon, "dipping down into matter"— the god made flesh in human form, a voluntary sacrifice, the image of suffering—the Egyptian deity is also sometimes pictured as a little child, maimed in his lower members and marred by the loss of his stolen eye, and the discerning reader is forced to recall some of the most moving words ever penned. Either Horus fulfills this Isaiah passage or, much more likely, the passage borrows from the earlier Horus myth. I like the James Moffat translation, which reads as follows:

He was despised and shunned by men,
a man of pain who knew what sickness was;
like one from whom men turn with shuddering,
he was despised, we took no heed of him.
And yet ours was the pain he bore,
the sorrow he endured!
We thought him suffering from a stroke
at God's own hand;
Yet he was wounded because we had sinned;
'twas our misdeeds that crushed him;
'twas for our welfare that he was chastised;

the blows that fell to him
have brought us healing.

And the Eternal laid on him
the guilt of all of us.
He was ill-treated, yet he bore it humbly,
he would never complain;
Dumb as a sheep led to the slaughter,
dumb as a ewe before the shearers.
They did away with him unjustly;
and who heeded how he fell,
torn from the land of the living,
struck down for sins of ours?
They laid him in a felon's grave,
and buried him with criminals,
though he was guilty of no violence
nor had he uttered a false word.

He shall succeed triumphantly,
since he has shed his life-blood,
and let himself be numbered among rebels,
bearing the great world's sins
and interposing for rebellious men.

Certainly this graphic description of the Christos who suffers for humanity was written long before the appearance of any historical Jesus. The Gospel "life" of Jesus, Isaiah's account of the suffering servant, the story of Job's afflictions, the pre-Christianism story of the suffering Christ, and the description of the pierced, wounded, crucified Horus of the ancient Egyptian records—all match each other with unmistakable fidelity, Kuhn says. It's the same story—as the familiar evangelical hymn puts it, "the old, old story"—indeed.

Sadly, as we have seen, the Christian third-century falsifiers, to cover up the fraud they committed in turning what was originally so allegorical and spiritual into history and literal fact, burned— along with the hundreds of thousands of other books already mentioned—the twenty-four volumes of the Gnostic theologian Basilides. The books, called *The Exegetica*, were his biblical studies, the very first commentaries on the Gospels by any Christian thinker. Since Basilides was steeped in all the ancient wisdom, his interpretation of the Gospels would have been of priceless value to the world and to would-be Christians today. Clement of Alexandria described Basilides as "the philosopher devoted to the contemplation of divine things." Like all the other Christian Gnostics, Basilides (who lived *c.* 140) expounded a fully spiritual, allegorical, and symbolic interpretation of the Christos based upon his knowledge of Greek, Hebraic, and Egyptian lore. We have an urgent need to recover his vision. One of the most hopeful outcomes for me as I read and reread the Gospel texts from the perspectives gained from the research discussed here is the continuous series of surprises I now get as I am able to accept the allegories, the metaphors, and the myths of the Bible and look behind or beyond them to the esoteric meaning buried deeply within.

For further strong parallels between Horus and Jesus, I would encourage readers to consult appendix B in this book. We have had only a partial peek at the scores of similarities I have seen.

By truly understanding the role of Horus as revealing the coming of ever-fuller divinity in every single human being, we are freed up to see the full meaning of the Jesus "player" in the Gospel dramas. Today's Christianity needs a cosmic yet inner Christ, not some personalized idol in a narrow cult that bids all the world to come to it—on its terms alone. People need and want a connection to God that has already been planted in the soil of their own minds and hearts. Knowing the Horus story is a sublime myth, we can penetrate once more—like Origen and the other earliest Christians—to the heart of the same eternal myth carried by the Gospels. That's where my hope for the future of the Church really lives—in the Christ within.

We are now ready, however, to tackle head-on the question of whether the Bible can in any sense be regarded as history.

7

THE BIBLE—
HISTORY OR MYTH?

The End of Fundamentalism

*In the cosmic economy, the divine must always
sacrifice its life for the lower ranks of existence. In every
religion a god is pictured as dying for man.*

There is not one iota of history as we know it *in the entire Bible!*

— ALVIN BOYD KUHN, Our Birth Is but a Sleep

False History?

THE LEAD ARTICLE in the March 2002 issue of the prestigious *Harper's* magazine, titled "False Testament," bluntly stated that archaeology now refutes the Bible's claim to history. Over the past several years, dispute over biblical historicity has marked scholarly conferences and been the focus of articles in *The New York Times* and *U.S. News and World Report*, a cover story in the December 2002 issue of *Maclean's* magazine, and a hard-hitting piece by the archaeologist Ze'ev Herzog in the Israeli newspaper *Ha'aretz*. But the *Harper's* exposé, by the journalist Daniel Lazare, was the most trenchant, current account I have seen yet.

Citing the most recent evidence (or rather, for the most part, the lack of it), Lazare pulled the foundation out from under almost every major historical beam in the edifice of accepted wisdom about everything from the existence of Abraham and the other biblical patriarchs to the Exodus from Egypt, the supposed glories of Kings David and Solomon, and even the reputed conquest of the Promised Land (Canaan).

For millions of Jews, Christians, and Muslims, the revelations came as an enormous shock. In the United States, clergy reported that many church members have had their faith severely shaken by the account. According to "Is the Bible Historical Hooey?," a leading article about the affair in the May/June 2002 issue of the widely circulated *Biblical Archaeological Review* (*BAR*), the ministers quoted said that people were demanding to know why, if the Bible is wholly unreliable as history, they should believe any of it. The absolutist, literalist approach has been so successful that the concept of Scripture as entirely allegorical and mythical is still virtually beyond comprehension for most traditional believers. Yet that is proving to be Christianity's Achilles' heel in the present crisis. The old literalism simply cannot withstand the probing of modern thought, research, and scholarship. What was never history to begin with can't masquerade as history any longer. This marks a major, decisive turning point in Christianity's overall story. It brings with it the hope of the recovery of a much more spiritual belief system and experience of God.

The old Bible view, Lazare noted, was that the Israelites started out in the middle of the second millennium B.C.E. as a nomadic band originating in Mesopotamia (Iraq); they migrated first to Palestine and then to Egypt; after years of enslavement, they escaped into the desert under Moses, eventually crossed the Jordan and, in a vicious conquest, took over what today constitutes modern Israel, the occupied territories, and (back in David's time) much more. [1]

Lazare stated baldly that on the basis of his research and a survey of current scholarship, he'd concluded that all of this is "bosh." In the past quarter century, he said, archaeologists have seen "one settled assumption over who the ancient Israelites were and where they came from proved false." Instead of a band of invaders who conquered Canaan, "the Israelites are now thought to have been an indigenous culture that developed west of the Jordan River around 1200 B.C.E."

The epic stories of Abraham, Isaac, and the other patriarchs "appear to have been spliced . . . out of various pieces of local lore." The whole account of David's empire is now viewed as "an invention of Jerusalem-based priests in the seventh and eighth centuries B.C.E. who were keen to burnish their national history," he wrote. (By the way, a study of comparative religions shows that all ancient peoples did the same.)

According to Lazare's findings, Jewish monotheism—that is, the exclusive worship of a Semitic deity called YHWA, or Yahweh (Jehovah)—didn't fully "coalesce" until sometime between an Assyrian conquest of the northern kingdom of Israel in 722 B.C.E. and the Babylonian conquest of the southern kingdom of Judah in 586. The Bible indicates this happened much earlier. As we shall discover, the true origins appeared in Egyptian religious thought.

The situation gets even more problematic for the traditionalists in every camp. Abraham, as Kuhn had long insisted, was utterly mythological. "Not only is there no evidence that any such figure as Abraham ever lived but archaeologists believe that there is no way such a figure could have lived given what we now know about Israelite origins," Lazare wrote. In other words, as Kuhn said much earlier, he was a leading figure in the larger myth.

And Lazare didn't stop there. The Exodus never occurred, he asserted, a conclusion he based upon a growing body of evidence about ancient Egyptian border defences, desert sites where the fleeing Israelites allegedly camped, and so on. The Old Testament description of the conquest of Canaan thus "turns out to be fictional as well."

King David, said by the Bible to have been a mighty potentate and empire builder, "was rather a freebooter who carved out what was at most a small duchy in the southern highlands around Jerusalem and Hebron." In fact, there are some archaeologists today who maintain, because of the absence of concrete evidence, that he too never existed. The name David appears on one lone inscription on a stone block, or stele, from the ninth century B.C.E., and that's all there is. As Lazare points out, "If David and Solomon had been important regional power brokers, one might reasonably expect their names to crop up on monuments and in the diplomatic correspondence of the day. Yet, once again, the record is silent."

Fundamentalists once took delight in evidence from the 1930s that the walls of Jericho had on one occasion fallen down, much as the Book of Joshua describes. However, Lazare reminds readers that the British archaeologist Kathleen Kenyon, in more recent times, has demonstrated from pottery shards in the ruins that the destruction occurred no later than 1300 B.C.E., almost a hundred years before the conquest (if there was one) could have happened. Joshua may well not have "fit the battle of Jericho" after all.

There was much more, and Lazare had plenty of hard data to support his devastating attack, including corroborative evidence from the recent best-selling book *The Bible Unearthed* by Israel Finkelstein, an archaeologist at Tel Aviv University, and the journalist Neil Silberman. Massey and Kuhn were strikingly far ahead of all of this present scholarship in their research and conclusions. In *Who Is This King of Glory?*, Kuhn mentions Massey's dismissal of the Pentateuch, or first five books of the Old Testament, as historical, quoting him in words that seem straight out of the Finkelstein-Silberman book. Massey derides the Pentateuch as an indistinguishable "mush" of myth and mystery. He said it had "neither head, tail, nor vertebrae." Had it been real history, particularly the detailed accounts of battles in the Book of Joshua, Palestine and Judea ought to be overrun with ancient implements of war and work, of Hebrew manufacture and of the conquered races. But outside of the Bible story, there's absolutely no evidence to be found of the numberless combats and the devastation of Jehovah's enemies in great battles. Also, the country of a people so rich that King David, in his poverty, could collect millions of pounds to build a temple is found to have been without art, sculptures, mosaics, bronzes, pottery, or precious stones. Similarly, Lazare writes, King Solomon was supposed to have been a master builder and "an insatiable accumulator" of luxurious items. "He drank out of golden goblets, outfitted his soldiers with golden shields, maintained a fleet of sailing ships to seek out exotic treasures, kept a harem of 1,000 wives and concubines, and spent 13 years building a palace and a richly decorated temple to house the Ark of the Covenant." Yet not one single goblet or one brick has ever been found to indicate that such a reign existed! Proofs of Bible history will not be found, says Massey, even if all of Palestine is dug up in the search. Indeed, how fatuous it is to think of digging in the earth to find proof of myths and allegories. *No amount of archaeology can ever prove a myth.*

The *BAR* response to Lazare's explosive tour de force was disappointing to anyone looking for a strong refutation. Indeed, I was struck more by the concessions it had to make to Lazare's case than by assurances of there being "another side." The piece, by one of the magazine's editors, charged that the *Harper*'s feature presented "only one side of a very hot debate in the field." In denying that Abraham ever existed, or that the Exodus from Egypt, the conquest of the Holy Land, and the grandeur of the empires of David and Solomon were solid facts of history, it didn't give any indication that there might be "another side."

It's true that Daniel Lazare didn't acknowledge that there are some conservative scholars who don't dismiss the biblical accounts as summarily as he does. Nevertheless, the case he presented was backed, as noted, by overwhelming evidence, and what was a real eye-opener for many traditional Bible readers was the extent to which the *BAR* editor had to agree with most of Lazare's most damning conclusions. He conceded, for example, that when it comes to the Exodus from Egypt—where Moses leads the Israelites across the Red (Reed) Sea into the somewhat absurd and obviously symbolic forty-year wilderness trek—"I doubt you'd find many scholars who'd accept the Biblical account at face value. We have no archaeological evidence of a man named Moses, of Israelites wandering in the desert or of the events at Mount Sinai." (Kuhn wrote a brilliant monograph, *The Red Sea Is Your Blood*, to show the true symbolic or allegorical meaning of the episode of the crossing of the Red—or, correctly translated, Reed—Sea.)

The *BAR* editor admitted as well that Lazare's argument that archaeology doesn't support the biblical story of the conquest of Canaan is based not on malice, as some fundamentalists have claimed, but on some very hard facts. He said, "The Biblical account of the conquest does have its problems—the picture formed by archaeology does not match the description in the Book of Joshua of a swift military victory by the Israelites." But the issue, he argued, is much more "complex" than Lazare describes.

The article was equally weak in its response to Lazare's debunking of the stories of the great kingdom of David. The editor wrote, "The paucity of archaeological remains from tenth-century Jerusalem is a problem. The capital of a significant empire should leave behind some artifacts for us to recover." But that's Lazare's point precisely. The evidence for a large Davidic empire simply isn't there. The *BAR* commentator is forced to concede that, "we are far from being able to offer a definitive history of David, one way or another."

Even on such an important topic as Abraham, there is little that can be said to dispute Lazare's claim that he never lived. The

BAR editor rather lamely points out that there are "some historical details" in the Bible stories that mesh with "details of treaties he made with local rulers and the price of slaves" and the "historical record." That proves nothing, however. He remains an extremely shadowy, mythical character. In *The Lost Light*, Kuhn makes some startling comments on Abraham, who he says categorically was never a historical figure. Kuhn even unlocks the meaning of the patriarch's name, A-Brahm, arguing it is a combination of the alpha privative (as in the words "amoral" and "anoxia" and Brahm (as in Vedic or Hindu), and means, therefore, "not Brahm." He writes that "Abraham the patriarch, or oldest of the emanations, was not Brahm, the Hindu supreme deity, Brahma, the Absolute, but the first emanation from Brahm. He was the first life that was not Absolute, but from the Absolute, a kind of demi-god, or sun God."

In the end, Lazare concludes, "Rather than a chronicle of genuine events, the history that Genesis (and other Old Testament books) set forth was an artificial construct, a narrative framework created long after the facts in order to link together a series of unconnected folktales like pearls on a string." All of this fully accords with the findings of the scholars we have met here. Myth certainly uses historical details at times, and there are many to be found in the Old Testament and the New. But ultimately a myth, as said earlier, has to do with eternal truths.

It's important to understand the kind of arguments used in reaching such conclusions. For example, Lazare's piece notes how the biblical stories of Abraham, Isaac, and Jacob make frequent mention of camel caravans. An instance is that of Genesis 24, where we read that Abraham's emissary, sent to find a wife for his son Isaac, "took ten of his master's camels and left taking with him all kinds of good things." But analysis of ancient animal bones "confirms that camels were not widely used for transport in the region until well after 1000 B.C.E.," that is, over five hundred years later than the Bible dating for the patriarchs. Nor is there any hint of mention of a person called Abraham in any of the non-biblically related inscriptions and other evidence available.

How Should We Interpret the Old Testament?

My own view, expressed in newspaper columns at the time, was that both sides in this ongoing debate should be aware of the salient truth about all ancient bibles and sacred texts insisted upon by Higgins, Massey, Kuhn, Northrop Frye, Joseph Campbell, and numerous others. These texts were never intended as history in the first place. They are almost purely allegorical, and their true meaning is to be sought beneath the surface. For example, the constant references to the various captivities of the Jews through-out the artificially constructed "history" of the Old Testament should be understood as the real "captivity" of the human soul in matter. The theme is really that of incarnation once again.

The following familiar Old Testament stories show that we need to look beneath the surface to know why they were told in the first place:

1. The crossing of the Red Sea is, according to the allegorical or symbolic meaning, really the entrance into matter. Water always stands for matter in the esoteric wisdom. The well-known story of the forty years the Jews spent wandering in the wilderness was a mythical construct that was symbolic of the soul's life in the body during its earthly sojourn. This insight is true of the Gospels also, as our exploration will show shortly.

2. The story of Daniel in the lion's den and the three faithful Israelites who survived the fiery furnace illustrate the central theme that life for the soul of each of us in matter is like being

exposed to wild beasts (our senses and passions) or being tried by fire (temptations and all forms of suffering). In each case, the trusting spirit within is given the courage and protection to survive. The divine soul is ultimately imperishable.

3. The strange, epic story of Samson makes little sense as a literal tale, but it simply glows once the allegorical and astronomical background is known. Samson in Hebrew means "solar," and he is plainly a sun-god figure (as the *Oxford Dictionary of the Christian Church* suggests and Kuhn affirms). Delilah, whose wiles eventually stripped him of his prodigious strength, is linked by Massey with the feeble, waning aspect of lunar light—the dark of the moon—a sign of the sun's weakening each month. In the saga, she shears off Samson's hair, symbolizing the sun's loss of its halo of powerful rays. As a result, Samson—like Horus—has his eyes put out. His "light" is extinguished temporarily. But in the conclusion, as he brings down the great theatre holding his enemies and kills three thousand Philistines, he wins victory over his foes.

4. The story of Gideon is another variation on the theme. He has his greatly outnumbered troops surround the enemy by night. Each soldier holds a candle hidden in an earthen pot or vase and then suddenly breaks it open to flash an encircling ring of light. His foes, hearing the cry "The sword of the Lord and of Gideon" from the hilltops surrounding their camp—and seeing the many lights—run for their lives. The hidden meaning is that the light within each of us (the Christ) can, as St. Paul says, overcome all things.

5. There are several perplexing passages in the Old Testament, and at least one in the New, where women far beyond the

age of child-bearing, women who have been barren their whole lives, suddenly and miraculously become pregnant and give birth. Sarah, the wife of Abraham, is one. Hannah, Samuel's mother, and Elizabeth, the mother of John the Baptist, are two others. What do these strange "miracles" really mean? Kuhn explains that each is a type, or symbol, of the evolutionary process. The mineral stage is followed by the vegetative, and that in turn is followed by the animal. Halfway through the age of the animal kingdom—in geology and biology, this would be billions of years after the big bang—the stage of incarnation (that is, the dawning of self-reflective consciousness) raises the animal to the human. "Late in time behold him come, offspring of the virgin's womb [matter]," as the carol says. The late birth of singular heroes such as Isaac, Samuel, and John the Baptist symbolizes the fact that our evolution as rational, soul-bearing animals has come well on in God's overall "plan" for this cycle or eon (age).

The Old Testament is not a historically accurate record of events but the story of a people's evolving understanding of God and of God's relationship with our humanity.

The New Testament

What about the New Testament, then? Surely here, if anywhere in holy writ, we are on historical terra firma. But once you realize, as I have been arguing, that ancient authors writing about God and God's ways with individuals and nations always use metaphor, myth, poetry, allegory, parable, and a host of other devices to describe eternal truths, you have to ask why they would suddenly stop at the beginning of the Christian era. The truth is that they didn't. The Gospels, in particular, may sound a little like history in places, but most biblical scholars today agree that they very are far from what we moderns understand by that concept.

The Gospels, however they originated, were religious dramas used for worship and as a form of evangelism. They were meant not to impart history but to buttress and convey belief. The editor of John's Gospel (the least historical of them all) boldly and honestly states his aims in the text itself when he says, "But these things are written so that you may come to believe that Jesus is the Messiah." The goal is to establish the faithful and to create new converts, not to create an authentic biography. [2]

Luke Tries to Make Myth into History

Luke's Gospel opens with the statement that he is adding his account to those already written by "many" others in order to set forth the "truth" about the Jesus story. This carries an appealing impression of concern for history. He names names and gives the illusion of firm dating. But the early chapters of this work are filled with non-historical, highly symbolic, mythical narratives.

For example, when Mary bursts into the soaring verses of the Magnificat upon hearing that her aged relative Elizabeth is also "with child," it is given as a spontaneous moment. But anyone of good sense can tell that this psalm is a well-crafted, well-studied piece of Midrashic writing (imaginative commentary) that nobody, let alone an untutored girl, could improvise. Scholars are quite aware that this psalm expands on and repeats Hannah's song in 1 Samuel, chapter 2. It has nothing historical about it.

Next, Luke tells how a decree went out from Augustus that "all the world should be registered." The trouble is that there is absolutely no trace—in a well-documented period—of such a decree. It's simply a means of getting Joseph and Mary to Bethlehem for theological reasons. The messiah had to be of Davidic descent, and thus from Bethlehem. Luke says the birth occurred while Quirinius was governor of Syria. That means it could not have happened before 6 C.E., the year we know he took office. At the same time, Matthew says Jesus was conceived while Herod the Great was in power in Judea. But Herod died in 4 B.C.E.! The authors of *The Jesus Mysteries* point out that Mary's real miracle, if both references are taken as genuinely historical, was "a 10-year pregnancy." For Matthew, Jesus' hometown was Bethlehem. For Luke, it was Nazareth.

As we have already seen, the stories of the angels and the shepherds, in Luke, and of the wise men, in Matthew, are rewrites of Egyptian mythical themes from at least two thousand years earlier. They are portrayed in the art at Luxor. There is no historical record of Herod's alleged edict regarding the "slaughter of the innocents" either. Common sense tells us that such an order was an impossibility in any case. Did Herod intend to kill the children of his friends, his soldiers, his civil servants, tourists passing through, and so on? You know for certain the whole matter is symbolic once you realize that an attempt to slaughter a holy child appears in all the ancient hero myths, from Moses to Horus to Sargon to Hercules. As noted earlier, the threat to the newly born Horus, the Egyptian Christ, came from Herut, the serpent.

Then there's the matter of the two genealogies of Jesus in Matthew and Luke. Clearly, they have nothing to do with history and everything to do with myth. Luke traces the family "history" to Adam because his story is universal. Matthew traces it to Abraham because he's interested in establishing the Jewish line of descent. But both accounts give the show away when they come to their conclusion. Both show clearly that on the father's side, Jesus was (as was compulsory for the Jewish story) a descendant of David. But they fail to point out how utterly irrelevant this really is, since, in their view, Joseph wasn't the real father at all—it was a virgin birth. The myth required this.

There is more. Historically, virgins don't have babies, but stories of virgin births abound in myths. Stars don't "stand" over houses or stables, and they don't lead people west (especially when they appear in the east!). But they do occur in every ancient myth. Every early messiah figure was heralded by a star. That's the point.

The Prodigal Son

This is one of the best-known stories told in the Gospels (found only in Luke). It has been preached about, dissected, and written about quite literally millions of times. In *Finding the Still Point*, I discussed it and tried to show that the point where the "lost" son "came to himself" was the central one that everything depended on. He realized his unique, inner self, and it turned him completely around. From the esoteric, allegorical viewpoint, however, the meaning lies even deeper yet. The story is actually a classic exposition of the incarnational theology I have been describing throughout. The Prodigal Son represents the hidden drama of the soul. When we enter into matter—taking upon us a body and embarking upon a lifetime of experience—we are truly going off into "a far country," to be tested, fed on scraps (compared with our true spiritual heritage), degraded, and alienated in many ways. One day, however, true enlightenment dawns. The divinity within is recognized, the "sleeping" Christ is awakened, and we return home to the waiting "Father." The welcome accorded the Prodigal Son is an allegorical reference to the ultimate rejoicing of the soul's glorious resurrection on the other side. Other details in the story, such as the carping of the elder son, were likely added later, either because of a failure to see its true esoteric sense or to score points in the early Christians' squabble with the synagogue.

The Sower

Another familiar parable is the one involving the sower who sows the Word—the Greek term is *logos*—on various soils. The true esoteric or allegorical meaning once again has to do with the theme of incarnation. The ancient Stoics believed there was a "seed" of the divine mind, or Logos, in every human being—they even called this the *spermatikos logos*, the "seed Logos"—and the Gospel story reflects a similar belief. God, the true "sower," casts the divine seed into every heart. But success is determined by the "soils"—that is, the kind of response and lives lived as a result. The message is: Be the best soil. In other words, wake up to who and what you really are. Become it.

A Case Study: The Raising of Lazarus

Since I want you to know as intimately as possible what was going on in my own mind as I wrestled with all of this material, I think it's useful to examine the most striking of all the New Testament miracles attributed to Jesus. The story of the raising of Lazarus is well known in some circles. But you need to be truly familiar with it for the discussion that follows. Here it is, then (John, chapter 11), taken from the King James Version.

> Now a certain man was sick, named Lazarus, of Bethany, the town of Mary and her sister Martha. . . . Therefore, his sisters sent unto him, saying, Lord, behold, he whom thou lovest is sick. When Jesus heard that, he said, This sickness is not unto death, but for the glory of God, that the Son of God, might be glorified thereby.
>   Now Jesus loved Martha, and her sister, and Lazarus. When he had heard therefore that he [Lazarus] was sick, he abode two days still in the same place where he was. Then

after that saith he to his disciples, Let us go into Judaea again. . . . These things said he: and after that he saith unto them, Our friend Lazarus sleepeth; but I go, that I may awake him out of sleep.

Then said his disciples, Lord, if he sleep, he shall do well. Howbeit Jesus spake of his death: but they thought that he had spoken of taking of rest in sleep. Then said Jesus unto them plainly, Lazarus is dead. And I am glad for your sakes that I was not there, to the intent ye may believe; nevertheless let us go unto him. Then said Thomas, which is called Didymus, unto his fellow disciples, Let us also go, that we may die with him.

Then when Jesus came, he found that he had lain in the grave four days already.

Now Bethany was nigh unto Jerusalem, about fifteen furlongs off. And many of the Jews came to Martha and Mary, to comfort them concerning their brother. Then Martha, as soon as she heard that Jesus was coming, went and met him: but Mary sat still in the house.

Then said Martha unto Jesus, Lord, if thou hadst been here my brother had not died. But I know, that even now, whatsoever thou wilt ask of God, God will give it thee. Jesus saith unto her, Thy brother shall rise again. Martha saith unto him, I know that he shall rise again in the resurrection at the last day. Jesus said unto her, I am the resurrection, and the life: he that believeth in me, though he were dead, yet shall he live: And whosoever liveth and believeth in me shall never die. Believest thou this? She saith unto him, Yea, Lord: I believe that thou art the Christ, the Son of God, which should come into the world. And when she had so said, she went her way, and called Mary her sister secretly saying, The Master is come, and calleth for thee. As soon as she heard that, she arose quickly and came unto him.

Now Jesus was not come into the town, but was in that place where Martha met him. The Jews then which were with her in the house, and comforted her, when they saw Mary, that she rose up hastily and went out, followed her, saying, She goeth unto the grave to weep there. Then when Mary was come where Jesus was, and saw him, she fell down at his feet, saying unto him, Lord, if thou hadst been here, my brother had not died. When Jesus therefore saw her weeping, and the Jews also weeping which came with her, he groaned in the spirit, and was troubled. And said, Where have ye laid him? They said unto him, Lord, come and see. Jesus wept.

Then said the Jews, Behold how he loved him! And some of them said, Could not this man, which opened the eyes of the blind, have caused that even this man should not have died?

Jesus therefore again groaning in himself cometh to the grave. It was a cave, and a stone lay upon it. Jesus said, Take ye away the stone. Martha, the sister of him that was dead, saith unto him, Lord, by this time he stinketh: for he had been dead four days. Jesus saith unto her, Said I not unto thee, that, if thou wouldest believe, thou shouldest see the glory of God?

Then they took away the stone from the place where the dead was laid. And Jesus lifted up his eyes, and said, Father, I thank thee that thou has heard me. And I knew that thou hearest me always: but because of the people which stand by I said it, that they may believe that thou has sent me.

And when he thus had spoken, he cried with a loud voice, Lazarus, come forth. And he that was dead came forth, bound hand and foot with graveclothes: and his face was bound about with a napkin. Jesus saith unto them, Loose him, and let him go.

Then many of the Jews which came to Mary, and had seen the things which Jesus did, believed on him.

Let me say from the outset that this entire chapter, with its detailed account of the raising of Lazarus, was always problematic to me, both as a student and later as a professor of the New Testament. It is set out in John as the last and crowning "Sign" of the series of seven signs, beginning with the changing of water into wine at the very outset of the Gospel, intended to convince the reader that Jesus is indeed the Messiah and the Son of God. In particular, it sets up the key saying about Jesus being the resurrection and the life. He is the one who can make the dead live again. Yet several things about the story had disturbed me long before I was made aware of its Egyptian antecedents.

First, the raising of Lazarus is presented in the Gospel as being the straw that broke the proverbial camel's back. Jewish authorities in the story are so shocked by it, and so afraid that the whole world will be convinced by it (to the point that the Roman authorities will be provoked and take violent, repressive action), that they immediately plot to get rid of Jesus once and for all. The raising of Lazarus, then, is purported to be the immediate cause of the crucifixion. Yet this flatly contradicts the picture given in the three Synoptic Gospels. There, Jesus' arrest, trials, and execution are quite plainly said to be the result of the angst and anger of the authorities over his cleansing of the temple. Mark puts it thus: "And the scribes and the chief priests heard it [about the temple cleansing and his remark about their having made God's house 'a den of thieves'], and sought how they might destroy him: for they feared him, because all the people were astonished at his doctrine." Both versions cannot be sustained together. The gap is too great. Interestingly, the temple cleansing comes right at the beginning of Jesus' public ministry according to John's Gospel but is placed right at the end of it by Matthew, Mark, and Luke.

Second, it has always seemed to me inexplicable that this spectacular story of Lazarus, had it been historical, would have been so thoroughly overlooked by the other three evangelists and their "schools." Yet the story appears solely in the Fourth Gospel. Such a momentous "proof" of superhuman, divine power could never have been kept hidden from others—indeed, as we have seen, it was its very celebrity, even among Jesus' enemies, that led to the cross, according to John. It seemed certain to me, then, that the miracle is not in Matthew, Mark, or Luke because those authors knew nothing whatever about it. It was not part of the common tradition. It bears the feel and character of allegory and myth.

Third, the secular witnesses were noticeably silent. If we recall the alleged opening of the tombs on that first Good Friday (recorded only by Matthew), when "the graves were opened; and many bodies of the saints which slept arose, and came out of the graves after his resurrection, and went into the holy city and appeared unto many," we must conclude that this kind of public wonder-working would certainly not have escaped the numerous secular chroniclers, historians, and other witnesses of the day. But there is not a word of secular or Jewish comment on it anywhere to be found.

It was thus all a serious puzzle for me when I took the widely accepted historical-critical approach to it as a New Testament scholar. However, once I came across the researches of Massey, Kuhn, and other scholars, with their deep knowledge of ancient linguistics and their insights into Egyptian mythology, the puzzle wholly disappeared. It became crystal clear to me that John's narrative at this point is lifted straight from ancient themes and then reworked to fit his own overall schema and purposes. Read allegorically, the way it is told in the Egyptian sources, this story is no problem. Read as history, it's a plagiaristic (though well-meaning) forgery. It creates insurmountable difficulties for reasonable, educated people today.

Consider this a form of detective work for a few moments and see how scholarly analysis reveals the true meaning of what is going on. In the Egyptian Book of the Dead, Anu, called Heliopolis in Greek (meaning "city of the sun"), was the theological name of an actual Egyptian city where the rites of the death, burial, and resurrection of Osiris or Horus were enacted each year. The name is a combination of *nu*, the name for "mother heaven" or primal, empty space, the "abyss of nothingness," and the alpha privative— hence, A-Nu, or "not nothingness," a world of concrete actuality, the world of substantial manifestation. In other words, Anu was precisely a place where units of divine consciousness (or souls) go to their symbolic "death" in every human (incarnation) and later rise again to glory. Anu was called, among other things, the place of "multiplying bread." (Significantly, Bethlehem, the birthplace of Jesus, means "the house of bread." We will not stop here, tempted though we may be, to show the intimate connections between this concept and the Gospel Christ who multiplies loaves and fishes for the crowds.) The Hebrews added their prefix for "house," *beth*, to Anu and produced Beth-Anu, or the House of Anu. But because the *u* and the *y* were interchangeable in antiquity, we ended up with the New Testament counterpart Bethany. The point here is that when we read the Egyptian text, we find that the Egyptian Christ, Horus, performed a great miracle at Anu, or Bethany. He raised his father, Osiris, from the dead, calling unto him in the cave to "rise and come forth."

These clues help us solve the question of who Lazarus was originally. According to Egyptologist Sir Wallis Budge, as well as my major sources and other eminent authorities on the texts, the ancient name for Osiris was Asar. The Egyptians regularly expressed their reverence by placing the definite article "the" before the names of their gods. Just as Christians say, or should say, "the Christ," the Egyptians said "the Osiris." But that was the equivalent of saying "Lord Osiris." When the Hebrews took up the name of the Osiris, or Lord Osiris, they used the Hebrew word for "lord," *el*—hence El-Asar.[3] Later on, the Romans, speaking Latin, of course, took El-Asar and added the *us* ending used for most male names. The result was El-Asar-us. In time, the initial *e* "wore off," as linguists describe it, and the *s* in Asar changed to *z*, its constant companion in language. Thus, we have Lazarus, the Osiris of the Beth-Anu story. So it is that, beginning with Massey, these scholars convincingly conclude that Jesus' raising of Lazarus at Bethany is "but a rescript of the old Egyptian dramatic mystery in which Horus, the Christ, raised his 'dead' father Osiris from the grave." It is written in the hieroglyphics that Horus followed the divine Meri to the place where Asar (Osiris) lay buried in his tomb, just as Jesus followed Mary, who had come forth to meet him on the way to Bethany. The most important point is that this Egyptian recital was in the papyri perhaps as long ago as five thousand years B.C.E.

Further evidence of similarities between the ancient myth and the Gospel account is found in the plentiful references in the Gospel story to mourning and weeping at the home and the grave of Lazarus. The "Jews" who were there to comfort the sisters were weeping, we are told, as was Mary. And then we have the ringing, famous words "Jesus wept." But the Bethany, or Beth-Anu, of the Egyptian story was known long before as "the place of weeping"! As Kuhn notes, "Isis and her divine sister, Nephthys, Jesus and Horus, Mary and Martha, all wept over the inert lord, El-Asar-us."

Those two divine sisters, Isis and Nephthys, are also significant. An old source-name for Isis was Meri, like the Latin word *mare*, "the sea" (the primitive source of all life). The Egyptian plural of Meri, however, was Merti. In the Latin feminine form, this became Mertae. In Hebrew, it resolved into what was rendered in English as Martha. So even in the ancient Egyptian transaction, there were also present the two Marys, or Mary and Martha, the sisters of Lazarus.

One final detail: in the Johannine account, Jesus makes the surprising assertion that Lazarus is not dead but only sleeping. The same thing was said many centuries earlier, in the ancient scripts of Osiris in Egypt: "That is Osiris who is not dead but sleeping in Anu, the place of his repose, awaiting the call that bids him come forth today." In the text of the Har-Hetep, the speaker, who personates Horus in the drama, is he who comes to awaken Asar (Osiris) out of his sleep.

What are we to make of this recondite but almost exact parallel between the two texts, the Egyptian and the Johannine? The conclusion seems inevitable to me. The Egyptian Ritual was certainly mythical in character—that is, it was intended to celebrate the eventual resurrection to radiant glory of the individual's true self, the inner Christ. Similarly, the author/editor of John had no intent to deceive the reader with "false history." The purpose, rather, was exactly the same—to convey, in the vivid context of a fictional story, the esoteric, spiritual truth of our own final victory over the grave itself, our resurrection. It was a vital part of the drama in this particularly Jewish version of the eternal myth. The thing that moves me most about such an approach, and that fills me with fresh optimism for a more profound understanding of the whole Jesus story, is that what is simply incredible as "history" suddenly becomes dazzlingly alive with spiritual meanings, as relevant as one's next breath. It was becoming increasingly obvious to me, as I read on, that what we need today is not a further rationalizing and de-mythologizing of the Bible accounts, but rather a re-mythologizing of them in order to see their eternal significance as we have never seen it before. The need is not to peel away the myth, as I used to think, but to use it to penetrate to the spiritual heart of what it has always been trying to tell us.

The Egyptians believed in the immortality of the soul and of its final glorious, spiritual resurrection from the very dawn of time. The story of Osiris/Lazarus dominated not just their religious thinking but that of the entire Greco-Roman world prior to what we now call the Christian era. To see it reflected in the Gospel, as we have done, is not to "debunk" the New Testament. Rather, it is to ground it, and the hope of the resurrection message, ever more firmly in the wider, more ancient wisdom of humanity's most gifted and learned sages. The mythical, symbolic meaning of the raising of Lazarus goes to the core truth that simple history can never touch. We shall all one day likewise rise again.

This, of course, is just a bare peek at the issues involved. But the evidence is mounting. The old literalist approach is dead in the water. Yet through this very necessary process, as we have already begun to see, something quite new and bracing and liberating is about to emerge.

8

SEEING THE GOSPELS WITH NEW EYES

Sublime Myth Is Not Biography

The evidence suggests that the New Testament is not a history of actual
events, but a history of the evolution of Christian mythology.

— TIMOTHY FREKE AND PETER GANDY, The Jesus Mysteries

From a hoary civilization [Egypt] comes the literature that
ends all debate by offering the incontrovertible evidence that the
Gospels are not and never were histories. They are now proven to have
been cryptic dramas of the spiritual evolution of humanity and of the
history of the human soul in its earthly tabernacle of flesh.

— ALVIN BOYD KUHN, Who Is This King of Glory?

B Y NOW, it is more than obvious that no part of this investigation is intended to take away from the enormous
importance of the Gospels to my own spiritual journey or
to any renewal of Christianity in our day. It is my deep conviction
and experience that the metaphorical/allegorical interpretation
given to them by the work of Massey and Kuhn, in particular,
greatly enhances their relevance to our lives—their power to
enlarge and uplift one's spiritual vision. At present, given the

prevalence of an overly literalist approach, I have come to realize that they are largely—indeed, one could say completely—misunderstood. To read them as history is to be forced to leave all sense of normal reality outside on the church steps. Taken literally, they present a world of abnormal events totally unrelated to people's authentic living today. When, in the liturgy, the Sunday Gospel is read, the reader says, "The word of the Lord," and the people respond with "Thanks be to God." But they usually have little sense of what it means.

As the scholars of the controversial California-based Jesus Seminar have pointed out, some twenty gospels of various kinds have come down to us either in whole or in pieces from the first three centuries of the common era, but only four ended up included in the New Testament. The seminar, founded in 1985 by Robert Funk, now consists of a group of over seventy-five internationally recognized biblical scholars who are experts in a wide variety of fields, from ancient history to archaeology. Sifting through the Gospels and the Book of Acts, grading the various sayings and deeds of Jesus according to their probability of authenticity, they have produced a very different "man" from the figure that is the icon of orthodox Christianity. In their findings, Jesus had a human father whose name may not have been Joseph; he was born not in Bethlehem but in Nazareth; he was an itinerant sage who liked the company of social outcasts; he healed many psychosomatic illnesses; he did not walk on water, feed the crowd with miraculous meals, change water into wine, or raise the dead. In their view, there was no empty tomb; belief in the Resurrection is based on the visionary experiences of Peter, Mary, and later, Paul. Jesus did not, in their view, preach that he would come again. The chief flaw in the entire Jesus Seminar approach, however, is that like the fundamentalists, the scholars of the Jesus Seminar seem stuck with the mistaken view that they are ultimately dealing with history. If they could only strip away all accretions and get back to the kernel or core! But myth treated as history invariably falls apart. Instead of a powerful spiritual message, they have ended up with scraps of "stones for bread."[1]

The truth is that the earliest documents available to the seminar scholars are some tiny fragments of a papyrus copy of John's Gospel, dating to about 130 C.E. The first substantial physical evidence for the four Gospels comes from near the end of the second century C.E., about 170 years after Jesus' demise. But even then, as the seminar's leaders point out, "hard information" is lacking as to how, when, and by whom they were actually composed or edited.[2]

The kind of exploration we have taken so far has shown that there is no question that the four Gospels contain material derived originally from ancient Egyptian sources. We have already seen plenty of evidence for this in the chapters on Horus and the Lazarus "miracle." But we must not think the borrowing was direct. Much of the material had undoubtedly been used and reused in the dramas and plays of the Greco-Roman Mystery Religions, and a great deal comes by way of what Christians call the Old Testament. Some of it, for example, much of the Sermon on the Mount, comes from a common store of ancient wisdom literature that was widely circulated in the Middle East and eventually found its way into Jewish Talmudic and Midrashic (imaginative) commentaries. With the possible exception of the saying about forgiving one's enemies (and even this is disputed), there is absolutely nothing in the sermon in Matthew, chapters 5 to 7—paralleled by Luke's Sermon on the Plain—that cannot be found in the Jewish sources. I already knew that according to the tradition of the Christian Fathers, the primary nucleus of the canonical Gospels was not the life of Jesus at all but a collection of Logia, or sayings, which were written down in Hebrew or Aramaic by Matthew, the scribe of the Lord. An early writer to bear testimony to Christian history is Papias, the bishop of Hieropolis in Asia Minor. Writing sometime around 120 C.E., he emphatically declares that the Christian Gospels were founded upon and originated in the Logia. (Papias also said that according to the tradition he received, Jesus died at home in bed of old age.) Notice that the Gospel of Thomas, discovered with other Gnostic writings at Nag Hammadi in Egypt in 1945, was purely made up of sayings attributed to Jesus. It had no Passion or Resurrection story. The same is true of the hypothetical document "Q," a "sayings" source believed to have been used by both Matthew and Luke.[3]

Papias is the earliest witness to name a written Gospel: Mark. He said that Mark, having become the interpreter for Peter, wrote down accurately what he remembered, but not in the correct order: "For he neither heard the Lord nor accompanied him." Matthew, he says, put the Oracles of the Lord in the Hebrew language, "and each one interpreted them as best he could." Kuhn notes that Papias knew of no other Gospels than those of Mark and Matthew at that time, and actually he had heard of such writings only from the elders at second hand. *He had not seen any himself.* Gerald Massey derives the word "myth" from the old Egyptian *mutu*, meaning utterance or sayings, and relates it to the Egyptian *mattiu*, which means "the word of truth" or "true sayings." The resemblance to Matthew here cannot be accidental.

Most significantly, key early Church Fathers—notably Clement of Alexandria, Origen, and Irenaeus—agree, following the witness of Papias (against Eusebius, the ever-dubious historian), that Matthew, and not Mark, was the primary Gospel. But there is plenty of evidence to show that these sayings, the admitted foundations of the Gospels, were not first uttered by Jesus or invented afterwards by his followers. Many of them were pre-existent, pre-historic, and therefore certainly pre-Christian. They were collections of Egyptian, Hebrew, and Gnostic sayings, and therefore cannot stand on their own as evidence that the Jesus of the Gospels ever lived as a man or teacher. These sayings were all oral teachings in the ancient Mysteries ages before they were written down. Most of the data included in the original Gospel of Matthew, in particular, were put in with the obvious motive of appearing to fulfill Old Testament prophecy. In other words, Jesus is made to fulfill what had already been written for a different context. Hence the frequent, almost tedious, refrain in that Gospel that events happened "according as it was prophesied by Isaiah" or some other prophet. You can check this aspect out for yourself by reading Matthew carefully and noticing how formulaic this process becomes. It's abundantly clear that the compiler was too uninstructed to know that these prophecies belonged previously to the astronomical allegory of ancient Egypt, and that they did not refer to human history and were not supposed to be fulfilled on the plain of objective event.

There is a huge amount of evidence that the core of the spiritual tradition handed down from earliest times was incorporated into collections of the most outstanding and vital utterances spoken by the Christos figure in the cryptic dramas and rituals of the past. These collations of "sacred utterances of the divine Son to humans" were circulated, in secret, all over the ancient world under the name the Logia, or "sayings of the Lord." Having thoroughly weighed the research, I now believe they were the root documents from which the canonical Gospels were extracted. Then, to cover deterioration and suit the various emerging communities of Christians, they were amended, interpolated, and edited by many scribes. I am convinced that this explanation is as near to being the truth of the source, origin, and nature of the Christian Gospels as can be determined.

It is worth remembering that most editors of such narratives felt fully at ease using that freedom which all antiquity was wont to allow itself in dealing with literary monuments. There were no copyright laws. Indeed, as difficult as this is for us to conceive of today, the concept of copyright was utterly foreign to the ancient mind. There was little hesitation in reshaping materials to exclude whatever did not suit the particular editor's point of view, or in substituting other formulae of his own composition and expanding or abridging after his own pleasure. The proof of this, for contemporary New Testament scholars and even the attentive lay student, can be seen in the somewhat cavalier way in which both Matthew and Luke treat the Gospel of Mark (which both, quite obviously, had before them as they compiled their own); they leave material out, make changes, and add to it at will. Elaine Pagels, author of *Beyond Belief: The Secret Gospel of Thomas*, reminds us that "what survived as orthodox Christianity did so by suppressing and forcibly eliminating a lot of other material."

What is more, we learn from Origen himself that as late as the early third century, there were different versions of Matthew's Gospel in circulation. Jerome, at the end of the fourth century, says the very same thing—he even says that there were as many different texts as there were manuscripts of the Latin version! It was an extreme fundamentalist's worst possible nightmare.

The Nativity Myth

When you recall that the birth narratives of Matthew and Luke are non-historical, made up as they are of pious legends and Midrashic-type invention (whose highly symbolic and spiritually meaningful character must nevertheless be stressed), and that the parables come from ancient "sayings sources," it becomes even more apparent that what we are dealing with in the Gospels are literary editions of allegorical and mythical themes that *have* a history of their own but contain little history themselves. All the legends about a virgin birth, a star in the east, three wise men bearing gifts, the evil power that tries to take a special child's life, and angelic messengers have, as we have seen, been enacted many times before in the myths of Egypt and other places too numerous to mention.

Bishop John Spong, members of the Jesus Seminar, and many other contemporary scholars have worked and reworked the birth narratives, sifting them like finely powdered flour, but none has, in my view, shown their full depth and significance as Massey and Kuhn have done.[4] Today's critical exegetes, I am persuaded, are still caught in the literalist, historical trap, even as they try to extricate the Jesus story from its mythical package. They are the rationalizers of the mythos against whom Massey in particular forewarned. Lose the myth and you lose everything.

The sad truth, as one reconsiders the conflicting nativity stories of Matthew and Luke, is that the resolution of the allegorical birth of the Christ into the delivery of a literal baby in a localized, historical Bethlehem has kept the rest of humanity from realizing the true meaning of the messianic fulfillment. With the third-century conversion of an age-old spiritual drama meant to depict the truth about each of us into the biography of a unique man-saviour, the great truth that a ray of the solar Logos was incorporated distributively into animal humanity faded out and was obliterated. Among other things, this has meant that the true, inner meaning of the annual celebration of Christmas for each individual person has been lost. I am reminded of the response made by Sir Wallis Budge, in his book *Osiris and the Egyptian Resurrection*, to a careless assertion by some of his contemporaries that the people of West Africa were "primitive savages." Budge wrote, "This is a great mistake, for they possess the remnants of a noble and sublime religion, the precepts of which they have forgotten and the ceremonies of which they have debased." Nowhere is this phenomenon of decline more visible than in what has happened to the religious treatment of Christmas. The story is not the literal account it seems to be on the surface; it is about the birth, in the heart of every human being, of the Christ. It is a supreme telling of the central myth of all religion—the incarnation of the divine into human flesh. As the quotation at the very beginning of our study says, "Though Christ a thousand times in Bethlehem be born, but not within thyself, thy soul will be forlorn; the cross on Golgotha thou lookest to in vain unless within thyself it be set up again."

The point is that while on the surface the Gospels appear to be a form of biography combined with proclamation, closer examination reveals that they are not biographies at all. They are extraordinarily imprecise or vague just at the places where we would most expect explicit details. We know nothing about Jesus' appearance from these texts—the colour of his skin or his eyes, his approximate height or size, whether he was bearded or clean-shaven, whether he had long hair or was balding, and so on. We're left wholly guessing about his date of birth and the year he died, even about whether he was married or single. Because of the vast silence about the years between his birth and the beginning of the ministry (apart from Luke's legend-like story about Jesus' visiting the temple at the age of twelve for his bar mitzvah, volumes have been filled with speculations that grow wilder with passing time. There are legends about supposed visits to England; mystical sojourns in Egypt, Tibet, India; and much more. Credulous souls who have great difficulty discerning evidence from fanciful conjecture flock to buy each latest embroidery on this theme.

Mark, the earliest Gospel, omits everything before Jesus' appearance as an adult man at the Jordan River to be baptized by John. It contains no birth narratives, no genealogies, no traces of childhood or youth whatever. This is a strange way to begin any attempt at a "life" of a person clearly regarded as spectacular. Mark's Gospel is so lean and spare, so lacking in details about Jesus' life that Jesus' ministry could only have lasted a little over one year, as we have seen. It is only from John that the case can be built for a three-year timespan. Long ago, I was struck by how Mark liked to link each anecdote to the next with the word "immediately" (*euthus* in Greek), which gives a breathless sense of pace but is actually a cover-up for the author's lack of knowledge of any specific time sequences. As Papias said, Mark did not have his account in any particular order. Scholars, myself included, have often described the Gospel as little more than a Passion narrative with an introduction.

However, the real centre of interest, and the place where the details start to flow, is not the birth but the events leading up to and culminating in the arrest, trials, and Crucifixion of Jesus, when the story nears its climax. It takes very little imagination indeed to see this entire Gospel as a ritual drama or mystery play. The divine teacher is called, is tested by the "adversary," gathers disciples, heals the sick, preaches the Good News about God's kingdom, finally runs afoul of his bitter enemies, suffers, dies, and is resurrected after three days. This is the total pattern of the sun god in all the ancient dramas, as we have already seen. What is different about Mark and the other, more complex Gospels is that it is all presented as if it was genuine history! Kuhn's marshalling of the evidence at this point seems to be beyond rebuttal. He shows that the stories of the arrest, trial, and Crucifixion are quite understandable as scenes in a mystery play but inexplicable as facts of history. He writes, "The trial is presented as lasting through one night when, as the great scholar Renan notes, an Eastern city is wrapped in silence and darkness—quite natural as scenes in a mystery play, but not as actual history."

The Passion Narratives

I have examined in detail how, in the Egyptian Ritual, a multitude of symbolic events are thrown into the night preceding the Passover of the spring equinox, March 21, the most important date in the Egyptian calendar and in all the various sun-based myths.[5] The spring equinox was, next to the summer solstice, the single most important cosmic event for all ancient cultures and religions, from the Druids at Stonehenge to the Native North Americans, from the heart of the African jungle to the fertile plains of Mesopotamia. It's the supremely symbolic moment when the sun's returning vigour actually draws equal to and then surpasses the forces of darkness. For the Egyptians, this particular night was symbolic of "the dark night of the soul" in incarnation, which ended with the soul passing over the boundary at Easter, just three days later. Kuhn writes, "All processes of transformation, purifying, perfecting, glorifying, reach their consummation on the last marge of the night period as it breaks into the dawn of Easter's spiritual Sun. In the Egyptian calendar this would be the night of the Passover of spring." It was for this reason that the Egyptian drama placed the crowning of every spiritual process on this eventful equinoctial night.

Remember, it was all purely symbolic, and so it was no problem to allocate to that night any number of representations of the soul's experience as it ends its earthly history. This is why in the Gospel accounts of the Passion, the various trials (before the high priest, Herod, and then Pilate) the Last Supper, Jesus' bloody sweat in the garden, his betrayal, his bearing the cross, his procession through the old city, his mockery and suffering, his crucifixion, his death and burial—and much else—could all be "staged" on this night. But it was not, and could not be, actual history.

Sadly, the final shapers of the Gospel materials in the second and third centuries were so blinded by their fanatical desire to crush Paganism and change spiritual allegory into history that they didn't pause to reckon with the difficulty of crowding this long series of varied events into the course of a single evening. Jesus, accordingly, as Kuhn wryly observes, was given an impossibly busy night to close his sad career. The literalizers of the drama didn't scruple to ask a credulous laity to believe that in one single night occurred the Last Supper with the disciples; the washing of the disciples' feet; the lengthy walk to the Mount of Olives;

the long watch in the Garden of Gethsemane; the disciples falling asleep when Jesus castigated them for not being able to watch with him one hour; the arrest, and the severing (and subsequent healing) of the ear cut off by Peter; then *three* distinct judicial trials involving the summoning of judges, juries, attendants, and officers, the populace always available *in the dead of night*; then the mockery of the soldiers, the parting of Jesus' garments, and the forcing on him of the crown of thorns; then the march along the Via Dolorosa and up the hill of Golgotha, "the place of the skull"; and the harrowing Crucifixion (which ran into the next morning). As I re-examined the details of the Passion texts (something that through overfamiliarity with the story, I had never really thought much about), I realized that there is an obvious, meagre limit to what can actually occur in the temporal span of one evening. The Gospels here stand helplessly vulnerable to the attack of plain reason. They are indeed exposed as the old manuscripts of the dramatized ritual of the incarnation and resurrection of the sun god, a ritual that was first Egyptian, later Gnostic and Hellenic, then Hebrew, and finally adopted ignorantly by the Christian movement and distorted into "history." The manuscripts were not history "until in Christian hands the esoteric meaning had been obscured and the wisdom needed to interpret them non-historically was wanting," says Kuhn.

It's important to be quite clear. Two levels of meaning are at stake in all of this. If my major sources and others of their school are correct, as I now am convinced they are, then in the ancient Egyptian (and other mystery) dramas and in the four Gospels, the central figure represents both the Christos (Divine Principle as he/it incarnates and dies only to rise again in self-offering on behalf of all humankind), *and also the soul of every individual in its journey to eternal life*. It came to me with unparalleled illumination that the story of Jesus is the story of each of us in allegorical form. As spirit-gifted animals, we are crucified on the cross of matter;

we are bearers of the Christ within and will one day be resurrected to a glorious destiny with God. Any soul is being crucified on the cross when it is alive in the physical body, according to the ancient esoteric wisdom.

It is highly significant that crucifixion was an integral component of many of the Mystery Religions, and it undoubtedly found its dramatic prototype there. In the Mystery ritual the candidate for initiation was symbolically bound or "nailed" to a cross and even, in some rites, put into a hypnotic coma, to be wakened from "death" after three days, on Easter morning. Indeed, some authorities see in this type of ritual the basis for Jesus' claim that Lazarus "is not dead, but sleepeth." The story originated in Egypt, then came to be a framework for a ritualistic dramatization of death and resurrection. One of the secrets of the transformative dynamic of the Mystery Religions was the regular use of very specific rituals, dramatizations, sounds, lights, and other effects *to recreate symbolically the inner changes of consciousness being portrayed*. This was the essence of their power.

Resurrection

It would take many books to deal fully with the Gospel narratives of the Resurrection. John Spong and dozens of other contemporary scholars have dealt in great detail with the intricacies of the texts, the stark inconsistencies between the different accounts, and the overall background. There's no need to repeat their work here. But I feel I must highlight certain key aspects. For example, in Matthew's story about the chief priests and the Pharisees coming to Pilate after the Crucifixion and demanding that the tomb be sealed and a "watch" of soldiers be set, they said, "We remember that that deceiver said, while he was yet alive, After three days I will rise again." As my old friend Professor Frank W. Beare noted in his commentary on Matthew, we are here asked to believe that

while the disciples had apparently forgotten all about any predic-
tion by their master—they are shown as totally unprepared and
disbelieving when presented with the *fact* of the Resurrection—
his enemies, the harshest non-believers, remembered it all. But
in any case, the whole Resurrection account by Matthew is rendered suspect as history because of his gratuitous embroidering
of the moments following Jesus' death. The King James Version of
Matthew 27:50ff reads, "Jesus, when he had cried again with a
loud voice, yielded up the ghost. And, behold, the veil of the temple was rent in twain from the top to the bottom; and the earth
did quake, and the rocks, rent; and the graves were opened; and
many bodies of the saints which slept arose, and came out of the
graves after his resurrection, and went into the holy city, and
appeared unto many."

I wish all fundamentalists would take special note that while
these quite public, literally stupendous events are alleged to have
taken place, not a single other contemporary source can be found
to corroborate or confirm them—even though this was at a time
and in a place where capable observers, recorders of remarkable
happenings, historians, and others were in no way lacking. There
is not a smidgeon of a trace of historicity to be found. Yet they are
stated in Matthew with every appearance of fact.

It's enough for our purposes to say that obviously the Gospels'
treatment of the Resurrection is similar to that already described
for Jesus' last night. In the ancient Egyptian lore, Osiris rose on the
third day, following lunar or cosmical symbolism. The inner meaning was that the germinal seed of divine consciousness, buried for
three ages (or "kingdoms") in lower matter—mineral, vegetable,
animal—then rose to incarnation in humans "in the fourth
watch."[6]

There can be no question that the literal misconstruction of the
Resurrection by Christian theology has been "most lamentably
serious and fatal," as Kuhn asserts. The imagery of the rent veil,

the discarded swathings, the rolled stone, and the opened tomb was converted into actual occurrence and mistakenly attached to a personal life. The figure of the Christos was nailed on a wooden cross (just as the mythical Prometheus was fastened to a rock in the Caucasus Mountains), and his body was consigned to a rocky tomb. And what may have been gained "in gruesome realism" by these manoeuvres has been erased by the loss of the universality of the experience and its ineffable beauty as a spiritual mystery. In Kuhn's view, one I soon came to share, there was no reason, justification, or need for the literalization of the Crucifixion and the Resurrection. People who were "children in intellect" took the grand parables and allegories of the esoteric wisdom and "fed them to infantile minds as veritable history." The Logos was declared to have come as the man Jesus, born as a baby in Judea and walking the lanes, lake strands, and hills like any peasant. Kuhn's own crusade was to "rekindle the lamp that once burned so luminously" of a truly spiritual faith. Taken literally, the stone said to have been rolled away by angels from the mouth of the tomb has all but suffocated the real spirit of what the myth is about— our own rising to immortality. The early Gnostics took a wholly spiritual view of Jesus' Resurrection, as indeed did St. Paul in 1 Corinthians 15 and scholars such as Origen. They regarded a belief in Jesus' physical resurrection as unlearned foolishness.

Nature

This is a good place to reassure the reader of a very important truth. Ancient religion was indeed deeply rooted in nature and nature symbolism, as we have seen, but these ancients were infinitely more sophisticated than our frequent, too readily assumed superiority allows most of us moderns to realize, especially Christian critics of Pagan thought. For example, the solar myth was not created to celebrate the sprouting of the corn; on the contrary, the sprouting of the grain was called upon to help the mind frame a more realistic conception of the divine seed that, like the grain, was buried in the earth of flesh and sensation. The ancient sages used nature to vivify spiritual processes. When Jesus says, "Except a seed fall into the ground and die, it abides alone and doesn't bear fruit," it is an eloquent example of this. As most poets have done, they worshipped spirit through its reflection in nature. Nature was the materialization of the thoughts of God—his panoply or garment. The ancients believed that a lively apprehension of the deeper aspects of truth would be facilitated by the contemplation of their universal counterpart in the physical world. The evidence is mountainous that *Pagan eyes pierced through the phenomena of nature to the truth of higher levels.* Everything in the environment of the early Egyptians, from the annual flooding of the Nile to the humblest creature, the dung beetle, held deep spiritual messages.

In other words, Pagan spiritual discernment was all the keener for its close beholding of the natural world. The assumption that in primitive infantilism the Pagan stopped at nature while the Christian went on to God is in reality a rank form of heresy. It's defied, I discovered, by all the facts of antiquity. This gratuitous, we might even say arrogant, depreciation of past civilization is belied by scriptures of the most exalted wisdom. The authors of such high revelations knew the realm of sublime truth that lay beyond nature, and they also knew the powerful reality that nature was the visible analogue of this other world of truth. Then, as now, esoteric genius grasped the distinction between outer and inner, but ancient wisdom recognized infinitely better than modern the essential kinship of the two. The lack of a deep connection between spiritual values and the natural world today contrasts sharply with what we have foolishly called "primitive" religions around the world, and accounts in no small measure for the dryness and overly cerebral nature of much of traditional Christian worship. It has contributed, in large measure, to our present

environmental crisis. Immediately, one thing is crucial to the
message of this book. Things are not true because they are in
the Bible. They were put in the Bible because they were spiritually true.

A Contemporary Comment: Insight from Earl Doherty

Earl Doherty, the author of *The Jesus Puzzle*, has played a prominent part in the recent debate over Christian origins. While I
don't agree with him on every point, I want to give a brief synop-
sis of some of what he has to say on his very active website on the
issues we're looking at here.[7]

Doherty explains that Jesus (Yeshua/Joshua) is a Hebrew
name meaning "saviour" (strictly speaking, "God saves"). At the
beginning of Christianity, he notes, it referred not to the name of
a specific human individual but, like the term Logos, to a concept—to a divine, spiritual figure who is the mediator of God's
salvation. As we have seen, the Christos, a Greek translation of the
Hebrew word *messiah*, is also a concept, meaning "the anointed
one of God." "In certain sectarian circles across the Roman
Empire, which included both Jews and Gentiles, these names
would have enjoyed a broad range of usage. Belief in some form
of spiritual Anointed Saviour . . . Christ Jesus . . . was in the air,"
Doherty writes. Paul and the Jerusalem brotherhood, he argues,
were simply one faction of this widespread phenomenon, albeit
an important and eventually very influential one. But later, in a
"myth-making process of its own," this group of missionaries
came to be regarded as the whole movement's point of origin. Did
the Evangelists see themselves as writing history? he asks, answer-
ing that it is now a maxim that the Gospels are "faith documents."
The Evangelists had no concern for historical research as we know
it; rather, they were engaged in a type of Midrash, an inspired

commentary. He confirms that in the minds of the Evangelists, the Gospels expounded new spiritual truths through a retelling of Scripture. "New Testament elements are simply a reworking of stories recorded in the Old Testament. Jesus was cast in tales like those of Moses, for example, presenting him as a new Moses for contemporary times." Mark, he says, might have thought there was some Joshua/Jesus figure who actually existed, but "in any event, before long, such Gospels came to be looked upon as purely factual records by gentiles who did not understand their Jewish roots, and scripture came to be seen as the prophecy of such real events rather than their source." Mark, he argues, brought to a head an already fledgling process and added those biographical elements he found in the "sayings" traditions. With the Old Testament open before him, he fleshed out his story of Jesus' ministry and passion.

Doherty reminds us too that the story of Jesus "resides in scripture more than in an assortment of isolated passages." The overall concept of the Passion, death, and Resurrection has emerged out of a theme repeated in tales throughout the Hebrew Bible and related writings. This is the story modern scholars have characterized as the Suffering and Vindication of the Innocent Righteous One. As we have already seen, we find it in the story of the suffering servant in Isaiah, in Tobit, in Esther, in Daniel, and in other places. All tell a story of a righteous man or woman who suffers, is convicted and condemned to death, gets resurrected at the last moment, and rises to a high position. "It is the tale of how the Jews saw themselves; the pious persecuted by the powerful, the people of God subjugated by the godless," he says. It was an image readily absorbed by the Christian sect, so the tale of Jesus also follows this pattern. Jesus' redemptive role was a paradigm for Jewish motifs of suffering and atonement and destined exaltation, brought into a potent mix with the Hellenistic son (Logos) and saviour-god philosophies. Thus, he concludes, "Christianity emerged as a genuine synthesis of the leading religious ideas of the ancient world particularly, and it set the course of Western faith for the next two millennia."

Most of what Doherty says here agrees with the major themes I have already raised. What he and many other more radical scholars today lack, however, is the deeper, earlier insight drawn by Kuhn and Massey from the fertile store of ancient Egyptian religion. That's what has been most surprising and enlightening for me. All of the Old Testament materials Doherty refers to themselves derive from Egyptian antecedents.

The question, then, is, If the Gospels are mainly allegorical and symbolic, have they any solid value for us at all as sources for religious and spiritual truth? Obviously, the two major authorities I have examined believe they do—and so do I. Ask yourself, Is a poem true? Can it contain truth of infinite value even though its content is symbolic or fictional? Are the plays of William Shakespeare true? Sublimely so, when it comes to matters of the human heart and human spirit. Yes, though fiction, they are supremely true. But they are not exact history, nor can they ever be. That precisely is the case with Matthew, Mark, Luke, and John. I find, in such an in-depth approach, excitingly fresh grounds for both faith and hope.

A Personal Note

I want to add a personal note to this look at the Gospels and the issue of their true value. The question of who wrote the Gospels (and when, how, and why) is extraordinarily complex. Indeed, a plethora of books on these and related themes exist all around us. But anyone who reads Massey and Kuhn will, I'm sure, reach the kinds of conclusions I have reached here. Yet it wasn't the research

I did in preparation for this book that first convinced me that the basic texts of the Christian faith, the four Gospels, had to be read in a manner quite different from that I had been raised on, and that I eventually taught to a subsequent generation of budding ministers in seminary. In fact, my understanding changed radically in the years after I left teaching in 1971. Anyone who wishes can check this by looking up my 1991 book, *Life After Death*. Chapter 12 of the book is titled "The Christ Myth as the Ultimate Myth of the Self." It drew sharp criticism from conservative-minded Christians at the time. I blame there a crude literalism for the way Christian thinking and teaching about an afterlife has become so distorted, irrelevant, and unreal. I wrote, "A story and a whole range of symbols meant to relate us to our own, inner selves have been taken as purely historical facts about a distant, inhuman person who was God-in-disguise. As Carl Jung argued, it makes Jesus Christ a monster figure to say that one can only become fully human in the presence of and through the death of one who is uniquely God-man. In that view, we can never be what he was. . . . He was so far unlike us and removed from us as to be of little real help. Pretending to live a normal, human life, he really always had 'four aces up his sleeve.'" (This is why, incidentally, Jung was so critical of the imitation of Christ as a way of moral development. He argued that only a "God within" had the much-needed psychological power to transform human personality.)

I, in that book, quoted Joseph Campbell, who wisely said, "A symbol, a mythic symbol, does not refer to something which is known or knowable in a rational way. It refers to a spiritual power that is operative in life and is known only through its effects." And I added that the purpose of religious myths is not to entertain but "to bring about a change of consciousness in each of us." With this as an introduction, I invited the reader to look at the Gospel story, or myth, of Jesus in a deeply personal way, as a story about the

inner meaning of his or her own life—from Virgin Birth to Crucifixion and Resurrection. I repeat that invitation with renewed
vigour today.

In the light of what I have learned since that time, both academ-
ically and spiritually, I am even more certain that this can be a vital
exercise for enhancing inner growth. We know how the Church
has for centuries insisted that Christ is every person and represents us all. But as we have seen, in the myth there is encapsulated
the profound reality that the opposite is true as well. As each of us
becomes aware of his or her true essence as a body-spirit entity
and awakens the Christ within, he or she too is Christ. No longer
is it a case of looking outside ourselves to emulate a remote
historical figure. Rather, it's a matter of knowing ourselves to be
wholly one with the very same energies and principles that in the
drama are shown driving him. Thus, as Carl Jung describes it,
each individual can discover that he or she is "imbued with a latent
divinity." What the ancient orthodoxy was trying to say in the
creeds about a literalized saviour figure, Jesus Christ, having "two
natures in one person" becomes an accurate description of you
and of me. It's the true definition of any human life. Full psychic
maturity and the only true hope of the greater evolution of genuine human community depends on it. I believe that all of this
makes the inner meaning of the Jesus story as relevant and life-
giving as our next heartbeat.

The Gospels, I have found, make sense today only when read
and understood from this spiritual point of view. That's why I'm
so certain that what is contained here is vital for the future of the
Christian faith and all humanity.

9

WAS THERE A JESUS OF HISTORY?

Where It All Began

Jesus of Nazareth and the Gospel story cannot be found in Christian writings earlier than the Gospels, the first of which [Mark] was composed only in the late first century. . . . There is no non-Christian record of Jesus before the second century.

— EARL DOHERTY, The Jesus Puzzle

When the conception of a purely spiritual Christ could no longer successfully be imported to the turbulent masses, who clamoured for a political saviour, it was found necessary or expedient to substitute the idea of a personal Messiah. . . . The swell of this tide carried the Church Fathers to the limit of recasting the entire four Gospels in terms of a human biography.

— ALVIN BOYD KUHN, The Lost Light

D
URING THE OPENING SEQUENCE of the Woody Allen film *Husbands and Wives*, Woody and his wife, played by Mia Farrow, are making final preparations to welcome lifetime friends over for dinner. Woody is neurotically fussing about and mumbles Einstein's saying that God doesn't "play

dice" with the universe. "No," Woody then intones, "he just plays hide-and-seek." There is a hide-and-seek quality to the profound question raised by all of our explorations thus far: in the light of everything we have examined, can we say with any authority that Jesus of Nazareth actually existed as a historical person? I have very grave doubts that we can.[1] It is abundantly clear to me that while there are indeed certain historical elements in the Gospel accounts—specific place names, actual persons (such as Herod, Pilate, and Caiaphas the High Priest, and alleged dates—these alone don't constitute a genuine history or biography in any modern sense. When we review the exact parallels between early saviour stories and the sayings and actions of Jesus, it's more than obvious that what we're dealing with is another variant of the overarching archetypal theme of the same mythos in all ancient religion—only this time in Jewish dress.

I hasten to assure the reader that I am fully aware that the discussion that follows will be at first quite intimidating for some, perhaps many. To claim that a historical figure who has inspired so much love and devotion over centuries is in fact a mythical copy of many preceding saviours is somewhat of a shock, I know. This was not something that I found easy to accept myself. But in matters of faith, as in all else, truth demands my allegiance over everything—truth acted upon in love. The reality is that God calls us to use his divine gift of reason, and we ignore this not just at our peril but to our ultimate loss. What we are considering now is the logical consequence of all we have been through so far. Be patient and hear the argument to its end. You will find, as I have promised from the start, that we are being called not to an impoverished vision but to one that radiates with fresh understanding and hope. Jesus lives on for us, but in a new way.

Reviewing the relevant literature I discovered that the mythical or spiritual as opposed to the historical interpretation of the Gospels has been set out repeatedly by such scholars as Dupuis, Drews,

Robertson, Smith, Renan, Strauss, Massey, Higgins, Mead, Kuhn and a score of others. In spite of a mass of scholarship on the topic, however, in spite of the evidence from the study of comparative religion in particular, the historical view of Jesus' life is still stubbornly maintained. Kuhn is correct when he says that all this scholarship "points with steady directness" to the truth that the events of the Gospel narratives are matched with amazing fidelity "by the antecedent careers of such world saviours as Dionysus, Osiris, Horus, Tammuz, Adonis, Atys, Orpheus, Mithras, Krishna, Bala-Rama, Vyasa, Buddha, Hercules, Sargon, Serapis, Marduk, Izdubar, Witoba, Apollonius of Tyana, Yehoshua ben Pandera, and even Plato and Pythagoras." We have seen for ourselves the clear reality of this view in our earlier detailed comparison of the lives of Horus and Jesus.

Matthew's technique of scouring the Old Testament for appropriate "prophecies" to act as a framework for his narrative gives that Gospel a surface feeling of authentic Jewish history. But this whole edifice collapses when you realize that these so-called prophecies were all fulfilled in the Old Testament and can be wholly explained without any future reference at all. Often, in the New Testament, they have been taken out of context and twisted beyond recognition. Hebrew prophecy, it must be remembered, was not about *fore*-telling but about *forth*-telling (i.e., about speaking out on issues immediately at hand). Their total artificiality is fully revealed when one realizes how they are used to make Jesus do exactly what his predecessors in the sun-god myths had already done centuries before. This is confirmed by the fact that the body of material regularly used in the ceremonial dramas of the widespread early Mystery Religions around 1200 years B.C.E. makes up in general the series of events narrated in the New Testament as if they were Jesus' personal life story.

Massey, near the end of his most important work, *Ancient Egypt: The Light of the World*, offers detailed proof that the literalizers of the legend and the "carnalizers" (historicizers) of the Egyptian–Gnostic Christ have but gathered up the "empty husks" of Pagan tradition, minus the kernel of the Gnosis (inner knowledge of the meaning of the higher spiritual truths). So when we have taken away from their collection all that pertains to Horus, there is nothing more than "the accretion of blindly ignorant belief" on which to base a Judean history. Then, Massey concludes, "Of all the Gospels and collections of sayings derived from the ritual of the resurrection in the names of Mattiu, or Matthew, Aan or John, Thomas or Tammuz or Tum, Hermes, Iu-em-hetep, Iusa or Jesus, those that were canonized at last as Christian are the most exoteric, and therefore the furthest away from the underlying, hidden and buried, but imperishable truth."

Massey testifies that neither Philo, the brilliant Alexandrian Jew who laboured so hard to effect a syncretism of Greek Platonism, Egyptian mysticism, and Mosaic Hebraism, and who was an exact contemporary of Jesus (*c.* 20 B.C.E.–50 C.E.), nor Irenaeus (*c.* 130–*c.* 200 C.E.), bishop of Lyons and one of the earliest Church Fathers, believed that the divine Word (Logos) could ever become incarnate in one man. Kuhn says that Philo no more knew of a Christ that could be made flesh than he knew of a Jesus in human form—and he lived at the time of the alleged historical Jesus! The same is true of Tatian, the Christian apologist and Gnostic (*c.* 160 C.E.) who wrote the first-ever attempted harmony of the four Gospels, the Diatessaron. He completely disclaimed the notion of the Christ having assumed an actual body, as did all the Gnostic Christians. They declared it impossible that he (the divine Logos) should suffer, since he was by nature both incomprehensible and invisible, a divine emanation of the one God.

The stark truth is that apart from the four Gospels (and their full witness is really established only from about 140 to 170 C.E.) and the Epistles, there is no hard, historical evidence for Jesus' existence coming out of the first century at all.[2] It must also be remembered that no autograph (original) manuscript of any one of the four Gospels has ever come to light, nor has any credible witness ever claimed to have seen such a manuscript.[3] Origen says the four Gospels were chosen out of a very large number (we know of at least twenty), and Irenaeus somewhat oddly says that the four were selected out of many because there were four winds and four quarters to the globe. Kuhn quotes Mead, in *Did Jesus Live 100 B.C.E.?*, when he writes: "It has always been an unfailing source of astonishment to the historical investigator of Christian beginnings that there is not one single word from the pen of any Pagan writer of the first century of our era which can in any fashion be referred to the marvelous story recounted by the Gospel writers. The very existence of Jesus seems unknown."

What is even more curious is that the closer one gets to Jesus' alleged time, the greater and more general is the denial or ignorance of his existence. But the further one draws away from it, the greater and more insistent are the "proofs" of it. This again entirely reverses the universal phenomenon of a historical recording. Most living characters are familiar entities during and immediately after their lives, and they wax romantic and are haloed only after centuries have elapsed. But Jesus was airy and ethereal in the first century and crystallized into quite a concrete personality only after several centuries. Something quite strange was going on.

Very sadly, a work of Celsus, a second-century Pagan philosopher, called *The True Logos*, which would have certainly thrown much light on all early Gnostic and esoteric interpretations of sacred writings of the time, was totally destroyed by literalist Christians. One intriguing fact, however, emerges from the mystery of the historicity of Jesus. Of the Church Fathers, Irenaeus seems never to have subscribed to the story of Jesus' death on the cross, or his death at all at the early age of about thirty-three. It is most curious—given the repeated claim by conservatives that Jesus' life was accepted as historical by the early Church—

that Irenaeus refers to a remarkable legend that flatly refutes the Gospel "history." The good bishop claims that Jesus was not crucified at the age of thirty-three but passed through every age and lived on to be an "oldish man," a claim he says is testified to by Church "elders" and was bequeathed to them directly from John. Papias, you remember, also said Jesus died in bed at an advanced age. Kuhn comments, "We are permitted to wonder how such a tradition, attributed to so accredited a source as John, could have lived on for so many years, if the general field was occupied by the factual acceptance of the Gospel narrative, or how it could have been purveyed by a bishop of such eminence in the Church as Irenaeus."

The truth is that both Massey and Kuhn have considered the question of the historicity of Jesus in the minutest detail, each spending hundreds of pages examining the evidence. What's more, they do not rest solely upon their own long years of labour in the field, drawing heavily on the work of scores of other eminent scholars in reaching their conclusion. In finally negating the historical Jesus, Kuhn cites not only such well-known philosophers as Kant and Hegel but the leading Jewish and Christian biblical experts of his era.

He quotes, for instance, Robert Keable, who in his book *The Great Galilean* says, "Nobody knows enough of the early life of Jesus to write a biography of him. For that matter, no one knows enough for the normal *Times* obituary notice of a great man. If regard were had to what we should call in correct speech definitely historical facts, scarcely three lines could be filled." In his challenging work *The Twilight of Christianity*, the Bible scholar Harry Elmer Barnes reviews the meagre number of non-Gospel mentions of Jesus—a sum total of twenty-four lines from Pliny, Tacitus, Suetonius, and Josephus—and states that, given that these passages are virtually all forgeries and interpolations, they constitute poor evidence of what the orthodox insist on calling one of the best-attested events in history. Barnes points out that even if this secular testimony was indisputably reliable and authentic, it would be "faltering support" for so great an edifice to rest upon. Add to all this the undeniable fact that there is, in the extant Jewish literature of the first century, not a single authentic reference to the founder of Christianity. For a detailed, critical look at the specific references in the four non-Christian authors just cited, I recommend Doherty's discussion in his book *The Jesus Puzzle*.

Commenting in his 1999 book *The Fabrication of the Christ Myth* on the well-known Gospel story of the Gadarene swine, which rushed down a steep cliff and were drowned in the Sea of Galilee, the Jewish scholar Joseph Leidner points out that because Gadera is actually several kilometres away from the sea, the whole incident is evidence of either ignorance or total lack of concern with veridical history.[4] Citing other similar examples, he writes, "From the evidence . . . the blunt conclusion emerges that the Gospel writers did not know the geography and customs of the Holy Land, and did not know Judaism itself. They were working with source materials having nothing to do with historical data of any kind."[5]

We must remember that very few periods in the history of the ancient world were so well documented as the period when Emperors Caesar Augustus and Tiberius reigned supreme. Yet one amazing fact must be faced: *no contemporary non-Christian writer even knew of Jesus' existence*. It's for this reason that Barnes was able to declare Jesus a mythical person, the product of the myth-making tendencies common to religious people of all ages, particularly the period of the early Roman Empire. He lists Bruno Bauer, Albert Kaltoff, Arthur Drews, J. C. Stendel, Emil Felden, Jensen, Lublinski, Bolland, Van der berg, Charles Virolleaud, Ryner Couchoud, Gerald Massey, Emilio Bossi, Georg Brandes, John M. Robertson, G. R. S. Mead, Whittaker, Edward Carpenter, and W. B. Smith among the eminent scholars and critics who have contended that Jesus was not historical.

Of the spate of new books on this theme, I would single out
Leidner's *Fabrication of the Christ Myth*. After a thorough investigation of the relevant Jewish sources for first-century Judaism and
history, he concludes: "There is not a particle of evidence that
'Jesus of Nazareth' ever existed. No detail of the story has been
confirmed beyond reasonable doubt." Leidner argues, in particular, that the Passion narratives are "a contrived and synthetic work"
derived from older, non-Christian sources. Significantly, he notes
that the Jewish historian Josephus, in his contemporary writings,
lists the name of Jesus/Yeshua "no less than 21 times referring to
different persons."[6] Jesus (or Joshua), he notes, is one of the com-
monest names in the index. Leidner sums up his "take" on the
whole issue in this way: "Jesus is a radically Christianized version
of the supernatural [hero] Joshua. We thus have an alternative for
Christian origins."

Certainly, a Jesus or Joshua/Yeshua character was already the
archetypal hero in Judaism in the Old Testament book that bears
his name many hundreds of years B.C.E. He was also the central
figure in the mystery dramas taken over by the Hellenized Jews.
The sages connected the Jewish Kabbalistic Yeshua-Jesus directly
with the biblical personification. They possessed the secrets of
the Mystery language, and it appears that this was the language in
which the Gospels were written. The Gospel editors thus did not
have to invent Jesus, or Yeshua. His name was already in the air.
He was already in the documents they had re-edited or tran-
scribed. But later ignorance changed him from a symbol (type) to
a personal entity or reality. Thus it happened that what had been a
combined astrological and mythical dramatization of every individual's total experience was turned into the story of one character
and set forth as a biography, or "life," Kuhn says. Nearly everybody
tends to think that Matthew, Mark, Luke, and John were citizens
of the first century C.E. who one day took pen in hand and wrote
the Gospels out of their heads. Not so. Kuhn enters a genuine

note of sanity here when he writes that the final staggering truth about the Bible books is that no "authors" ever sat down and wrote them the way Walter Scott wrote the Waverley novels. The longer I researched this issue, the clearer his judgment became. The books of the Bible were in existence long before ink ever met paper to record and preserve them. They were the spoken lines, or sayings, of the great spiritual drama; they were the esoteric oral tradition, extant many thousands of years before they were ever written down. But at some epoch, as Kuhn says, "The sages . . . did at last commit them to writing, lest in some degenerate age they be lost." The Evangelists then, I am convinced, simply brought out to more popular knowledge hidden Gospels that already had a Joshua/Jesus central figure and had previously been concealed inside the depths of Essene and Mystery cult secrecy. They were an exoteric popularization, not a fresh literary or religious creation.

Significantly, the controversial founder of Theosophy, Madame H. P. Blavatsky, who has been maligned by her detractors, had unquestionably a deep insight into the nature and meaning of ancient, esoteric wisdoms. She writes, in *Isis Unveiled*,

> It is a poor compliment paid the Supreme, this forcing upon him four Gospels, in which, contradictory as they often are, there is not a single narrative, sentence or peculiar expression whose parallel may not be found in some older doctrine of philosophy. Surely the Almighty—were it but to spare future generations their current perplexity—might have brought down with Him, at His first and only incarnation upon earth, something original, something that would trace a distinct line of demarcation between Himself and the score or so of incarnate Pagan gods, who had been born of virgins, had all been saviours, and were either killed or were otherwise sacrificed for humanity.

She says, with respect, that neither she nor anyone else honestly looking at the question has put the divine son of God in the position of a poor religious plagiarist. The blame falls squarely on the Christian Fathers and their successors in the Church.

Theosophists aside, the renowned genius and humanitarian Dr. Albert Schweitzer, in *The Quest for the Historical Jesus*, says that after years of careful study, he concluded there was no *traditional* Jesus of Nazareth as a historical person. Prophetically, he saw that the Jesus figure of the theologians was the dramatized, ritualized, symbolic figure of our divine nature—grossly mistaken after centuries of ignorance for a man of flesh. Schweitzer writes, "There is nothing more negative than the result of the critical study of the life of Jesus. The Jesus of Nazareth who came forward publicly as the Messiah, who preached the ethic of the Kingdom of God, who founded the Kingdom of heaven upon earth, and died to give his work its final consecration, never had any existence. This image has not been destroyed from without, it has fallen to pieces, cleft and disintegrated by the concrete historical problems which come to the surface one after another."[7] In our day, the labours of the California-based Jesus Seminar have afforded ample proof of Schweitzer's convictions. They have stripped away almost everything mythical and reduced Jesus to a wandering Cynic philosopher who came finally to a criminal's end. Marcus Borg appears to be the most positive to me, but his demythologized Jesus of history nevertheless still seems to be in a radical "disconnect" from his Christ of faith.

St. Paul

The earliest writings in the New Testament, which make up more than one-quarter of its total content, are the letters of the Apostle Paul. What is absolutely striking about them is their virtual silence on the whole subject of a historical Jesus of Nazareth. There is no question that this is the datum that ultimately stares down the proponents of historicity. Before it, all glib sophistry fails and even the most subtle argument goes dumb. There is no adequate answer to this testimony, in my view. If Jesus lived as claimed, and Paul—who definitely was historical—lived and wrote as claimed, I believe it is unthinkable that the Apostle would have left a total blank on the subject. Traditionalists can offer a wide variety of specious reasons to "explain" Paul's silence about his master. But when they have exhausted all their arguments, they have not laid to rest the ghost of this utterly insistent question or reduced by one iota the pressure of its threat to the prevailing orthodox position. "It haunts the claim of Jesus' existence like a stalking specter and no trickery can exorcise it," Kuhn asserts. Paul never once mentions the man Jesus, in the full historical sense. Yet, as stated, he is the earliest witness among all the Bible writers, the one nearest Jesus in actual time. His earliest letters antedate the appearance of Mark by at least a generation.

Of course, a critic will argue that Paul does occasionally speak of Jesus by name. This is quite true. But today, most Bible theologians agree that even when he does so, he is not talking about a man of flesh and blood, a historical person, any more than the Egyptians were when they spoke of Iusa millennia earlier. Paul's Christ is nowhere called Jesus of Nazareth, nor is he born in Bethlehem. The Jesus Paul dilates upon repeatedly is in reality the spiritual entity in the core of each human's inner being. He is the spiritual Christ principle (the eternal Christos), not the man. As Benjamin Bacon, of the Yale Divinity School, says in his book *Jesus and Paul*, "Paul is the first Bible writer in the first century and he definitely knows no Christ except one he describes as 'not after the flesh.'" Yes, Paul does talk about "this Jesus whom we have seen," and at times he gives the impression he has an interest in an actual person, but closer examination shows that he really is speaking always of mystical visions of an exalted, spiritual being whom he calls Christ. When, in 1 Corinthians 15, he describes his experience of the risen Christ, he says that "last of all he was seen by me also." But the Greek word he uses for this, and all the other apostolic encounters he describes there, is *ophthe*. It was the word regularly used by the Mystery religionists to describe a visionary "seeing."

As a matter of fact, as Bacon says, Paul expressly disavows even having any interest in a "Jesus after the flesh," i.e., a historical Jesus, and his letters bear this out because—and this is highly significant—they contain not a single reference to any of the great miracles, teachings, and other events related in the Gospel narratives as integral to Jesus' life and ministry. I have looked myself in detail at what scholar after scholar has discovered—that all the miracles, parables, and other teachings of Jesus' ministry are either unknown to Paul or a matter of complete indifference to him. Stunning though it may be, Paul apparently knew nothing about or cared nothing for the Gospel story that had allegedly founded the very faith he had so enthusiastically embraced. The conservatives cry out that he simply took all that for granted. But their argument here is, to my mind, unbelievably weak. It is indeed commonly assumed in Christian circles that Paul knew everything the Gospels describe, and that this body of history was the basis of his espousal of the faith. But my own study, in addition to that of my other sources, makes it clear to me that, as George Bernard Shaw makes clear in his preface to *Androcles and the Lion*, the Epistles are in no way an outgrowth of Gospel "history." They are clearly prior, independent, and would undoubtedly still be in the biblical literature if no personal Jesus had ever lived. They are about a spiritual Christ presence within.

Some have argued that Paul didn't have to mention Jesus because everybody already knew of his existence. Such knowledge was so commonplace that there was no reason even to mention it, this line of reasoning says. Because he was so obviously a definite, historical character, his life and personal doings never needed to be spoken of. I can readily see why Kuhn has so little time for such a devious tack. He says, with justified impatience, that it is impossible that Paul could discourse at length upon the fundamentals of the religion that Jesus assumedly founded and feel no need to speak of the founder himself. Jesus was the source and inspiration of the greatest religion on earth—a man whose life was so epochal that history was redated from his birth, a man whose bold preaching of the divine wisdom granted to men was to free the human race from the bondage of sin and evil, a man whose mission was so mighty that stars led the way and angels choired and heavenly hallelujahs mingled with earthly songs to celebrate the descent of deity to the planet—and yet when Paul "descants with holy enthusiasm upon the marvels of this world-changing message," he found no occasion to speak directly of the man who was the genius of it all. He concludes, "For Paul to write fifteen Epistles, basic treatises on the religion that this man founded, and find no reason to refer even once to anything he said or did would be on the order of one's writing a thorough treatise on the American Revolution and never once mentioning George Washington!"

Since Paul was, above all things, a communicator par excellence, he spoke to the people of his time in the mystical language they understood—the vernacular of the Mystery Religions. He uses their phraseology, their symbols, their whole philosophy of personal redemption and immortality through identification with and absorption into the dead and resurrected Christhood of God's Logos, or son. All his language about being "in Christ" or having "Christ in you" reflects the current Hellenic theosophy and philosophy. It is really Orphic-Platonic-Mystery cultism, almost pure Hindu or Vedic yoga mysticism, with no immediate reference to the Gospel life of Jesus at all.[8] It is the universal Good News of the incarnation of the divine in every human being.

The clincher to all of this for me comes in Colossians, where the Apostle, or someone relying heavily upon his thought, comes right out and declares bluntly that the secret of the whole Christian "mystery" is this: "Christ in you, the hope of glory." This is indeed a mystical, spiritual reality akin to that of ancient Egypt, and it has nothing whatever to do with a presumed historical Jesus. The same is true of his famous saying "You have the mind of Christ."

Several noted scholars have remarked upon the obvious fact that even when Paul does mention Jesus by name, he lacks the features given him in the Gospels that render him so human and so real. Noting this phenomenon, Kuhn wonders when it will dawn upon the orthodox mind that Paul's Jesus lacks any human quality for the very reason that in Paul's understanding, he was not a human person at all. Only by use of an elaborate metaphor could Paul's description of a principle of mystic exaltation be clothed in terms of touching human appeal. "This is the one substratum which explains and resolves all the puzzles and conundrums of the argumentative problem, yet it is the last one the apologists will look at," Kuhn says.

Paul's Conversion

What are we to make, then, of Paul's conversion on the road to Damascus? I have become fully convinced that strange as this may sound to orthodox ears, there is more than enough solid reason to suspect that the whole episode of Paul's great vision was the rescript of a portion of Mystery dramatism. For Paul says that the sudden, blinding radiance of Christly glory threw him with his face to the ground, after which a voice out of the light spoke to him and said, "Stand on your feet, Paul." This hardly seems like personal history; in the Mystery philosophy, the descent of the divine soul into incarnation in the early human beginning stage sent it first into the bodies of animals, who walked on all fours with face to the ground. As the Christ consciousness gradually asserted its rulership, the humanized animals slowly rose to their feet. For the god-soul to incarnate at the beginning of the cycle was for it to fall to earth with its face to the ground; then the divine voice within spoke and bade it stand up on its feet as the upright human-divine! It is not hard to presume that an age saturated with mythical typology would have readily introduced in the Mystery ceremonial such a dramatized representation of the soul's descent into lowly animal body and its resurrection to eventual upright human status. The initiate acted out the entire consciousness-raising rite.

Let's take a closer look at the description of Paul's conversion in the New Testament. Most are unaware that the Book of Acts, the major source for this life-changing Pauline experience, has two distinct versions of it. What's more, the two descriptions do not entirely agree. In Acts 9:1ff, we have the first telling of the story—in the third person. Here is the core of it from the KJV:

> And as he journeyed, he came near Damascus: and suddenly there shined round about him a light from heaven:
>
> And he fell to the earth, and heard a voice saying unto him, Saul, Saul, why persecutest thou me?
>
> And he said, Who are thou, Lord? And the Lord said, I am Jesus whom thou persecutest: it is hard for thee to kick against the pricks.
>
> And he trembling and astonished said, Lord, what wilt thou have me to do? And the Lord said unto him, Arise, and go into the city, and it shall be told thee what thou must do.
>
> And the men which journeyed with him stood speechless, hearing a voice, but seeing no man.

Those with him, it says, "stood speechless"; in this telling, they heard a voice but saw nothing. Then, almost at the end of Acts

(26:1–20), Paul retells the experience in the first person—his own words. There are some minor variations, but the most blatant is the statement that they "were all fallen to the earth"—in other words, his companions also saw the blinding light, otherwise their falling to the ground is without explanation. But the voice, in this version, is heard only by Paul himself. It was a purely inner experience. In any case, Paul's words of conclusion are what is truly important here. He says, "Whereupon, O King Agrippa, I was not disobedient to the heavenly vision." Paul describes his encounter with the Christ as a mystical, visionary experience. It was by no means some kind of objective encounter with the resurrected Jesus of Nazareth of the Gospels. Paul was a mystic, and he knew only the mystical Christos, Christ not "after the flesh" but after the spirit. As he says, "The Lord is that Spirit."

F. W. Conybeare, in *Myth, Magic and Morals*, corroborates my own (as well as Kuhn's and Doherty's) position on Paul when he says that Paul's Christ is an a priori construction owing little or nothing to the historical man of Nazareth, and to those who allegedly knew that man and cherished his memory. The most that Paul owed to him was the ancient name Jesus/Joshua. Paul's Jesus, he says, is an ideal supernatural, superhuman saviour, destined from the beginning of the world to play a cosmic role. Paul, surprisingly, shows no acquaintance with the Sermon on the Mount or with the parables (or with the Virgin Birth and the empty tomb, for that matter). Elsewhere, Paul also describes what happened to him as God revealing his son "in me" instead of "to me," thus indicating an inner mystical vision rather than an external event. Twice in 1 Corinthians (12ff), he says he can't really describe or remember whether certain visions occurred to him "in the body or out of it, I know not; God knoweth." There is no doubt that this can serve as the legitimate foundation for the suggestion that Paul's ecstatic vision may well have been one of those super-conscious experiences that many people have had, an experience so detached from objective reality that it cannot be related to actual events in the world at all.

When Paul designates the "figure" appearing to him with his phrase "the Lord Jesus Christ," it can be seen to stand for a generic name of such a type of radiant manifestation, with no connection to any former or present living personality. Ancient Egyptian necrological science, as I have learned, predicated that the gods and the elect of perfected humanity could appear to men in whatever garments of solid or etheric matter they chose. They could appear in many different forms, clothed in flesh or clothed in light. Paul, with his Mystery Religions associations, must have been familiar with these possibilities. There's a perfect example of this phenomenon in the Book of Acts itself (14:11–12). In Lystra, a mob cried out that "the gods have come down to us in human form." They called Barnabas, Paul's associate, Zeus and Paul himself Hermes because "he was the chief speaker."

What has genuinely amazed me, in reading Massey and Kuhn, is how fully they anticipated—by over fifty years, at least—the results of current scholarship on Paul's commitment to the mystical, Gnostic view of the Christ and his avoidance of the literalist, "personal saviour" point of view. The authors of *The Jesus Mysteries*, who never once mention Kuhn's name (not even in their bibliography), come to exactly the same conclusion he reached in *Who Is This King of Glory?* long ago. As he wrote then, "Paul had striven to describe and colour in the most graphic language available, which evidently he judged to be the phraseology of the Mystery Religions, the only Christ he knew, the power and the grace of the Christ of the inner chamber of human consciousness."9

I am compelled, therefore, by my own independent research to agree that Paul's Christ was not Jesus of Nazareth. Paul himself tells us in Galatians, "I made known to you brethren, as touching the Gospel which was preached by me, that it was not after man [i.e., of human origin]. For neither did I receive it from a man, nor was I taught it, save through the revelation of the Christ revealed within me." His was the mystical Christ known down through the ages, the so-called Pagan Christ, the ray of the cosmic Logos, who was and remains non-historical, having neither beginning of days nor end of life.

In the end, then, it became extremely difficult—in fact, impossible—for me to withstand the cumulative force of reasoning on either the Gospels or Paul and the "historical Jesus." Kuhn sums it up most succinctly when he says that Paul's silence about the parables and miracles and other details of the Gospel Jesus is quite incredible. "No amount of sophistry or mental chicanery can set aside the verdict of common sense," he concludes.

Paul, it seems clear, was a Gnostic "in his essential leanings," and the reason he makes no mention of and shows no interest in a historical Jesus—he uses the mystical term "Christos" roughly 270 times—is that he had never heard of him. Obviously, he knew the Greek name Jesus as the equivalent of Joshua, and knew that the Hebrew or Jewish version of the Christos myth had Yeshua-Christos, or Jesus Christ, as its "Lord," but that is a far cry from believing in or knowing of a flesh-and-blood saviour. Paul could no more have believed in a personal Logos than could Philo, who as we have observed was just about contemporary with him. The ultra-conservatives keep insisting on a "physical" resurrection of Jesus. Paul, whose work pre-dates the first Gospel, insists on the exact opposite. His fifteenth chapter of 1 Corinthians could not possibly be clearer. I invite you to read or reread that passage for yourself. The passage is almost pure Platonism. Paul knows only a spiritual resurrection. He says, "It is sown a natural body; it is raised a spiritual body." Corruption cannot inherit in corruption. As in the Egyptian theology, only the Sahu, the spiritual body, enters into bliss. He certainly believed—as I do—in a future resurrection, but he did not believe in the resuscitation of corpses.

What's really important is that Paul's spiritual view of Christ (his Christology) and Gnostic Christianity held the early Christian movement up to a truly high standard of intellectual and philosophical excellence. Later literalizing and popularizing trends turned the Church away from "the higher and fuller concept of the Christ as the ever-coming world Messiah of a divine spirit transfiguring humanity," to what Kuhn calls the "winsome-but-gruesome personal Jesus." Before anyone becomes too upset by the use of the adjective "gruesome" here, it should be said that no offence is intended to the traditionalist mind. In referring to it, I am thinking expressly of certain extreme forms of both Protestantism and Catholicism, where in hymns, art, and a myriad other forms so much is made of "the blood," the bleeding wounds, and the supposedly pierced heart of the personal saviour on a cross. To a total outsider, unfamiliar with all of this, the sudden introduction to so much religious gore can, as I myself have witnessed, be a traumatizing experience. It is both unnecessary and wrong, a mistaking of myth for historicity. [10]

No doubt it will come as a great surprise—and may well bring, at first, a sense of loss—to those who, over their years of traditional-style learning and worship, have become attached to a "personal Jesus" to discover that his historicity is in question. It was the same for me some years ago, when I first began to look hard at the Jesus-of-history/Christ-of-faith dichotomy. But I have come to realize just how totally luminescent and freeing the position argued by Massey, Kuhn, and many others really is. The personal Jesus concept is truly a limiting, and deeply divisive, dead end. The historical evidence simply isn't there. It's a classic example of the emperor's having no clothes. What is more, it commits idolatry by making a flesh-and-blood man into God—thus forever alienating Jews, Muslims, and believers of a host of other religions, and making full religious harmony on the planet a perpetual impossibility. It has, most notably in the United States, created a kind of passive-dependent Jesus cult totally prone to extreme magical thinking. It restricts Christhood to one person in all of history, instead of acknowledging the deep, archetypal power of a universal—yes, cosmic—principle and ideal. There is no doubt that by exalting Jesus in a unique magnificence, the Church has too often let the divinity in every human heart—yours and mine—lie fallow. Kuhn is right. The deity that needs exaltation is that struggling "within the breasts of the sons and daughters of Earth. Jesus' enthronement is the disinheritance of the common human being. . . . The historical Jesus blocks the way to the spiritual Christ in the chamber of the heart."

The truth, I have discovered, is that this inner experience of the presence and power of God as the Christ within our own consciousness is the best proof of the authenticity of true Christianity. As a scholar friend of mine puts it, "I don't need an external, allegedly historical figure to experience God. But I do need the story of Jesus, the mythos, to bring home to me in power the meaning of the struggle and destiny of my own soul. I don't need the crumbs of assumed but largely incomprehensible 'events' in the past, but rather the feast of a living parable that illuminates my spiritual journey today. It's the allegorical or metaphorical interpretation of the Gospel story that makes God relevant and real to me."

I am today wholly convinced that a Christianity that embodies and proclaims a spiritual Christos, or Jesus Christ, available in every heart will hold once more the intellectual and moral dynamism first experienced by St. Paul and the other earliest Christians. Once again, I am filled with a firm hope for the future.

10

THE ONLY WAY AHEAD

Cosmic Christianity

*The historical Jesus as a civilizing influence has now been
tried for nearly twenty centuries. With a weird irony, not only
has it not in large measure elevated humanity in the West above
an earlier barbarism, but it has in fact been used as a cloak for the
worst atrocities and inhumanities that history records. The foulest
cruelties were perpetrated in the very name of the gentle Nazarene!
It well behooves humanity in the West now to try the concept
of the indwelling Christ, the hope of our glory.*

— ALVIN BOYD KUHN, The Root of All Religion

IT WOULD BE MISLEADING to leave you with the overall
impression that the conclusions we are about to examine
came at me like some bolt from the blue. Faithful readers of
my previous books, and of my columns over the years, will know
that I have been steadily and inexorably pushed by the Spirit
toward an independent realization of many of the truths expressed
much more boldly and fully in this volume. This is especially the
case with my previous book, *Finding the Still Point*, where I made
my strongest case yet for the indwelling presence of the divine
(Incarnation) in the life and soul of every human being. That book
was already at the printer before I had read even a line of my

major source authors in this present book. Those who remember
my much earlier *Life After Death* may recall that in the chapter
titled "The Christ Myth as the Ultimate Myth of the Self," I rea-
soned that the story of Jesus was indeed the story of every person,
and it gains its true meaning and relevance for us only if it is seen
in that light. Whether there ever was a so-called historical Jesus
really makes no difference to the meaning of his story, or mythos,
for our lives. Significantly, I began that passage, written over a
decade ago, with the following words of Joseph Campbell: "The
biography of a spiritual teacher is not an account of historical
facts. . . . It is a symbol of the spiritual biography of that man, and
all the elements of the biography are symbolic. Just through reading them properly, you learn the message." These are words every
seminary student should be required to memorize.

I only wish I had known at the beginning of my working life and
ministry, nearly fifty years ago, what I know now. What's much
more important, though, is the inescapable conclusion that the
entire course of Western history over the past eighteen hundred
years would have been far different if a more spiritual understanding of the Christ and Christianity had prevailed at the outset,
instead of what Paul called "the letter that kills" (i.e., flat literalism). The Church's deplorable record of persecutions, wars, and
other atrocities would never have taken place. Uncounted millions would have been encouraged to nurture and bring to fruition
their own moral and spiritual Christhood, instead of always pas-
sively waiting for a perfect saviour from outside to do the job for
them. That, of course, would not have suited ecclesiastical authorities bent on maintaining control of both bodies and souls.

From the outset, in writing *The Pagan Christ*, I had a number of
crucial goals in mind. In particular, I wanted to address the future
of the Church and of Christianity, long a major passion and concern. It is only in the past few years, and then particularly during
the researching and writing of this book, however, that I have

come to understand the full nature of the problem—and to see clearly a transforming path ahead. There is no doubt whatever that the Church of the late second, third, and fourth centuries scored a great triumph in winning over the uneducated masses. But by literalizing and making a pseudo-history out of the Jesus story—by making all the ancient wisdom exoteric and commonplace—the Church turned that triumph into a pyrrhic victory of staggering proportions. Ignorance and an unquestioning faith were championed, frauds were passed for sacred truths, dissent of any kind was labelled heresy, and within a short time, all of Europe was plunged into the Dark Ages. Only a much later return to the so-called Pagans, Plato and Aristotle, injected sufficient rationality and philosophy into Christian theology to keep it alive at all.

Today, we have a situation where the ultra-conservative wing of the Church has, as a prime specimen of its devotion to credulity, U. S. President George W. Bush, the leader of the most powerful nation on earth. Bush, who has said that Jesus Christ is his "favourite philosopher," was once asked at a press conference what he thought about the ongoing debate in some American educational circles over creationism and the theory of evolution. The leader of the world's only superpower replied that in his considered view, "The jury is still out on that one." Ignorance is bliss, indeed, it seems. He is surrounded by like-minded born-again Christians—and the Pentagon is filled with them—who believe that an apocalyptic armageddon, or final battle between good and evil, is currently in God's plans, and that it will be fought in and around Jerusalem. I wonder whether he has ever even heard of the concept of a self-fulfilling prophecy. [1]

However scary that product of a literalist reading of the Bible, and of Revelation especially, may be, there is little reason for joy even when we look to the liberal wing of Christianity. Take, for example, the Jesus Seminar, the California-based scholars who for years now have been subjecting the New Testament to the most rigorous of scrutinies to determine what is bedrock and what is not. Though obviously they are the opposite of fundamentalists, they share the same basic assumption that behind the whole Jesus story, there is a historic kernel—if they can only find it. What they have found is so meagre that it frankly will not serve as sustaining, energizing spiritual food for today's men and women. Once you assume historicity and train the full glare of historical research on the Bible, the entire edifice begins to crumble. As I have argued, it is not about history, unless by that you mean the inner story of the human mind and heart in its dealings with the divine.

To realize that Jesus was, and still remains, the supreme dramatic symbol of the divinity within us all; to understand that the Christ is the divine essence of our nature; that his story is a dramatic representation of a deep element of human consciousness; to see the symbolic quality of all Scripture—all of this has made me deeply aware of the tremendously significant message I had to try to clarify and make as widely known as possible. Religion does not have to continue to be the sadly divisive part of the world's problems. As we shall see in a moment, the doctrine of Incarnation I have described here at some length gives us a basis for universal recognition of one another as brothers and sisters in God.

I trust that in arguing this case and presenting the evidence, I have succeeded in bringing to a much wider audience the work of a man I have come to regard as one of the single greatest geniuses of the twentieth century, Alvin Boyd Kuhn. From my own lengthy experience and background, I can safely say that he towers above all others of recent memory in intellect and his understanding of the world's religions. Kuhn has, I believe, more to offer the Church just now than all the scholars of the Jesus Seminar together. More than John Spong, much more than his contemporary C. S. Lewis, more than Joseph Campbell or Matthew Fox. I remain stunned at the silence with which his writings have been greeted by scholars.

Ordinary laypeople can be forgiven. He is anything but an easy read. By everyone else, his work has been deliberately, though subtly, ignored or suppressed. I hope *The Pagan Christ* will play a strong role in changing all that.

Here, then, are the nine areas where my thinking has been challenged and transformed—the areas I believe are most pregnant with hope for the future.

1. Makes the Bible Come Alive

The enigma of the Bible has been largely solved. Dark passages, cryptic narratives or events—all have been shot through with a new, though long-lost, light because of this awareness that the key to all Scripture is to be found in the doctrine of Incarnation. Once you really understand that all the myths, legends, stories, "histories," allegories, parables, and symbols are a kaleidoscope of variations on this one central theme, the Bible comes alive in a wholly new way, I have found. This is a theme I plan to explore in much greater detail someday. In the meantime, it is particularly important to remember that the Bible books were never "written" in any normal, modern sense. From the beginning, they were preserved in memory only. They made up the body of what is known as the great oral tradition, a set of ritual formulas, ceremonial rites, allegorical depictions of truth, myths, number graphs, and pictorial symbols of the realities and the phenomena of human spiritual history that had been handed down from generation to generation in unwritten form. Only here and there, chiefly to avoid their being lost, forgotten, or too badly corrupted by change, they were set down in writing and so, at last, came to later ages as books, presumably "written" or edited and revised by somebody. Kuhn says—and he documents this thoroughly—that once written, they became subject to the usual human proclivities of tampering, altering, and religious skulduggery of many kinds. The fact that they met with this treatment not only is admitted by historians of Christianity in its early stages, as we have seen, but is boasted of by the scribes and some of the Church Fathers, who thus resorted to unholy means to achieve holy ends. I quote again for emphasis a letter from St. Gregory Nazianzen, one of the most respected theologians of the early centuries, to his close friend St. Jerome, in which he said, "Nothing can impose better on a people than verbiage: the less they understand the more they admire. . . . Our Fathers and Doctors have often said, not what they thought, but that to which circumstances and necessity forced them." It really changes our understanding profoundly to realize that the books of the Bible were never written in the modern understanding of literary authorship. They were largely the final deposit on vellum or papyrus of formulas acted out and retold down through the ages. They were often direct transcriptions of the lines recited by actors in the great Mystery plays of the ancient religion.

Not only are former Bible riddles solved when we reach this new understanding, but the texts make sense as never before. Take, for example, that well-known Gospel incident of Jesus' walking on water and stilling a storm. If you see this not as some supernatural trick but as a powerful symbolic representation of the Christ within calming the "troubled ocean" of our inner fears and instilling a sense of peace, you are released from the intellectual impossibility of believing in a god-man who defies gravity and is wholly beyond our emulation today. If we see the various "miraculous" healings as a dramatic, mythical reference to the healing power of the Christ within each one of us, and if we see such otherwise incomprehensible and magical events (such as the feeding of thousands by multiplying bread or turning water into wine) as symbolizing God's gift to each of us of the divine energies by which we live and grow, the passages hit home in an entirely new way. As Kuhn says, the Gospels are the story of our souls. "The birth, the awakening of intellectual power at age twelve, the temptation or stress of conflict between the body and the soul, the development of the soul's divine potency to heal the ills and weaknesses of the flesh, the overcoming and casting out of the demonic forces of the natural man by the Christ's influence, the symbolic raising of the dead inert spiritual power to a new birth of life . . . the whole experience of the soul under the long domination of the animal instinct being itself the essence of crucifixion on the cross of matter, the final victory in the soul's radiant transfiguration of the mortal man by the spirit's light, the ultimate resurrection of the soul out of its death under the suffocating heaviness of the life of sense." There is no doubt that this utterly transforms our entire understanding of the ancient text.

There is indeed, then, a potent wisdom in the Bible, hidden though it is in necessary imagery, that bites on our personal and communal lives today as nothing else can do.

2. Inspires Fresh Hope for a Cosmic Faith

All of the research done for this book has helped me bring to my faith a fully spiritual comprehension of what was once bogged down in utterly outmoded credal and other accumulations. I really believe that applying the truths so clearly revealed by our study means that the original, more truly spiritual Christianity of the first two centuries can be recovered. For the first time, something I have been searching for all my adult life—namely, a basis for a universal, cosmic Christianity—has been rendered a possibility. The view of faith outlined here is one that knows no boundaries of sect or creed because it is based on the universal truth of the "light that lighteth every person coming into the world"; it belongs to all, regardless of ethnicity, colour, or clime. Significantly, it applies to the millions of humans who were born and died long before Christianity as a religion was ever thought of; it belongs to the now, and to the future as well. Whatever the defenders of orthodoxy have to say, and I am well aware it will be plenty, they cannot deny that the literalist, exclusivist Christianism held by the majority of Churches—"Our Church and our view of Jesus remain the only way"—is extremely divisive and will never lead to the solidarity of all humanity. It remains a serious source of global disharmony and, at times, vicious open conflict. The theologian Hans Kung has said repeatedly that there will never be global peace until there is harmony between the world's great religions, especially Islam and Christianity. But this will never happen while Christians claim to hold a monopoly on divine truth. I am not pleading here for one totally homogeneous faith to replace the current religious pluralism. Not at all. Rather, I'm urging the adoption of a profoundly unifying basis to transcend the divisive outlook that so often accompanies our traditional differences. As the poet W. H. Auden has warned us, we must either learn to love or die. Using the words "the Christ" is important for would-be Christians. But if other religions use other terms—atman, spirit, soul, the higher self—we must realize they're still speaking of the same inner reality.

As Kuhn says in his most recent book, *A Rebirth for Christianity*, "If Christianity will now recognize that the time has come to join with the other great living religious traditions, and direct its vision to the reawakening of the divine spirit, the Christos in man, it may yet vindicate its right to call its message the true religion of humanity." If you recognize the divine presence in another person, you cannot harm him or suffer your brother to endure injustice.

The words of Northrop Frye, whom I quoted near the beginning of our exploration, resonate with fresh power for me now. Just before his death, he wrote, "I think immense changes could be brought about by a Christianity . . . that was no longer crippled by notions of heresy, infallibility, or exclusiveness of a kind that should be totally renounced and not rationalized to the slightest

degree. Such a Christianity might represent the age of the Spirit."[2]
That's the new vision.

3. Clarifies the Ancient Symbols

For the first time for me, a spiritual and mystical understanding of
the Christ myth has made powerfully relevant the whole doctrine
of the Cross, the Crucifixion, and the Resurrection of the Christ.
All the old business about blood and sacrifice and suffering gods
finally comes into focus and grasps hold of both mind and heart.
The love of God is seen more clearly than ever in the "sacrifice,"
or constant outpouring of his divine nature, to secure our share in
it forever. The mythical, allegorical meaning of the Passion of
Jesus Christ as an enactment of God's role in our creation and
our incarnation as embodied "fragments of deity" is far more profound than some imagined transaction where God's wrath is nullified by the literal death of an only son.

The above point leads to my renewed awareness of the power
and the symbolism of the Eucharist itself. It is no longer a crude,
barbarous echo of some kind of cannibalistic rite, nor is it a purely
polite symbolic recalling of a two-thousand-year-old event. It
graphically and powerfully offers an immediate experience of
inwardly "feeding" upon the facts that the divine has poured out
its energies and life as our spiritual bread and drink. And it is a
dramatic experience of "re-membering," in the sense of bringing
back together all the various fragments of the "body" of God. It is
a potent symbol of the restoration of the whole family of humanity as the child of God.

4. Underlines the Dangers of Literalism

Once the literalist approach to the Gospels and the rest of the
Bible has been seen for the great blunder it has been—and in

some places remains today—the pernicious habit of targeting specific groups and lacerating them by quoting "proof texts" loses all its presumed authority. Most of the atrocities committed by the Church and its more rabid followers down through the ages have been directly inspired by literalist thinking. The lies, for example, behind all the anti-Jewish bigotry and hatred that has so tragically marked the history of Christianity almost from its inception, and that culminated in the Holocaust. The Church did not kill six million Jews, obviously. But centuries of a literal reading of the Passion narratives—especially the words, in Matthew, "His blood be upon us and our children"—and the anti-Jewish teachings of a continuous train of Christian theologians down to and including Martin Luther himself, made it possible for the Holocaust to occur. Even at present, hatred toward Jews, homosexuals, Muslims, and others is still being encouraged in some quarters by extreme biblical literalists. The biblical exposition given here, I repeat, utterly destroys this dangerous fundamentalist exegesis once and for all. We will never have peace on earth as long as literalism controls religions.

As Origen, the vigorous foe of literalism, rightly said so long ago, "Very many mistakes have been made [interpreting Scripture], because the right method of examining the holy texts has not been discovered by the greater number of readers."[3]

5. Emphasizes Our Responsibility for Our Own Evolution

The kind of spirituality of which I have written here offers a full response to what I believe to be the cardinal quest of contemporary human beings in their hunger for God. It offers living experience in the place of dry dogma. It offers an emphasis on experiencing the God within in the "now," instead of a wistful looking back over two thousand years to an unreachable ideal, a hero who, as

Carl Jung warned, appeared unique and therefore forever un-repeatable.

Rather than encouraging the belief that all we have to do is to depend on the works and moral perfection of a peerless wonder-worker from long ago, such a spirituality calls for the individual to take fullest responsibility for his or her own moral struggle. He or she is aided, to be sure, by the constant presence of the Christ spirit within, but the call is—as St. Paul often reminds us—to work out our own salvation "in fear and trembling." In other words, it stimulates vigorous moral effort rather than dampening it. The point is that no literal, historical son of God was ever sent to earth to transfigure and transform each of us by some remote magic and thus save us from the evolutionary task of transfiguring ourselves. Human beings will never really be successfully oriented toward this task until they realize that within their own minds and bodies dwells the divine power that is to be raised up and glorified in us. Paul reminded his followers at Corinth, "Don't you know that you are the temple of God and that the Spirit of God dwells within you?" God has called us to full responsibility for our own evolution, our own actions. It is only when this knowledge becomes a certainty that the individual can truly begin to focus his or her psychic energies upon stirring into full awakening the latent nature of the God within. It's the only effective way forward, morally and spiritually.

I am reminded here of what Carl Jung said about the weakness of the old Imitatio Christi approach. Jung obviously had nothing against people trying to be loving and kind. But, he said, "The Imitatio Christi will forever have this disadvantage: we worship a man as a divine model, embodying the deepest meaning of life, and then out of sheer imitation we forget to make real the profound meaning present in ourselves. If I accept the fact that a god is absolute and beyond all human experience, he leaves me cold. I do not affect him, nor does he affect me. But if I know, on the other hand, that God is a mighty activity within my own soul, at once I must concern myself with him." If we follow a Christ "out there," in other words, while ignoring the kingdom of God or the Christ within, authentic transformation never occurs.

6. Highlights Nature's Guiding Role

Nature and the material world are far more integral to the spirituality outlined here. While literalist Christianism tends to rely on a supernatural, magical, or otherworldly view of life and the universe, the ancient wisdom presented here as the matrix out of which true, spiritual Christianity emerged is entirely holistic and rooted in a natural reality that comprehends the entire cosmos. The solstitial-equinoctial basis of Christmas and Easter alone provides a natural symbolism for the deepest truths of each individual's spiritual life. The heavens do indeed "declare the Glory of God," as the Psalmist says. The first thing that strikes a novice studying ancient Egyptian religion is the huge part played in it by a daily awareness of nature and its role everywhere around us as teacher and guide. There are deep implications here for our urgent environmental concerns and a host of other current issues. I now never look at the clear night sky without recalling that Orion is the timeless figure of the heavenly Christ. The three stars of the belt have been known for millennia as the three kings, or wise men. I never see the moon now without being reminded of its reflecting the solar glory and its monthly telling of the story of our incarnation and ultimate resurrection.

The ideas of the ancients regarding the evolution of the universe in general and of humanity (especially individual humans) in particular resonate so closely with contemporary scientific thought. What ignorance once called primitive religion taught that at a certain point in evolution—when the mineral had given rise to the vegetable, then to the animal—the process could go no further.

What was needed was a metaphorical "stooping down," the "descent" or the "sacrifice" of spirit to inject a fresh and higher impulse to the process. Symbolically, the God "died" in order to be fragmented and then incarnated into the highest (humanoid) animal souls. That is the evolutionary "moment" described in the first two chapters of Genesis, when the human was made in God's likeness (mythically speaking) and Adam became "a living soul." Soon after, in the myth, Adam and Eve's "eyes were opened" and moral awareness was born. With this kind of an understanding, all the years of conflict between religion and science are seen for what they were—sheer nonsense and a sad waste of both time and lives.

7. Explains What the Jesus Story Really Means to Us

While showing the deep relevance of the Jesus story, and the persona of Jesus for the life and spiritual growth of every Christian, this fresh view of the faith leads to an escape from the false religion involved in the current idolatrous cult of a "personal" Jesus. By showing him to have been deeply true in the mythical sense rather than literally as God, the vast theological offence currently given to the majority of other faiths, particularly Islam and Judaism, is not simply mitigated—it is entirely removed. Thus lies open a way to interfaith understanding that otherwise can never exist. This has enormous potential for world peace, since there is currently an underlying religious dimension to almost every conflict on the face of the globe.

I have found that seeing the Jesus story for what it is—a profoundly spiritual allegory of the soul—in no way detracts from the moral and social teaching that for so many centuries has been so deeply connected with his assumed deeds. Unquestionably, this story has produced an infinite outpouring of compassionate activity through down the ages. I would never for a moment question the positive contributions to human welfare of traditional Christianity. But whatever the source of the teachings in the Gospels (see, for example, Luke 4:17–19, which is clearly direct from the Old Testament, however much it in turn owed to Egypt), their relevance and urgency for the human conscience remain precisely the same. They are wholly unchallenged or weakened in any way. Justice is always justice, whether expressed in hieroglyphics, Hebrew, Greek, or English. The inspiration of Jesus Christ as portrayed in the Gospels is in no way lessened by the knowledge that each of us has the potential for birthing the Christ within, and for living that out to ever fuller maturity. Quite the contrary. As Paul told the Galatians, the aim of all his efforts and teachings was that the Christ might be fully "formed in you."

8. Gives Our Rituals More Potency

Let me try to allay one possible source of alarm. Once it is realized that what formerly passed as historical—and thus to so many made little sense—is to be taken in a symbolical or allegorical manner, the fear may be that all the old pageantry, ritual, and celebration will have to go. Nothing could be further from the truth. In reality, those who celebrate Christmas knowing that the Bethlehem baby is an image of something remote from the physical and not an event in the usual sense at all will still find the stable, the manger, the ox, and the star radiantly alight with a transferred meaning poured down upon them from above. "The whole pageantry and accoutrement of meaning can be heartily entertained and in no sense (save the historical) rejected, when a reference to a reality beyond it is accepted and one that it cannot carry is rejected. It becomes translucent with beauty through simply being the agency of the mind's grasp of the supernal beauty beyond it," Kuhn asserts.

Since this is a seismic shift in thought for most people, it's essential to let the scholar himself be heard. "It may be a paradox," he explains, yet it is thoroughly true that religious imagery and pageantry exercise a far stronger dynamism when they are known to be allegorical than if they are believed to be memorials of fact. The symbol helps the mind to grasp greater reality over in the subjective world; from that clearer vision the mind can swing back and embrace the symbol as an integral part of the great treasure of light caught by its aid." This is to refute the charge that if the events of religious festivity are thrown out as non-historical, Christmas and Easter and ceremonies like them will lose all their gripping impressiveness. On the contrary, Kuhn affirms, *the symbols will exert a far weightier significance when they are envisioned truly as symbols and not falsely as events*. I can only add that this has been my personal experience too. The celebrations of Christmas and Easter have become infinitely more potent for me as I have learned to penetrate beyond the externals to the realities within. As Origen says, taken in its literal, allegedly historical sense, "Christ crucified is teaching for babes." Or, to quote St. Paul, "But, when I became a mature man, I put away childish things."

9. Enhances Belief in Life After Death

My belief in a glorious dimension of life yet to be revealed—a life beyond death—is even stronger now than it was when my book on the subject appeared over a decade ago. What the scholarship explored has done is to deepen and enrich that belief in more ways than I can fully describe.

If you believe in the truths of the most ancient of human wisdom—the wisdom expounded by the Egyptians, the Orphics, the Pythagoreans and Plato, as well as by St. Paul, the Gnostics, Clement of Alexandria, Origen, and a host of others—we are all "sparks of divine fire struck off from the flint of the Eternal," immortal souls clad in mortal bodies. You can begin to understand how allegorically, in the minds of these illuminati, death changes its meaning entirely. Death meant simply the end of our life in the body now. That's why St. Paul could say, "Who will deliver me from the body of this death?" Or, again, "We have this treasure— the Christ within—in vessels of clay." The Greeks, with a play on words, said *soma sema*, "the body is a tomb." So Kuhn can argue that you and I, in a profound sense, are never going to be more "dead" than we are right at this moment. He says, "Right now our deific souls are at the very bottom of the arc of death and can never be as dead again as they are now and have been." As we live our lives here, immersed in matter, we are gaining experience and expanding consciousness. But we are, in a deep sense, alien- ated from, or "dead" to, the spiritual realm whence we originally came and to which we shall one day return. That's a belief that changes how you look at everything and everyone.

This view of life and death also transforms the way ancient sacred texts should be read, including the various Books of the Dead. What we call physical death is really the moment of our rebirthing and return to glory. At that point, depending on how spiritually mature we have become through our "death in matter," we either move on to "heaven" (to take on new responsibilities) or come back in the "cycle of necessity" (to reincarnate and grow further).

I have thought a lot about reincarnation since I argued the case against it in *Life After Death*, but I have been challenged to examine that theory much more closely through this latest research. I still have not made up my mind. Certainly some of the brightest lights of the early Church believed in it, and that belief persisted for sev- eral centuries in the face of growing opposition. Indeed, the fact that there was so much resistance to it from the third century on leads me to suspect it was a serious threat to the paternalism and authoritarianism that Rome had come to espouse so heartily. Not surprisingly, Rome didn't want the masses doing what Paul had so strongly urged: working out their own salvation with fear and trembling. The Church wanted passive obedience, not karmic self-responsibility.

I was thrilled when I first read how the ancient Chaldean Oracles said, "All things are the progeny of fire." This ultimate symbol for the divine is where we all originate. But we walk about in near-total forgetfulness of who we really are. As Plato said, "Humans are on Earth like beings stricken with amnesia." This led to his theory of reminiscence—that all learning ultimately is a form of remembering. The relevance of this for religion, and spiritually in general, is tremendous. Kuhn says evocatively, "Salvation, the whole aim of religion, is by way of rekindled memory of slumbering divinity." I love that. Sacred literary composition for the ancient sages had one supreme aim: to reveal the heroic struggle of the soul-fire of humanity to overcome its prison in matter and free itself to transform mortality into immortality.

In short, my faith that the Christ within us is indeed "the hope of glory" still to come has been fortified by the sweep of Kuhn's vast knowledge and the razor edge of his logic and reason. As he has said so well, "Beneath the superficial consciousness, wrapped up with the concerns of ordinary existence in each mortal, there slumbers the unawakened energy of a divine nature."

Such a faith, so very far from being escapist or life-avoiding, arms us with the moral and intellectual courage to live our lives to the fullest for the advancement of all, *sub specie aeternitatis*—in the light of the eternal.

EPILOGUE

The historian Edward Gibbon, in his *Decline and Fall of the Roman Empire*, writes, "The practice of superstition is so congenial to the multitudes that, if they are forcibly awakened, they still regret the loss of their pleasing vision." Gibbon was echoing one of the most well-known passages from Plato's writings, the great Myth of the Cave, from the *Republic*. There, Plato tells the story of captives in a cave, forced to look at mere shadows reflected on the wall for their only glimpse of life and ignorant of the sunlit world beyond their confines. He says that if somebody were to come to free them and lead them up to the light, they might well prefer to stay in darkness. The point is that I am fully aware that there will be great resistance in some quarters to the ideas set forth in this book. Nobody likes to change, and religious views are held to more tenaciously than any others. All a person can do is try to set forth the truth as clearly as he sees it and let the Spirit take it from there.

Having spent twenty years preparing and writing his *Anacalypsis*, Godfrey Higgins writes in the preface that he had some strong trepidation over how it would be received. "I will not deny that I feel cowardly," he wrote. He foresaw the loss of some of his friends. I can identify with those feelings. But I also identify with his commitment to honour "and establish truth."

Like Higgins, I quote in conclusion, therefore, some sage words of the freed slave and Stoic philosopher Epictetus (first century C.E.) on this issue:

If you resolve to make wisdom and virtue the study and business of your life, you must be sure to arm yourself before-
hand against all the inconveniences and discouragements that
are likely to attend this resolution. I imagine that you will
meet with many scoffs and much derision; and that people
will upbraid you with turning philosopher all on the sudden.
But be not you affected or supercilious; only stick close to
whatever you are in your judgment convinced is right and
becoming; and consider this as your proper station, assigned
you by God, which you must not quit on any terms. And
remember, that if you persevere in goodness, those very men
who derided you at first will afterward turn your admirers.
But if you give way to their reproaches, and are vanquished
by them, you will then render yourself doubly and most
deservedly ridiculous.

It is my firm conclusion, at the end of this study, that Christianity did indeed take a tragically wrong turn at the end of the
third century and the beginning of the fourth. It is high time to
reverse that. A better story has taken its place!

May the Christ in each of us give us the courage to see and live
the truth.

Easter 2004

Our birth is but a sleep and a forgetting:
The Soul that rises with us, our life's Star,
Hath had elsewhere its setting,
And cometh from afar:
Not in entire forgetfulness,
And not in utter nakedness,
But trailing clouds of glory do we come
From God, who is our home.

— WILLIAM WORDSWORTH,
"Ode: Intimations of Immortality"

APPENDIX A

Background on Three Experts on Mythology, Religion, and Ancient Egypt

Godfrey Higgins (1771–1834)

Higgins, whose father was a "gentleman of small, though independent, fortune," went to Trinity Hall, Cambridge. He had a grounding in Greek and Latin and early on wrestled with the works of Euclid, John Locke's *On the Understanding*, and the writings of Varro, Macrobius, and Cicero. He preferred the philosopher Epictetus to the Greek poets, and he gained familiarity with a impressive range of other classical authors. As soon as possible he turned his attention to the "evidence upon which our religion was founded," and was both shocked and intrigued by what he discovered. He then widened the inquiry to include the origin of all religions, nations, and languages. He taught himself languages ancient and modern; visited libraries in France, Rome, and Naples; and wrote a book on the Druids in the process. One of his earliest discoveries, he says, was that it was "impossible" to look on the supposed histories of ancient empires or peoples, or on the old mythologies, as having anything whatever to do with actual events. This led eventually to his conviction that a high civilization had existed prior to all recorded history. He became convinced that there was a most ancient and universal religion from which all later creeds and doctrines everywhere sprang. He believed that this primordial religion possessed accurate knowledge of universal and cosmic phenomena, and that it positioned no person or institution as intermediary in man's communion with the divine.

Higgins soon realized that nothing he had been taught as a youth about faith and religion could be relied upon at all. Once he had taught himself Hebrew, he says he "very soon discovered that no translation of the Book of Genesis, either by Jew or Christian, could be depended upon." In fact, he remarks that "almost all the latter part of my life has been spent in unlearning the nonsense I learned in my youth." This has been largely my experience too.

Higgins set out on what he regarded as the most valuable contribution to progress one man could make. He says he shortly saw that in his arduous labours, he "was striking the hardest blow that ever was struck at the tyranny of the sacerdotal [priestly] order— that I was doing more than any man had ever done before to disabuse and enlighten mankind, and to liberate them from the shackles of prejudice in which they were bound." Not surprisingly, his work was constantly attacked and suppressed by outraged religious opponents.

Higgins was convinced he had proved, among many other things, that the Celtic Druids were originally priests who emigrated from India, and that they were both the introducers of the Cadmean system of letters (from Cadmus, the legendary founder of Thebes) and the builders of Stonehenge, Carnac, and other cyclopean works found in Asia and Europe.

Here is my favourite Higgins quotation: "Had Jesus considered any symbol or confession of faith necessary, he would have given one. As he has not given one, and as he did not take it upon himself to legislate in the case, on every principle of sound reasoning it must be held that he did not think a belief in this or that faith, as it is called, was necessary to salvation."[1]

Gerald Massey (1828–1907)

Relatively little is known of Massey's career. His humble birth at Gamble Wharf, Hertfordshire, England, in May 1828, held scant promise for the future. His parents were illiterate and his education was meagre. From the age of eight, he laboured twelve hours a day, first at a silk mill, breathing a rank atmosphere amid the deafening roar of incessant machines, then as a straw-plaiter in the marshes, an even unhealthier environment. For three years, he suffered from tertian ague, a disease acquired from this.

In later life, Massey said, "Having to earn my own bread by the eternal cheapening of flesh and blood so early, I never knew what childhood meant. Ever since I can remember I have had the aching fear of want, throbbing in heart and brow. The child comes into the world like a new coin with the stamp of God upon it, and in the manner in which rich people sweat down sovereigns by hustling them in a bag to get gold dust off them, so is the poor man's child hustled and sweated down in this society to get wealth from him. . . . So blighting are the influences which so surround thousands in early life, to which I can bear bitter testimony."

But Massey improved his life at every opportunity, and in his spare time, he read voraciously. Books were scarce, however, and he memorized several chapters of the Bible, read *Robinson Crusoe* and John Bunyan. He discovered English, Roman, and Greek history, and a ravishing awakening ensued—the wonders of a new world. "Till then," he says, "I had wondered why I lived at all. Now I began to think that the crown of all desire and the sum of all existence was to read and get knowledge. Read! Read! Read! I used to read at all possible places—and in bed till three in the morning."

Massey became increasingly interested in Egyptology. Finally, after years of study, he wrote a series of brilliant scholarly works on the religion and mythology of ancient Egypt. In 1881 he published, in two volumes, *A Book of the Beginnings. The Natural Genesis* followed in 1883, and finally, in 1907, he published the two-volume *Ancient Egypt: The Light of the World.*

Dr. Alvin Boyd Kuhn acknowledged that Gerald Massey had been a great inspiration to him. In *A Rebirth for Christianity*, Kuhn called specific attention to the enormous value to him of Massey's research on Christian origins. He writes, "With brilliant scholarship and insight he pierced Egypt's enigmatic scriptology, and documented the provenance of both Old and New Testament literature from remote Egyptian sources. He forced us to ask how the four Gospels of the Christian canon could be the biography of any Messianic personality living in the first Christian century, when he traced their texts back to Egyptian documents that must have been venerable even in 3500 B.C.E."

To Gerald Massey, it was an unforgivable pretense for the clergy to continue to preach that man was a fallen creature doomed to plead for God's salvation. Every advance made by science for humanity was the result of research and perseverance, not praying to "a jealous God." Massey proclaimed, "It is a sad farce for you to pray for God to work a miracle . . . when you are doing all you can to prevent it."

The death of Jesus could not save man from himself, he argued. Massey was adamant in his belief that man, as the old Egyptians taught, was what he was as a result of what he had done. There was no dodging the law of cause and effect.

One of Massey's greatest contributions was his lecture "The Coming Religion." It is poignant with sincerity. He asserted that each person must do his own thinking and have absolute freedom of expression. He stressed that the new religion about to be born must have "sincerity of life, in place of pretended belief; a religion of science, in place of superstition." This religion, he predicted, will proclaim man's ascent rather than his fall. It will be a religion of fact in the present, not of faith for the future. The temple will be what it was intended to be—the human form—rather than an edifice of brick and stone. It will be a religion of accomplishment rather than of worship, and in place of the many narrow creeds, it will be a religion of life. Above all, it will be a joyous religion, Massey affirmed, a cosmic path for all. [2]

Alvin Boyd Kuhn (1880–1963)

His brief obituary in *The New York Times* on September 15, 1963, is most notable for what it misses and leaves out. [3] But its brevity and opacity are symbolic of the severely muted response that greeted the man and his monumental achievement.

Kuhn was born on September 22, 1880, on a farm in Franklin County, Pennsylvania. While in high school, the future scholar of comparative religions was able to take two years of classical Greek—an experience he later realized was hugely important for his "true life's work." He gave a graduation valedictory address called "The Lyre of Orpheus," which dealt with Jason and the Argonauts in their search for the storied Golden Fleece. It was this speech that Kuhn felt presaged his later fascination with the Orphics and with

Platonism. He became convinced early on that his role would be to reawaken the "supernal wisdom," and to be the one who recovered the Golden Fleece of ancient truth for the good of the modern world.

Kuhn resembles his mentor, Gerald Massey, in that he did a prodigious amount of reading and research on his own. After a couple of years of teaching elementary school, he obtained a B.A. degree at the age of twenty-three. He taught for twenty-five years, but at the same time, he pursued his more serious academic search into the origins of religious symbols and meanings. At the age of forty-six, he was able to study philosophy at Columbia University and obtain a Ph.D. Finally, the cherished dream of writing and lecturing opened up. He was offered several posts at universities but he preferred to remain free to lecture and continue his research. He continued his career up to the week he died.

Kuhn founded his own publishing firm and produced a number of his own books and monographs himself. This might have been a mixed blessing, in my view. I know from my own experience how much a book's success depends upon marketing and promotion, and this self-publishing aspect (in addition to the religious hostilities already mentioned) might well have a lot to do with the lack of attention his work was to receive.

Apart from his almost unbelievable erudition, Kuhn had the energy and capacity for the work of three men. His nearly two thousand public lectures—always lengthy, detailed, and delivered to packed houses, according to eyewitnesses with whom I have spoken—represent by themselves a huge outpouring of vitality and strength. He was a frequent visitor, for example, to Toronto, where his annual week-long lecture series drew capacity crowds for years.

APPENDIX B

More Similarities between the Egyptian Christ, Horus, and Jesus

- Horus in ancient Egyptian wisdom comes as "the Lord of life and freedom"; Jesus in the Gospels comes that we might have life and "have it more abundantly." Horus comes with the title of "the Deliverer," for those who are "in their prison cells" (i.e., entombed in matter). Jesus comes to set the captives free and to liberate the oppressed. Horus is the Egyptian prototype of the chosen one (called the Servant by Isaiah), who came for "a light to lighten the gentiles, to open blind eyes, to bring out the prisoners from their dungeons, and them that sit in darkness out of the prison-house." His earthly father was Seb, or Joseph. Seb was also of royal descent.

- Jesus came as the Messiah, the Christos, the anointed one. Horus, according to a passage in the Egyptian Ritual where he addresses his father, Osiris, also likened this blessing to "the gift of grace and of spiritual unction." He tells Osiris, "I have strengthened thy existence. . . . I have given thee thy soul, thy strength, thy victory. I have anointed thee with offerings of holy oil." It is no coincidence that the word *messiah* comes from the Hebrew word for "anointed one." The Greek equivalent is *christos*, from a root also meaning "to anoint." (The hidden esoteric meaning of all this talk about anointing is that in each human being, the guardian angel, the spirit—the divine element or fragment or spark—and the "animal human" anoint each other according to the ancient wisdom. The union of spirit with flesh gives spirit the opportunity for experience and flesh the opportunity for glory to come. Neither is inferior to the other in the grand evolutionary plan.)

• The Christ of the Gospels is the coming one, "he that should come," while "he that cometh"—bringing peace—was the Egyptian Jesus, Iu-em-hetep. According to the earliest Greek historian, Herodotus, the father of secular history, this Jesus was to be found eighteen thousand years earlier in Egyptian religion. In the New Testament, it is said of the future manifestor, "Then shall they see the Son of Man coming in a cloud with power and great glory. But when these things begin to come to pass, look up, and lift up your heads; because your redemption draweth nigh." And of Osiris coming in the clouds of heaven, we read, "The Osiris passes through the clouds, turns back the opposers, gives life to the ministers of the sun. The face of the Osiris [or Horus] is rendered great by his crown. Lift up your heads! Pay ye attention! Make way for your Lord."

• In the famous *kenosis*, or "emptying," passage in Paul's Letter to the Philippians, the Apostle says that the Christ "emptied himself." In the Egyptian Ritual, we learn that Horus (Iusu, Iusa, or Jesus) "disrobes" to reveal himself while he presents himself to earth. In ancient esoteric thought, the entire process of the god or the soul coming down to incarnation often involved his taking off layers of glorious apparel on the one hand while assuming ever more dense garments at the same time—signifying immersion in the opacity of matter. Obviously, a humiliation, the taking-on of the role of a less glorious being, was being depicted; it was an emptying-out of glory. At one stage or another of the myth, all three persons of the Egyptian Trinity, Isis, Osiris, and Horus, are represented "descending" to this earth in humble, human form.

- Ra (or Osiris/Horus) manifests as "the burning one," "he who sends his fire into the place of destruction," "he who sends fire upon the rebels." Christ also comes in the person of the burning one and the sender of destruction by fire. He is proclaimed by Matthew to be the baptizer with fire. He says, in another pronouncement, "I am come to send fire upon the earth."

- Osiris/Horus is the god who opens pathways in the highest heaven, and as the risen god, "his form is of the eternal essence . . . he shines and he sees his mysteries." He is also referred to as the splendid one who lights up the sarcophagus (tomb) and raises the soul of the deceased. Jesus is the resurrection and the life, the door, the tomb-breaker, and the establisher of a foothold in the heavens. In the vanishing vision of the risen Christ in the Gospels, "he was taken up, and a cloud received him" as the inhabitant of the empyrean above.

- Horus says in the Egyptian Ritual, "I am Horus, the Prince of Eternity." John's Jesus tells the disciples that he was with the

Father before all worlds. In the Ritual, Horus says, "Verily before Isis was, I grew up and waxed old, and was honoured before those who were with me in glory."[1]

- According to the Synoptic Gospels, Jesus' ministry lasted only one year; you have to examine John's version to get a ministry of almost three years. Horus, because of the nature of the solar cycle, typically reigned for one year. (By the way, both Clement of Alexandria and Origen held the view that Jesus' ministry lasted only one full year.)

- Regarding the Transfiguration, the Egyptian Ritual says: "Horus gives thee the gods, he makes them come to thee, they illumine thy face." On the Mount of Transfiguration (Mt. Tabor), Jesus' face "did shine as the sun and his garments became as white as the light." Both these stories teach the illuminative power of solar deity, and thus of God behind and through it all.

- Like Jesus in the Gospels, Horus was the raiser of the dead. Kuhn, following Massey, contends that the story of the paralytic who was let down through the roof and was told by Jesus to take up his bed and walk is an actualization of a passage in the Ritual where the deceased is told, "Horus causes thee to stand up at the risings. Thou art raised up; thou art not dead." The Lazarus story is another example of this.

- Jesus dies between two thieves. But in Egyptian lunar lore, "two thieves of the light," who happened to be the minor deities Anup and Aan, are at one point drawn up on either side of the sun god. The inner message was that incarnation steals away the divine light—only to add to its brightness. Here, indeed, would appear to be the authentic pre-

Christian prototype of the Gospel Crucifixion between two thieves.

• The first Palm Sunday, Jesus' triumphal but strangely inconclusive ride through Jerusalem in the Gospels, is really a literalized but mishandled part of the ancient myth where Horus, too, rides on the back of a donkey. The real meaning in both cases—though obscured in the New Testament rendition—is that the divine element, or the god, in every person rides into glory on the back of the animal self. It's to mark the final triumph of the soul in man over his lower world. Massey, with typical erudition, points out that palm leaves were thrown in front of Jesus because the palm tree is an arcane symbol of the lunar month. It was widely believed to be the only tree to produce an additional branch every twenty-eight days!

• The familiar story of the man who asked Jesus to permit him to enter into a nearby herd of pigs and then rushed them headlong to their destruction over a cliff and into the sea seems at first sight to be original to the Gospels. But in the ancient Egyptian judgment scene, when the person whose life marked him as evil was condemned and rejected, he was delivered to a being called the Typhonian beast—a combined crocodile/hippopotamus/pig. The esoteric meaning here is quite plain. He was not released but sent down again into incarnation in the body of a beast, thrust back into the animal body for more learning experience. In the Gospel account, the entry of the rejected "evil spirits" into the pigs, plus the rush down into the water (symbolizing matter), is thus this same reality—the return to indwelling of an animal organism by souls in need of further moral evolution.

- Horus says he has come with empowerment and certitude to offer the comfort that he "lives on amidst all overthrow." This is a sort of a "Rock of Ages" certitude that abides amidst all flux. In his turn, many centuries later, Jesus says, "In this world, you face persecution. But, take courage; I have conquered the world!"

APPENDIX C

Two Strange Passages

There are two oddities from the text of the New Testament itself. They fully support the thesis that the true background of the Jesus story is the eternal, spiritual Christ myth. Both come from the Book of Revelation—the book that Gerald Massey contended holds some of the earliest material in the entire corpus of New Testament writings.

a) Revelation 1:13, in the King James Version, says, "And I saw in the midst of the seven candlesticks one like unto the Son of Man, clothed with a garment down to the foot, and girt about the paps with a golden girdle." "Paps" is the archaic word for a woman's breasts. In the Greek, the word used is the plural *mastos*, which the lexicon defines as "the breast, esp., of the swelling breast of a woman." Rarely, the plural was used to refer to a man's breasts, but the prevailing sense is female. The fact that the figure in this passage from Revelation wore a "girdle," or cincture, about the breasts—the modern equivalent would be a brassiere—confirms that the breasts in question are female. Indeed, the New English Bible translates the plural as though it were a singular —"with a golden girdle round his breast." The New Revised Standard Version tries to avoid any embarrassment by wrongly translating it as "chest." True, the word in Greek here for "girdle" is the same one used to describe John the Baptist's girdle. But there it plainly says that it was wound about his loins, not his chest.

What makes me come down on the side of the KJV's take—though preferring the translation of breasts to paps—is that something more than the surface meaning is at play here. Among the ancients, for centuries before the Christian era and contemporaneously with it, it was common to picture divinities with features of the opposite sex, denoting wholeness. For example, Horus was at times depicted with "the locks of girlhood." The male gods Bacchus and Serapis often appear with breasts, and Venus, goddess of love for the Romans, is sometimes depicted with a beard!

A deep esoteric point was being made. In ancient philosophy and religion, before Creation, God—all life—was seen as Father and Mother in one. Only by slow development did God become Mother and Father separately. The belief was that human beings too were androgynous before a bifurcation took place and they split into separate sexes. Since there are many other references in Revelation that betray the author's deep knowledge of so-called Pagan symbolism, it's quite possible that the Son of Man figure with breasts echoes this primal oneness theme. In any case, this figure of the Christos is by no means any historical man. It's an archetype of the spiritual, timeless Christ of the myth.

b) In Revelation 11:8, there is a most puzzling passage in which two "witnesses" are to be killed. "And their dead bodies shall lie in the street of the great city, which spiritually *pneumatikōs* is called Sodom and Egypt, *where also our Lord was crucified*," reads the text [my emphasis]. Once again, it must be stressed that the author is clearly concerned not with any historical events, or a "Jesus of history," but with symbolism and allegory. Jerusalem, and not Sodom or Egypt, clearly is the location for the death of Jesus in all four Gospel accounts. Sodom and Egypt here are an esoteric, "spiritual," or symbolic way of speaking of this earth and of time (as opposed to the heavenly realms and eternity). "Our Lord" here is once more not a "personal" Jesus but the eternal Christos.

GLOSSARY

Allegory and Allegorical

Allegory is an extended figure of speech, a continuous metaphor. St. Augustine defined allegory as a mode of speech whereby one thing is understood by means of another. It's very important to notice that the term itself is used in one of the earliest New Testament writings by Paul. In Galatians 4:24, he says: "Which things [the story of Abraham and Sarah] contain an allegory." In other words, what seems like a historical narrative is not one at all. *The Cambridge Encyclopedia* calls allegory "a literary device by which another level of meaning is concealed within what is usually a story of some kind." We are so used to the literal approach to Scripture that we fail to remember that the greatest scholars of the first two Christian centuries employed the allegorical method almost entirely. For Origen, for example, the allegorical method was for spiritually mature Christians. He called the literalists "somatic" (i.e., physically oriented) believers. Allegory, he said, takes one from the level of simplistic "belief" to actual heart-and-mind knowledge, or "gnosis." On the other hand, sheer literalism, he said, leads only to a popular, irrational faith. It is the allegorical method of interpretation that marks the approach the first compilers of the New Testament habitually took toward the Old Testament. My thesis here is that all Scripture is by nature allegorical, and that to treat it otherwise is to conclude in serious error.

Esoteric and Exoteric

Esoteric means "inner" or "hidden." It's a kind of spiritual wisdom kept from crass outsiders with no spiritual ambitions. In the Gospels, Jesus applies the esoteric principle sharply when he warns the disciples not to throw "pearls before swine." Exoteric is, of course, the opposite, meaning "external" and "open." Christianity began as an esoteric religion but was changed within three centuries into one almost wholly exoteric.

Incarnation

Quite literally, the word means "in the flesh." It comes from two Latin words, *in* and *carne*. The central, orthodox Christian doctrine of Incarnation is limited to the presumed historical person of Jesus, or Yeshua/Joshua, the "Word made flesh." But as the scholars referenced here have proved beyond a shadow of doubt, this doctrine has from earliest times been applied not to one individual but to every member of our species. The Egyptians taught this; the Greeks, especially the Orphics, Pythagoras, and Plato, taught this; and so did the Mystery Religions of the Greco-Roman world. Dr. Alvin Boyd Kuhn's major thesis is this: "There is but one central theme to the drama of human life, i.e., the interrelated history of the two components of man's life—soul and body, god and animal." The term "incarnation" is used throughout this book to refer to the God within each of us—the "Light which lighteth every person coming into the world." To quote the great American transcendentalist Ralph Waldo Emerson, "Man is a god in ruins."

Metaphor

The Concise Oxford Dictionary defines a metaphor as the "application of a name or descriptive term or phrase to an object or action to which it is imaginatively but not literally applicable." Examples of metaphors include "the fog was a grey cat prowling across the harbour" and "the moon was a lighthouse to the wanderers lost in the forest's gloom." In short, a metaphor is the imaginative use of one term to describe another to which it does not normally apply. Scripture is filled with such figures of speech. Jesus, for example, says, "I am the door," "I am the vine," and "I am the bread of life." All language about God must of necessity be a metaphor, since he/she is beyond any literal description. Religion forgets this at its peril.

Mystery Religions

This refers to a range of religious rites and cults spread throughout the ancient Greco-Roman world. Full admission was limited to those with genuine spiritual aspirations; they went through elaborate secret initiation rituals, or "mysteries." The most famous of these religions were the mysteries of Demeter at Eleusis, in Greece, but those of Dionysus, Isis, and Mithras (which was remarkably like Christianity) were all similar. They involved deeply moving experiences aimed at awakening to full consciousness the reality of the god within, and they held forth the promise of eternal life. All of them are traceable in one form or another to Egyptian—or, in the case of Mithras, Persian—sources. Plutarch tells us they arrived in Rome about 70 B.C.E. Mithraism, with its baptism, eucharist, and other rituals, gave Christianity a close "run" as a rival for about two hundred years. Christianity, in its earliest days, also had its "mysteries"—the doctrine of the Trinity, the Eucharist, and so on. Paul often uses terms taken from the Mystery Religions, showing much more kinship with them than orthodoxy has acknowledged.

Symbol, Symbolic, and Symbolism

The American philosopher and educator John Dewey (1859–1952) says in his book *The Quest for Certainty*, "The invention or discovery of symbols is doubtless by far the greatest single event in the history of man. Without them no intellectual advance is possible; with them, there is no limit set to intellectual development except inherent stupidity." Dewey is right. It is a truth, however, often forgotten by critics of religion, and by religious people themselves. There are, as the scholar Thomas Masson noted in his book *Ascensions*, many things, those utterly beyond the power of words to convey, "which can be only indicated by symbols understood by the few and reinterpreted for wider circles." Kuhn, commenting on this phenomenon, quotes Emerson: "A good symbol is a missionary to convince thousands." In our present culture, with its tendency to be overawed by science and technology, and thus prone to the error that only the "scientific method" results in true knowledge, we need to be reminded that it is not just religion that relies upon symbolism in its thinking. The physicist James Jeans, in his book *The World around Us*, says, "When we try to discuss the ultimate structure of the atom, we are driven to speak in terms of similes, metaphors, and parables." Today we cannot be reminded too often of the power of imagery and symbolism of every kind to change our awareness and our lives. Almost the whole of contemporary advertising is based upon the use of symbols. All language about God is, in the end, symbolic.

Notes

1 Christians and others assume that the Greek name Jesus was the original name of the saviour. This was impossible. The name Jesus did not
exist, and would not have been spelled with the letter *J*, until about six
hundred years ago. There was no *J* in any language prior to the fourteenth century in England. The letter did not become widely used until
the seventeenth century. *The Encyclopedia Americana* contains the following on the letter *J*: "The form of J was unknown in any alphabet until
the 14th century. Either symbol J or I used initially generally had to be
the sound of Y as in year. Gradually the two symbols J and I were differ-
entiated, the J usually acquiring consonantal force and thus becoming
regarded as a consonant, and the I becoming a vowel. It was not until
1630 that the differentiation became accepted in England." In the 1611
King James Version of the Bible, there was no *J* letter. James was spelled
Iames and Jesus was spelled Iesous. In the ancient Latin and Greek
languages, Jesus was spelled with the letter *I*. In Hebrew we know there
was no *J* either, so Jesus was originally spelled Yeshua. But the *ua* ending
in Yeshua's name, when transliterated into Greek, is feminine singular,
which presents a problem. The Church simply changed *ua* to *u*; thus
Jesus became a male saviour. What most people do not understand is that
the *us* ending to Jesus' name was set up to denote male gender. The *ous*
and the *us* ending in the Greek name Iesous and the Latin name Iesus also
denote the masculine singular. Where did the name Jesus originate? Simply put, it was derived from the Latin Iesus, which was derived from the
Greek Iesous, which in turn was derived from the Egyptian Iusa. "Jesus"
has Egyptian roots. See also Kuhn's *Who Is This King of Glory?*, page 264.

2 *The Secret Lore of Egypt*, p. 60.

3. Richard Holloway, *Doubts and Loves* (Edinburgh: Canongate Books, 2001).

4. Kuhn's first book, *Theosophy: A Modern Revival of the Ancient Wisdom*, published by Henry Holt and Co. in New York, in 1930, was his Ph.D. thesis at Columbia. It was the first and only time that any university in Europe or America had ever permitted anyone to win the degree with a thesis on Theos [or God], a thesis for which the Society later criticized him. Here again we can discern possible problems for him in terms of reception by the wider public. Theosophy is an honourable and learned branch of philosophy dealing with hidden or mystical teachings of the past, but there were some messy controversies involving Madame H. P. Blavatsky, one of the founders of the movement, which no doubt cast some clouds over the entire subject in some circles. At any rate, as a debut title it was bound to give Kuhn's critics and enemies a tool with which to oppose his challenging ideas. Kuhn's *Lost Light* was followed by scores of books and printed lectures, all of which focused on the background and meaning of religious symbolism in general and that of the Christian religion in particular. *Who Is This King of Glory?: A Critical Study of the Christos-Messiah Tradition*, one of his most important works, was published in 1944; *Sex as Symbol* came out in 1945; and the real shocker, *Shadow of the Third Century: A Revaluation of Christianity*, a book that exposed the Church's use and abuse of Pagan sources (and that every seminarian and cleric should read at the earliest opportunity), appeared in 1949. *India's True Voice* was published in 1955, and in 1970 there appeared, posthumously, his smaller but prophetic volume *A Rebirth for Christianity*, which is still in print and selling today. Because of greatly renewed interest in Kuhn's findings today, Kessinger Publishing, in Montana, a specialist in rare esoteric books, has been reprinting all his major works. In addition, Health Research of Makulumne Hills, California, has brought out *Hark! Messiah Speaks* and Kuhn's last-completed book on nature, *The Ultimate Canon of Knowledge*. It has also published two of his insightful monographs: *Christ's Three Days in Hell* and *Case of the Missing Messiah*. Kuhn also left behind his unfinished autobiography, *Great Pan Returns*, and a book titled *Krishnamurti and Theosophy*. Other unpublished Kuhn manuscripts include "Rudolph Steiner's 'Mystery of Golgotha'" and several untitled pieces. See the bibliography for further details.

5. Northrop Frye, *The Double Vision: Language and Meaning in Religion* (Toronto: University of Toronto Press, 1991), p. 58.

6. See the explosive 1999 book *The Jesus Mysteries*, by Timothy Freke and Peter Gandy.

2: SETTING THE STAGE

1. See glossary.

2. See Galatians. 4:24–25.

3. "Mystery of Solar Neutrinos Solved at Underground Site," *Toronto Star*, November 25, 2003.

4. I am indebted here in part to the Reverend Larry Marshall, a learned colleague who has immersed himself in ancient spiritualities and philosophies, especially the writings of Massey and Kuhn, for many years.

3: CHRISTIANITY BEFORE CHRISTIANITY

1. Eusebius, *Ecclesiastical History*, chapter 17 of Book 2.

2. Godfrey Higgins, *Anacalypsis*, p. 441.

3. Gerald Masey, *The Natural Genesis*, vol. 1, p. 313.

4. Incidentally, Horus says the same thing in the same role, and Lord Krishna, in Hinduism, cries, "I am the letter A, I am the beginning and the end," while the Christ of Revelation says, "I am the Alpha and Omega." Like Jesus, Krishna tells his disciples he will dwell in them and they in him. He says he is the light and the life and the sacrifice.

5. Egyptologist Erik Hornung says on page 34 of *The Secret Lore of Egypt*, "The roots of Hermeticism might reach back to the beginning of the second millennium B.C.E.

6. I am indebted to Kuhn for most of the research here, but for a more recent examination of the same subject, see Marcus Borg, *Jesus and Buddha: The Parallel Sayings*.

7. See William Stewart, "The Egyptian Secret," in *Quest* magazine, May–June 2003.

8. In the Book of Enoch, written before or about 170 B.C.E., the Christ is spoken of as already existing in heaven and is referred to at times as the Son of Man. There are echoes of Enoch in Revelation and in Paul's letters, as well as in the Gospels.

9. In Montfaucon's *Antiquities*, a statue of a hierophant of the Mysteries

depicts a woman dramatizing the role of the Syrian goddess Cybele. She is shown wearing an Episcopal-type mitre on her head, a tunic or cassock like a Catholic priest down to her ankles, and a surplice, with overall an Episcopal cope with the twelve signs of the zodiac along the borders. The similarities to later Christian robes are startling.

10. See the dozens of citations in the index of *Massey's Ancient Egypt, The Light of the World, Volume II*, page 927 under Iu, Iu-em-hetep. Egyptologists today call him Imhotep.

11. See John 15:1–8.

4: THE GREATEST COVER-UP OF ALL TIME

1. Edward Gibbon, *The Decline and Fall of the Roman Empire* (New York: Modern Library, 1995), p. 502.

2. For a detailed account, see Joseph Wheless's *Forgery in Christianity*.

3. Eusebius, who died *c.* 340, together with the other shapers of the emerging orthodoxy, was aided enormously by Emperor Constantine's claim that Christianity was the glue with which to hold the empire together. The surge toward centralism and conformity was now backed by the might of Caesar.

4. Anselm was the archbishop of Canterbury at the time. He lived from *c.* 1033 to 1109.

5. *Catholic Encyclopedia*, vol. 5, p. 10.

6. Origen, *Commentary on Matthew*, XV, p. 14.

7. Ad. Haeres (Against Heresy), 26:2

8. For further reading on this, see not only Kuhn but Mead, *Fragments of a Faith Forgotten*.

9. See Erik Hornung's *The Secret Lore of Egypt*, p. 186: "Christian zealots had . . . made it a tabula rasa."

10. *Oxford Dictionary of the Christian Church*, edited by F. L. Cross, former Professor of Divinity in the University of Oxford.

11. On October 16, 2002.

5: IT WAS ALL WRITTEN BEFORE——IN EGYPT

1. There are many excellent sources for this subject, including *Conceptions of God in Ancient Egypt* by Eric Hornung and others mentioned in the bibliography. Hornung defines "Egyptosophy" as the belief that the land of the Nile was the fount of all wisdom. Once the discipline of "Egyptology" made its appearance in 1822, the relationship between the two has been problematic and there had been a reluctance to treat the topic. He says that though Egyptosophy often imagines itself to be far superior to any discipline that is blind to its true wisdom, Egyptology is often all too hastily inclined to ignore anything having to do with Egyptosophy, forgetting that it represents a hunger for hidden truths that is not satisfied by the scientific discipline and is in this respect entirely legitimate. He says "And while we in Egyptology take the picture of Egypt in classical antiquity quite seriously, we have trouble taking its continuation down into modern esoteric movements and its unbelievable wide spread equally seriously. . . . Scholarly concern with the esoteric tradition is still in its infancy and stands in inverse proportion to the immense importance of the esoteric among the general public. Even today there is only one professorship of esoteric lore in all the world, at the Sorbonne in Paris."

2. Compare this to Genesis 2:7: "And the Lord God formed man of the dust . . . and breathed into his nostrils the breath of life."

3. Hornung, *The Secret Lore of Egypt*, p. 75.

4. Mark 9:2–8.

5. In the catacombs of Rome are many pictures of the baby Horus being held in the arms of his mother, Isis—the original Madonna and Child. Other images, supposed by some of the pious to be likenesses of baby Jesus, are actually of the infant Horus and include a solar disk.

6. See the excellent article on the number twelve in *The Interpreter's Dictionary of the Bible*, vol. 4.

6: CONVINCING THE SCEPTICS

1. 1 Corinthians 3:16.

2. New Revised Standard Version.

3. Luke 1:80.

4. Didron, *The Book of Iconography*, Figure 124.

5. The book *The Jesus Mysteries* has a very full description of the nature and influence of what Freke and Gandy call the Osiris/Dionysus Mystery Religions and, in particular, the role of Dionysus/Bacchus as the god of the vine and wine.

6. Modern Egyptologists dispute this, but according to Gerald Massey, Karast, "the deceased," was anointed, hence the transition to the concept of Christos, which of course, means "anointed" in Greek.

7. The June 2003 issue of *Bible Review* carried a lead article on the Egyptian roots of Moses' name, and on Egyptian–Hebrew overlappings in general.

8. Mark 6:47–51.

9. *The Ritual* (Egyptian Book of the Dead), Chapter 170.

10. *The Ritual*, Chapter 131.

7: THE BIBLE——HISTORY OR MYTH?

1. See the Book of Joshua for the story of the mayhem allegedly committed in the name of Yahweh.

2. For a very scholarly treatment of the inconsistencies and flat contradictions of the New Testament documents when taken from a historical perspective, see *Can We Trust the New Testament* by G. A. Wells.

3. Rénan in his *Life of Jesus* says that in the late middle ages the name Lazarus was rendered, Eleazar. Bethany in the same period was Elazarie.

8: SEEING THE GOSPELS WITH NEW EYES

1. See Robert Funk and the Jesus Seminar *The Acts of Jesus: What Did Jesus Really Do?* (Harper San Francisco, 1998).

2. Ibid., pp. 1–2.

3. See Elaine Pagels *Beyond Belief: The Secret Gospel of Thomas* (New York: Random House, 2003) and B. L. Mack *The Lost Gospel: The Book of Q and Christian Origins*.

4. In their thick 1998 report, "The Acts of Jesus: What Did Jesus Really Do?," the scholars of the Jesus Seminar conclude that of all the sayings attributed to Jesus in the Gospels, only 18 percent are "actual or probable." Regarding the 176 "events" described as happening to or with

him, they conclude that only 16 percent fall in these same categories. They, of course, take a historical/critical approach, one that leaves them in the end with very little indeed. Jesus is simply an itinerant sage who comes to a grisly end. See *The Acts of Jesus*, pp. 1–8.

5. *The Ritual*, Chapter 19.

6. In the Gospel story of Jesus walking on the sea, it is highly symbolic that he is said to come during the fourth watch of the night! That's when the Christ appears.

7. See www.jesuspuzzle.org.

9: WAS THERE A JESUS OF HISTORY?

1. I refer the reader again to jesuspuzzle.org and to the wide-ranging, heated debate that has been going on there for several years now. Earl Doherty, the author of the website and a recent book by the same name, has compiled all scholarship on this contentious and deeply controversial issue for all to see. As was to be expected, the work has been greeted with derision and catcalls from the conservative wing of the Church. But when taken along with the exhaustive studies of the antecedent Egyptian materials, it makes what seems to me to be an incontrovertible case. One champion of the conservative position is the American journalist Lee Strobel; he has published a book of interviews with conservative scholars, *The Case for Christ*. Doherty, at the time of writing, had just published a compelling rebuttal of Strobel's chief arguments called *Challenging the Verdict*.

2. There was a great furor in the world's media and among scholars in the fall of 2002 when an ossuary alleged to have once held the bones of James, the brother of Jesus, came to light in Jerusalem and eventually was displayed in museums around the world, including the Royal Ontario Museum in Toronto. It was hailed as the first archaeological evidence for a historical Jesus. However, as I predicted in a column in the *Sunday Star* at that time, after a few months, a group of fourteen experts pronounced the ossuary a complete fake. It dated to the first century C.E., but the inscription in Aramaic was obviously forged. It had been scratched on only a couple of years ago and then covered by a doctored varnish to give the appearance of age.

3. Fundamentalists often make the claim that the Bible is inerrant and hence infallible in the "original autographs." They neglect to add that

we don't have a single autograph of any book in the entire Bible.

4. Joseph Leidner, *The Fabrication of the Christ Myth*.

5. The one possible exception to Leidner's argument is found in the Fourth Gospel. One of the sources relied on by the author/editor does show some detailed knowledge of Jerusalem.

6. In the Loeb edition of Josephus' words.

7. Schweitzer concluded that Jesus was an apocalyptic preacher whose message turned out to be wrong.

8. I refer the reader here to my book *Finding the Still Point*, and the discussion in the section titled "The God Within." It expresses the very same spiritual philosophy.

9. For those wishing to explore this further, I would recommend the work of Elaine Pagels on the Gnostics and the Gospels, and especially her book on Pauline Gnosticism. See the bibliography for details.

10. See Donald Akenson, *St. Saul* (Montreal: McGill University Press, 2000), p. 171.

10: THE ONLY WAY AHEAD

1. The kind of wisdom Kuhn and Massey are talking about is a form of Hermetism. The Egyptologist, Erik Hornung, ends his book *The Secret Lore of Egypt* with these words: "All Hermetism is by its very nature tolerant. Hermes Trismegistus (the Greek version of the Egyptian Thoth) is a god of harmony, of reconciliation and transformation, and he preaches no rigid dogma. He is thus an antidote to the fundamentalism that must be overcome if we desire to live in peace."

2. Frye, *The Double Vision*, p. 58.

3. Origen, *Philocalis* 1.8.

APPENDIX A

1. Higgins, *Anacalypsis*, p. xviii.

2. Through those long years of devoted study at the British Museum, Massey enjoyed the friendship and wise counsel of Dr. Samuel Birch, an outstanding Egyptologist. He attracted a following of dedicated students, who later assisted in his research. Two of his most prominent co-workers were George St. Clair, who authored *Creation Records Discovered in Egypt*, and Dr. Albert Churchward, who wrote *The Origin and Evolution of the Human Race*. Gerald Massey so impressed the novelist George Eliot that she made him the hero of one of her famous romances. Thus Massey became immortalized in literature as "Felix Holt the Radical." Among Massey's American friends and admirers was a prominent New York journalist and publisher, D. M. Bernett. On page 967 of the second edition of his *World's Sages, Thinkers and Reformers*, Bernett says, "Gerald Massey is a warm-hearted, genial man, and as a companion and friend he has few superiors. His interests and incentives are decidedly in the direction of science and rationalism. He has for many years been freed from the old binding and blinding theological creeds and obligations. He regards priestcraft as one of the great evils which mankind for thousands of years has been compelled to endure and support; and holds it as one of the most important works that men of the present time can engage in to demolish the idols of the past dark ages." Though a poet, Shakespeare scholar, and renowned Egyptologist, Gerald Massey is best remembered for his courageous convictions. His research led him to the conclusion that in Africa alone could be found the origins of myths, mysteries, symbols, languages, and religions. Egypt was the mouthpiece. In his lectures, Massey often repeated his contention that the gnosis, or central mystery, of Christianity was primarily derived from Egypt through various lines of descent—Hebrew, Persian, Greek, Alexandrian, Essenian, and Nazarene. These converged in Rome, where the history was manufactured from identifiable matter recorded in the ancient Book of Wisdom. It was during this period that he delivered his famous lectures on Gnostic and historic Christianity. He clearly depicted the origin of Christianity and said unequivocally that it was not derived from Buddhism, as some then held. Long before man uttered a verbal prayer, he expressed himself by actions or gesture-language, Massey said. He discussed this at length in "Man in Search of His Soul during 50,000 Years and How He Found It." Present-day psychologists

recognize gesture-language as an indication of man's true unexpressed attitudes; unconsciously, he assumes gestures revealing his thinking. In "The Seven Souls of Man," Massey said, "The modern manufacture of ancient mysteries is a great imposition and sure to be found out. The mysteries called Christian . . . I look upon them as the greatest imposition of all." His own meditation on facts of abnormal or extraordinary nature proved to him that mind existed and operated invisibly. He did not trouble about "the other world" at all, for it was in this world that people needed assistance. Life to him was not worth living if something was not done to further its work. "It is only in helping others that we can truly help ourselves," said Massey in the lecture "The Devil of Darkness in the Light of Evolution."

3. Here is Alvin Boyd Kuhn's obituary notice, as it appeared in *The New York Times* on September 15, 1963: "Elizabeth, N.J., Sept. 14. Dr. Alvin Boyd Kuhn, author, lecturer and former teacher of languages, died today at Morristown Memorial Hospital. He was 82 years old. Dr. Kuhn wrote ten books and twenty booklets [monographs] on religion, philosophy, semantics and Bible interpretation. He gave 1,945 lectures in the United States and Canada, discussing, among many subjects, the Dead Sea Scrolls. Dr. Kuhn, who received his Doctor of Philosophy degree from Columbia University, taught Latin, Greek, French, German, Spanish and English in high schools in Chambersburg, Harrisburg and elsewhere in Pennsylvania. He studied Hebrew and hieroglyphics for his work in Bible interpretation. His works include: *The Lost Light*; *Shadow of the Third Century*; *Who Is This King of Glory?*; *India's True Voice*; *The Lost Key to the Scriptures*; *Man's Two Births*; and *The Red Sea*. Dr. Kuhn received a B.A. degree from Franklin and Marshall College, where he was for a time secretary to the president. He is survived by a son, Dr. Alvin Kuhn, a professor at the University of Cincinnati; a daughter, Mrs. William Caulwell, wife of a faculty member at Millersville State College (Pa.), and four grandchildren."

APPENDIX B

1. In the Hindu Bible, the Bhagavad-Gita, Lord Krishna, the Hindu Christ, says to the warrior Arjuna, "I am the beginning, the life-span, and the end of all. . . . I am the beginning, the middle and the end in creation. . . . In the alphabet, I am the A [alpha]."

Bibliography

Assman, Jan. *Moses the Egyptian: The Memory of Egypt in Western Monotheism*. Cambridge, MA: Harvard University Press, 1998.

————. *The Search for God in Ancient Egypt*. Ithica, New York and London: Cornell University Press, 2001.

————. *The Mind of Egypt*. New York: Metropolitan Books, Henry Holt & Company, 1996.

Barnes, Harry Elmer. *The Twilight of Christianity*. New York: Richard R. Smith, Inc., 1931.

Beard, Mary, and John North. *Pagan Priest: Religion and Power in the Ancient World*. London: Duckworth Press, 1990.

Boardman, Griffin, and Oswyn Murray. *The Oxford History of the Classical World*. Oxford: Oxford University Press, 1986.

Borg, Marcus. *Jesus and Buddha: The Parallel Sayings*. Berkeley, CA: Ulysses Press, 1999.

————. *The Heart of Christianity: Rediscovering a Life of Faith*. San Francisco: HarperCollins, 2003.

Brandon, S. G. F. *Religion in Ancient History: Studies in Ideas, Men and Events*. London: Allen and Unwin, 1969.

Budge, E. A. Wallis. *Egyptian Religion*. New York: Citadel Press, 1997.

————. *Gods of the Egyptians*. New York: Dover Publications, 1969.

————, trans. *The Egyptian Book of the Dead*. New York: Dover Publications, 1967.

Burckhardt, Jacob. *The Life of Constantine*. Munich: Deutsche Verlags-Anstalt, 1929.

————. *The Age of Constantine the Great*. New York: Dorset Press, 1949.

Burkert, Walter. *Greek Religion: Archaic and Classical*. Oxford: Blackwell Publishers, 1985.

————. *Ancient Mystery Cults*. Cambridge, MA: Harvard University Press, 1987.

Campbell, Joseph. *The Hero with a Thousand Faces*. London: Paladin, 1949.

————. *The Power of Myth*. Charlotte, NC: Anchor Publishing, 1991.

Carpenter, Edward. *Pagan and Christian Creed: Their Origin and Meaning*. Kila, MT: Kessinger Publishing, 1997.

Carpenter, Thomas, and Christopher Faraone. *Masks of Dionysus*. Ithaca, NY: Cornell University Press, 1993.

Churton, Tobias. *Gnostics*. London: Weidenfeld and Nicholson, 1987.

Cross, F. L., ed. *The Oxford Dictionary of the Christian Church*. Oxford: Oxford University Press, 1958.

Crossan, John Dominic. *The Historical Jesus: The Life of a Mediterranean Jewish Peasant*. San Francisco: HarperCollins, 1991.

————. *Who Killed Jesus?: Exposing the Roots of Anti-Semitism in the Gospel Story of the Death of Jesus*. San Francisco: HarperCollins, 1995.

————. *The Birth of Christianity: Discovering What Happened in the Years Immediately After the Execution of Jesus*. San Francisco: HarperCollins, 1998.

Doane, Thomas William. *Bible Myths and Their Parallels in Other Religions*. Kila, MT: Kessinger Publishing, 1997.

Doherty, Earl. *The Jesus Puzzle: Did Christianity Begin with a Mythical Christ?*. Ottawa: Canadian Humanist Publications, 1999.

Dunand, Francois, & Zivie-Coche, Christiane. *Gods and Men in Egypt: 3000 BCE to 395 CE*. Ithica, New York: Cornell University Press, 2004.

Dunlap, Samuel F. *Sod: The Mysteries of Adoni*. London: Williams and Norgate, 1866.

Eliade, Mircea. *The Myth of the Eternal Return: Or, Cosmos and History*. Princeton: Princeton University Press, 1974.

Ellerbe, Helen. *The Dark Side of Christian History*. Bellingham, WA: Morningstar Books, 1995.

Eusebius. *The History of the Church from Christ to Constantine*. New York: Penguin, 1965.

Faulkner, Raymond O., trans. *The Book of the Dead*. London: British Museum Press, 1972.

Feldman, Louis H. *Josephus, the Bible and History*. Detroit: Wayne State University Press, 1989.

Fideler, David. *Jesus Christ, Sun of God: Ancient Cosmology and Early Christian Symbolism*. Wheaton, IL: Quest Books, *1993*.

Finkelstein, Israel, and Neil Asher Silberman. *The Bible Unearthed: Archeology's New Vision of Ancient Israel and the Origin of Its Sacred Texts*. New York: Touchstone Books, *2002*.

Frazer, James George. *The Golden Bough*. London: Wordsworth Reference Books, *1922*.

Freke, Timothy, and Peter Gandy. *The Complete Guide to World Mysticism*. London: Piatkus Books, *1997*.

————. *The Wisdom of the Pagan Philosophers*. Boston: Journey Editions, *1998*.

————. *The Jesus Mysteries: Was the "Original Jesus" a Pagan God?*. New York: Random House, *1999*.

————. *Jesus and the Lost Goddess: The Secret Teachings of the Original Christians*. New York: Harmony Books, *2001*.

Frye, Northrop: *The Double Vision: Language and Meaning in Religion*. Toronto: University of Toronto Press, *1991*.

Funk, Robert, and the Jesus Seminar. *The Five Gospels: The Search for the Authentic Words of Jesus*. San Francisco: HarperCollins, *1997*.

————. *The Acts of Jesus: What Did Jesus Really Do?*. New York: HarperCollins, *1998*.

Gadalla, Moustafa. *Historical Deception: The Untold Story of Ancient Egypt*. Erie, PA: Bastet Publishing, *1996*.

Gibbon, Edward. *The Decline and Fall of the Roman Empire*. 5 vols., *1776–88*. Reprint. New York: Modern Library, *1995*.

The Gnostic Bible: Gnostic Texts of Mystical Wisdom. Willis Bornstone and Marvin Meyer, eds. Boston: Shambala Publications, *2003*.

Graves, Kersey. *The World's Sixteen Crucified Saviors: Christianity before Christ*. Kila, MT: Kessinger Publishing, *1999*.

Graves, Robert. *The Greek Myths*. London: Penguin Books, *1992*.

Gregory, John. *The Neoplatonists: A Reader*. London: Kylie Cathie, *1987*.

Hall, Manly P. *Mystics and Mysteries in Alexandria*. Los Angeles: Philosophical Research Society, *1981*.

Harnack, Adolf von. *Mission and Expansion of Christianity*. 2 vols., *1908*. Reprint. New York: HarperCollins, *1962*.

Harpur, Tom. *For Christ's Sake*. Toronto: McClelland and Stewart, *1986*.

————. *Life after Death*. Toronto: McClelland and Stewart, *1991*.

————. *Finding the Still Point: A Spiritual Response to Stress*. Kelowna, BC: Northstone Publishing, *2002*.

Higgins, Godfrey. *Anacalypsis: An Inquiry into the Origin of Languages, Nations and Religions*. *1833*. Reprint. Kila, MT: Kessinger Publishing, *1997*.

Hoeller, Stephan. *Gnosticism: New Light on the Ancient Tradition of Inner Knowing*. Wheaton, IL: Quest Books, *2002*.

Hoffmann, R. Joseph, trans. *Celsus on the True Doctrine: A Discourse Against the Christians*. Oxford: Oxford University Press, *1987*.

Hollroyd, S. *Gnosticism*. Boston: Element Books, *1994*.

Hornung, Erik. *Conceptions of God in Ancient Egypt: The One and the Many*. Ithaca, NY: Cornell University Press, *1982*.

————. *The Secret Lore of Egypt*. Ithica, New York: Cornell University Press, *2001*.

Johnson, Sarah Iles, Editor: *Religiions in the Ancient World: A Guide*. Cambridge, London, & Massachusetts: Harvard University Press, *2004*.

Josephus, Flavius. *The Jewish War*. New York: Penguin, *1959*.

————. *The Antiquities of the Jews* (Loeb Classical Library). 9 vols. Cambridge, MA: Harvard University Press, *1965*.

Kallen, Horace M. *The Book of Job as a Greek Tragedy*. Kila, MT: Kessinger Publishing, *1997*.

Kennedy, H. A. A. *St. Paul and the Mystery Religions*. London: Hodder and Stoughton, *1969*.

Kingsford, Anna Bonus, and Edward Maitland. *The Perfect Way: Or the Finding of Christ*. Kila MT: Kessinger Publishing, *1996*.

Klausner, Joseph. *From Jesus to Paul*. *1934*. Reprint. Boston: Beacon Press, *1961*.

————. *Jesus of Nazareth: His Life, Times and Teaching*. *1922*. Reprint. Boston: Beacon Press, *1964*.

King, C. W. *Early Christian Numismatics*. London: Bell and Dalby, *1873*.

Knight, Christopher. *The Hiram Key: Pharaohs, Freemasons and the Discovery of the Secret Scrolls of Jesus*. London: Arrow Books, *1997*.

Koester, Helmut. *Ancient Christian Gospels: Their History and Development*. Philadelphia: Trinity Press, *1990*.

Kuhn, Alvin Boyd. *A Rebirth for Christianity*. Theosophical Publishing House, *1970*.

————. *The Root of All Religion.* 1944. Reprint. Kila, MT: Kessinger Publishing, 1993.

————. *The Lost Light: An Interpretation of Ancient Scriptures.* 1940. Reprint. Kila, MT: Kessinger Publishing, 1997.

————. *Prayer and Healing.* Kila, MT: Kessinger Publishing, 1997.

————. *The Red Sea Is Your Blood.* Kila, MT: Kessinger Publishing, 1997.

————. *Shadow of the Third Century: A Revaluation of Christianity.* Kila, MT: Kessinger Publishing, 1997.

————. *Who Is This King of Glory?.* Kila, MT: Kessinger Publishing, 1997.

————. *Mary Magdalene and Her Seven Devils.* nd. Available at http://www.members.tripod.com/~pc93/mmag7dev.htm.

————. *Let There Be Light on Genesis.* nd. Available at http://www.members.tripod.com/~pc93/ltblongn.htm.

————. *The Great Myth of the Sun-Gods.* nd. Available at http://http://members.tripod.com/~pc93.kuhn.htm.

————. *Christ's Three Days in Hell: The Revelation of an Astounding Christian Fallacy.* nd. Available at http://members.tripod.com/~pc93.kuhn/htm.

————. *Easter: The Birthday of the Gods.* Courtice, ON: Canadian Theosophical Society, nd. Available at http://members.tripod.com/~pc93/kuhn.htm.

————. *The Tree of Knowledge.* Vancouver: Canadian Theosophical Society, nd. Available at http://members.tripod.com/~pc93.kuhn/htm.

————. *Creation in Six Days?.* Vancouver: Canadian Theosophical Society, nd. Available at http://members.tripod.com/~pc93.kuhn/htm.

————. *Our Birth Is But a Sleep.* Olcott Foundation Lecture, 1959.

Lane Fox, Robin. *Pagans and Christians.* New York: Penguin, 1986.

Leedom, Tim C. *The Book Your Church Doesn't Want You to Read.* San Diego: Truth Seeker, 2001.

Leidner, Harold. *The Fabrication of the Christ Myth.* Tampa, FL: Survey Books, 1999.

Loisy, Alfred F. *The Birth of the Christian Religion: The Origins of the New Testament.* New Hyde Park, NY: University Books, 1962.

Ludemann, Gerd. *Heretics.* Norwich, UK: SCM Press, 1995.

Lund, Nils Wilhelm. *Chiasmus in the New Testament: A Study in the Form and Function of Chiastic Structures.* London: Hendrickson Publishers, 1992.

Lundy, John P. *Monumental Christianity: Or the Art and Symbolism of the Primitive Church*. Kila, MT: Kessinger Publishing, 2003.

Mack, Burton L. *The Lost Gospel: the Book of Q and Christian Origins*. New York: HarperCollins, 1993.

Martin, Luther H. *Hellenistic Religions: An Introduction*. Oxford: Oxford University Press, 1987.

Martin, Raymond. *The Elusive Messiah: A Philosophical Overview of the Quest for the Historical Jesus*. Boulder, CO: Westview Press, 1999.

Massey, Gerald. *Ancient Egypt, the Light of the World: A Work of Reclamation and Restitution in Twelve Volumes*. Vols. 1 and 2. Kila, MT: Kessinger Publications, 2001.

———. *The Historical Jesus and the Mythical Christ*. Kila, MT: Kessinger Publications, 2002

———. *The Natural Genesis*. Kila, MT: Kessinger Publications, 1999.

Mead, G. R. S. *Fragments of a Faith Forgotten*. Kila, MT: Kessinger Publications, 1997.

———. *Pistis Sophia: A Gnostic Gospel*. Kila, MT: Kessinger Publications, 1998.

———. *Thrice Greatest Hermes: Studies in Hellenistic Theosophy and Gnosis*. 1906. Reprint. Kila, MT: Kessinger Publications, 1997.

Meyer, Marvin. *The Ancient Mysteries: Sacred Texts of the Mystery Religions of the Ancient Mediterranean World*. San Francisco: HarperCollins, 1987.

Morenz, Siegfried: *Egyptian Religion*. Ithica, New York: Cornell University Press, 1996.

Mosheim, Johann Lorenz von. *History of the Christian Religion*. 2 vols. New York: South Converse, 1854.

Pagels, Elaine. *The Gnostic Gospels*. New York: Vintage Books, 1981.

———. *The Gnostic Paul: Gnostic Exegesis of the Pauline Letters*. Philadelphia: Trinity Press, 1992.

Powell Davies, A. *The First Christian: A Study of St. Paul*. New York: New American Library, 1959.

Price, Robert M.: *Deconstructing Jesus*. New York: Prometheus Books, 2000.

Riley, Frank L. *Biblical Allegorism: A Key to the Mysteries of the Kingdom of God*. Kila, MT: Kessinger Publishing, 1997.

Robinson, James M., ed. *The Nag Hammadi Library*. New York: HarperCollins, 1978.

Rushkoff, Douglas. *Nothing Sacred: The Truth about Judaism*. New York: Crown Publishing, *2003*.

S, Acharya. *The Christ Conspiracy: The Greatest Story Ever Sold*. Kempton, IL: Adventures Unlimited, *1999*.

Schuon, Frithjof. *In the Face of the Absolute*. Bloomington, IN: World Wisdom Books, *1994*.

Schweitzer, Albert. *The Quest of the Historical Jesus. 1910*. Reprint. New York: Macmillan, *1964*.

Segal, Robert A., ed. *The Gnostic Jung*. New York: Routledge, *1992*.

Smith, Jonathan Z.: *Drudgery Divine: On the Comparison of Early Christianity's & the Religiions of Late Antiquity*. Chicago: University of Chicago Press, *1994*.

Spong, John Shelby. *Why Christianity Must Change or Die: A Bishop Speaks to Believers in Exile*. San Francisco: HarperCollins, *1998*.

——————. *A New Christianity for a New World: Why Traditional Faith Is Dying and How a New Faith Is Being Born*. San Francisco: HarperCollins, *2003*.

Taylor, Thomas, trans. *Iamblichus on the Mysteries of the Egyptians, Chaldeans and Assyrians*. San Diego: Wizards Bookshelf, *1997*.

——————. *Eleusinian and Bacchic Mysteries*. San Diego: Wizards Bookshelf, *1997*.

Thorburn, T. J. *The Mythical Interpretations of the Gospels*. Kila, MT: Kessinger Publishing, .

Turcan, Robert. *Cults of the Roman Empire*. Oxford: Blackwell Publishers, *1992*.

Ulansey, David. *The Origins of the Mithraic Mysteries: Cosmology and Salvation in the Ancient World*. Oxford: Oxford University Press, *1989*.

Waite, Charles B. *The History of the Christian Religion to the Year Two Hundred*. Chicago: C. V. Waite, *1900*.

Weiss, Johannes. *Earliest Christianity: A History of the Period A.D. 30–150. 1914*. Reprint. New York: Harper's, *1959*.

Wells, G. A. *Can We Trust the New Testament: Thoughts on the Reliability of Early Christian Testimony*. Chicago: Open Court, *2004*.

——————. *Did Jesus Exist?*. Pemberton Publishing, *1975*.

West, John Anthony. *The Traveler's Key to Ancient Egypt: A Guide to the Sacred Places of Ancient Egypt*. Wheaton, IL: Quest Books, *1995*.

Wheless, Joseph. *Forgery in Christianity: A Documented Record of the Foundations of the Christian Religion. 1930*. Reprint. Kila, MT: Kessinger Publishing, *1997*.

Suggested Websites

www.crosscurrents.org/. An online magazine for those dedicated to current discussions of wisdom/faith.

www.homestead.com/tomharpur/. Global thinking about religion and spirituality.

www.jesuspuzzle.com/. A source for following the ongoing discussions raised by the book of the same name.

www.newadvent.org/. Resources such as the Catholic Encyclopedia, Church Fathers, etc.

www.tcpc.org/. The site for Progressive Christianity, a growing, inclusive, non-dogmatic form of the Christian faith.

www.theosophical.ca. The home page leads to a wide range of esoteric authors, including Massey and Kuhn.

www.tomharpur.com/. An emerging site dedicated to cosmic spirituality.

www.truthbeknown.com/. The highly provocative, often shocking insights of a remine scholar and free thinker, Achary S.

www.webcom.com/~gnosis/search_form.html/. The Gnosis Archive. All Nag Hammadi and many other Gnostic texts are available here.

www.wisdomworld.org/. The world of theosophy explained and explored. A guide to ancient wisdom.

www.medmalexperts.com/POCM

Index